Lecture Notes of the Institute for Computer Sciences, Social Informatics and Telecommunications Engineering 189

More information about this series at http://www.springer.com/series/8197

Antonella Longo · Marco Zappatore
Massimo Villari · Omer Rana
Dario Bruneo · Rajiv Ranjan
Maria Fazio · Philippe Massonet (Eds.)

Cloud Infrastructures, Services, and IoT Systems for Smart Cities

Second EAI International Conference, IISSC 2017 and CN4IoT 2017
Brindisi, Italy, April 20–21, 2017
Proceedings

 Springer

Editors
Antonella Longo
Department of Engineering for Innovation
University of Salento
Lecce
Italy

Marco Zappatore
Department of Engineering for Innovation
University of Salento
Lecce
Italy

Massimo Villari
Faculty of Engineering
University of Messina
Messina
Italy

Omer Rana
Cardiff University
Cardiff
UK

Dario Bruneo (iD)
Dipartimento di Ingegneria
Università di Messina
Messina
Italy

Rajiv Ranjan
Newcastle University
Newcastle upon Tyne
UK

Maria Fazio
DICIEAMA Department
University of Messina
Messina
Italy

Philippe Massonet
CETIC
Charleroi
Belgium

ISSN 1867-8211   ISSN 1867-822X   (electronic)
Lecture Notes of the Institute for Computer Sciences, Social Informatics
and Telecommunications Engineering
ISBN 978-3-319-67635-7   ISBN 978-3-319-67636-4   (eBook)
https://doi.org/10.1007/978-3-319-67636-4

Library of Congress Control Number: 2017956067

Printed on acid-free paper

This Springer imprint is published by Springer Nature
The registered company is Springer International Publishing AG
The registered company address is: Gewerbestrasse 11, 6330 Cham, Switzerland

Preface

On behalf of the Organizing Committee, we are honored and pleased to welcome you to the second edition of the EAI International Conference on ICT Infrastructures and Services for Smart Cities (IISSC) held in the wonderful location of Santa Chiara Convent in Brindisi, Italy.

The main objective of this event is twofold. First, the conference aims at disseminating recent research advancements, offering researchers the opportunity to present their novel results about the development, deployment, and use of ICT in smart cities. A second goal is to promote sharing of ideas, partnerships, and cooperation between everyone involved in shaping the smart city evolution, thus contributing to routing technical challenges and their impact on the socio-technical smart cities system.

The core mission of the conference is to address key topics on ICT infrastructure (technologies, models, frameworks) and services in cities and smart communities, in order to enhance performance and well-being, to reduce costs and resource consumption, and to engage more effectively and actively with their citizens.

The technical program of the conference covers a broad range of hot topics, spanning over five main tracks: e-health and smart living, privacy and security, smart transportation, smart industry, and infrastructures for smart cities. The program this year also included:

- A special session about challenges and opportunities in smart cities, which cut across and beyond the single field of interests, such as socio-technical challenges related to the impact of technology and smart cities evolution.
- A showcase, which represents the other pulsing soul of the conference: a place where industrial partners, public stakeholders, scientific communities from the pan-European area can share their experiences, projects and developed resources. We hope to provide a good context for exchanging ideas, challenges, and needs, gaining from the experiences and achievements of the participants and creating the proper background for future collaborations.
- Two exciting keynote lectures held, jointly with CN4IoT, by Prof. Antonio Corradi and Prof. Rebecca Montanari from the University of Bologna, Italy

During the conference, the city of Brindisi opened the Brindisi Smart Lab, a vibrant incubator of creativity and ideas, for prototyping and sustaining new start-ups, which will positively impact on the local smart community.

The second edition of EAI IISSC attracted 23 manuscripts from all around the world. At least two Technical Program Committee (TPC) members were assigned to review each paper. Each submission went through a rigorous peer-review process. The authors were then requested to consider the reviewers' remarks in preparing the final version of their papers. At the end of the process, 12 papers satisfying the requirements of quality, novelty, and relevance to the conference scope were selected for inclusion in the conference proceedings (acceptance rate: 52%). Three more papers were invited by the TPC owing to the appropriateness of the presented topics.

We are confident that researchers can find in the proceedings possible solutions to existing or emerging problems and, hopefully, ideas and insights for further activities in the relevant and wide research area of smart cities.

Moreover, the best conference contribution award was assigned at the end of the conference by a committee appointed by the TPC chairs based on paper review scores.

We would like to thank all the many persons who contributed to make this conference successful. First and foremost, we would like to express our gratitude to the authors of the technical papers: IISSC 2017 would not have been possible without their valuable contributions.

Special thanks go to the members of the Organizing Committee and to the members of the Technical Program Committee for their diligent and hard work, especially to Eng. Marco Zappatore, who deserves a special mention for his constant dedication to the conference.

We would like also to thank the keynote and invited speakers and the showcase participants for their invaluable contribution and for sharing their vision with us. Also, we truly appreciated the perseverance and the hard work of the local organizing secretariat (SPAM Communication): Organizing a conference of this level is a task that can only be accomplished by the collaborative effort of a dedicated and highly capable team.

We are grateful for the support received from all the sponsors of the conference. Major support for the conference was provided by Capgemini Italia and University of Salento.

In addition, we are grateful to the Municipality and the Province of Brindisi, the institutions, and the citizens and entrepreneurs of Apulia Region for being close to us in promoting and being part of this initiative.

Last but not least, we would like to thank all of the participants for coming.

September 2017

Antonella Longo
Massimo Villari
Daniele Napoleone

Preface

The Second International Conference on Cloud, Networking for IoT systems (CN4IoT) was held in Brindisi, Italy on April 20–21, 2017, as a co-located event of the Second EAI International Conference on ICT Infrastructures and Services for Smart Cities.

The mission of CN4IoT 2017 was to serve and promote ongoing research activities on the uniform management and operation related to software-defined infrastructures, in particular by analyzing limits and/or advantages in the exploitation of existing solutions developed for cloud, networking, and IoT. IoT can significantly benefit from the integration with cloud computing and network infrastructures along with services provided by big players (e.g., Microsoft, Google, Apple, and Amazon) as well as small and medium enterprises alike. Indeed, networking technologies implement both virtual and physical interconnections among cooperating entities and data centers, organizing them into a unique computing ecosystem. In such a connected ecosystem, IoT applications can establish a elastic relationship driven by performance requirements (e.g., information availability, execution time, monetary budget, etc.) and constraints (e.g., input data size, input data streaming rate, number of end-users connecting to that application, output data size, etc.)

The integration of IoT, networking, and cloud computing can then leverage the rising of new mash-up applications and services interacting with a multi-cloud ecosystem, where several cloud providers are interconnected through the network to deliver a universal decentralized computing environment to support IoT scenarios.

It was our honor to have invited prominent and valuable ICT international experts as keynote speakers. The conference program comprised technical papers selected through peer reviews by the TPC members and invited talks. CN4IoT 2017 would not be a reality without the help and dedication of our conference manager Erika Pokorna from the European Alliance for Innovation (EAI). We would like to thank the conference committees and the reviewers for their dedicated and passionate work. None of this would have happened without the support and curiosity of the authors who sent their papers to this second edition of CN4IoT.

IISSC 2017 Organization

Steering Committee

Imrich Chlamtac	CREATE-NET and University of Trento, Italy
Dagmar Cagáňová	Slovak University of Technology (STU), Slovakia
Massimo Craglia	European Commission, Joint Research Centre, Digital Earth and Reference Data Unit, Italy
Mauro Draoli	University of Rome Tor Vergata, Agenzia per l'Italia Digitale (AGID), Italy
Antonella Longo	University of Salento, Italy
Massimo Villari	University of Messina, Italy

Organizing Committee

General Chair

Antonella Longo   University of Salento, Italy

General Co-chair

Massimo Villari   University of Messina, Italy

Technical Program Committee Chair

Marco Zappatore   University of Salento, Italy

Workshops Chair

Beniamino Di Martino   University of Naples, Italy

Workshops Co-chairs

Giuseppina Cretella	University of Naples, Italy
Antonio Esposito	University of Naples, Italy

Publicity and Social Media Chair

Massimo Villari   University of Messina, Italy

Sponsorship and Exhibits Chair

Alessandro Musumeci   CDTI: Association of IT Managers, Italy

Publications Chair

Mario Alessandro   University of Salento, Italy
  Bochicchio

Local Chair

Antonella Longo   University of Salento, Italy

Web Chair

Marco Zappatore   University of Salento, Italy

Panels Chair

Dagmar Cagáňová   Slovak University of Technology (STU), Slovakia

Panels Co-chairs

Natália Horňáková   Institute of Industrial Engineering and Management, MTF, Slovakia

Viera Gáťová   Slovak University of Technology (STU), Slovakia

Smart City Challenges and Needs Special Event Program Chair

Daniele Napoleone   Capgemini Italia, Italy

Conference Manager

Lenka Koczová   EAI, European Alliance for Innovation, Slovakia

Technical Program Committee

Aitor Almeida	Universidad de Deusto, Spain
Christos Bouras	University of Patras, Greece
Dagmar Caganova	MTF, Slovak University of Technology, Slovakia
Antonio Celesti	University of Messina, Italy
Angelo Coluccia	University of Salento, Italy
Giuseppina Cretella	University of Naples, Italy
Marco Del Coco	ISASI, CNR, Italy
Simone Di Cola	The University of Manchester, UK
Beniamino Di Martino	Second University of Naples, Italy
Yucong Duan	Hainan University, China
Gianluca Elia	University of Salento, Italy
Antonio Esposito	University of Naples, Italy
Maria Fazio	University of Messina, Italy
Viera Gáťová	MTF, Slovak University of Technology, Slovakia
Julius Golej	Institute of Management, Slovak University of Technology, Slovakia
Natalia Horňáková	MTF, Slovak University of Technology, Slovakia
Verena Kantere	Université de Genève, Switzerland
Vaggelis Kapoulas	Computer Technology Institute and Press Diophantus, Greece
Diego López-de-Ipiña	Universidad de Deusto, Spain
Luca Mainetti	University of Salento, Italy

Johann M. Marquez-Barja   CONNECT Centre for Future Networks
                             and Communications, Trinity College, Ireland
Kevin McFall   Kennesaw State University, USA
Nicola Mezzetti   University of Trento, Italy
Gianmario Motta   Università di Pavia, Italy
Pablo Orduña   Universidad de Deusto, Spain
Luigi Patrono   University of Salento, Italy
Andreas Pester   Carinthia University of Applied Sciences, Austria
Maria Teresa Restivo   University of Porto, Portugal
Manfred Schrenk   CORP, Competence Center of Urban and Regional
                             Planning, Austria
Juraj Sipko   Institute of Economic Research, Slovak Academy
                             of Sciences, Slovakia
Luigi Spedicato   University of Salento, Italy
Daniela Spirkova   Institute of Management, Slovak University
                             of Technology, Slovakia
Emanuele Storti   Università Politecnica delle Marche, Italy
Luciano Tarricone   University of Salento, Italy
Mira Trebar   University of Ljubljana, Slovenia
Thrasyvoulos Tsiatsos   Aristotle University of Thessaloniki, Greece
Jekaterina Tsukrejeva   Tallinn University of Technology, Estonia
Lucia Vaira   University of Salento, Italy
Massimo Villari   University of Messina, Italy
Isabella Wagner   Centre for Social Innovation (ZSI), Austria
Krzysztof Witkowski   University of Zielona Góra, Poland
Stefano Za   eCampus University, Italy

CN4IoT 2017 Organization

Steering Committee

Steering Committee Chair

Imrich Chlamtac   CREATE-NET, Italy

Steering Committee Members

Antonio Celesti   University of Messina, Italy
Burak Kantarci   Clarkson University, NY, USA
Georgiana Copil   TU Vienna, Austria
Schahram Dustdar   TU Vienna, Austria
Prem Prakash Jayaraman   CSIRO, Digital Productivity Flagship, Australia
Rajiv Ranjan   CSIRO, Digital Productivity Flagship, Australia
Massimo Villari   University of Messina, Italy
Joe Weinman   Chief IEEE Intercloud Testbed, Telx, NY, USA
Frank Leymann   IASS, Stuttgart University, Germany

Organizing Committee

General Chair

Massimo Villari   University of Messina, Italy

Technical Program Committee Chairs

Omer Rana   Cardiff University, UK
Dario Bruneo   University of Messina, Italy
Rajiv Ranjan   Newcastle University, UK

Website Chair

Antonio Celesti   University of Messina, Italy

Publicity and Social Media Chair

Luca Foschini   Bologna University, Italy

Workshops Chair

Giuseppe Di Modica   University of Catania, Italy

Sponsorship and Exhibits Chair

Massimo Villari   University of Messina, Italy

Publications Chairs

Maria Fazio   University of Messina, Italy
Philippe Massonet   CETIC, Belgium

Local Chair

Antonella Longo   University of Salento, Italy

Technical Program Committee

Rui Aguiar   University of Aveiro, Portugal
David Breitgand   IBM Haifa Research Lab, Israel
Clarissa Cassales   Huawei European Research Center, Munich, Germany
  Marquezan
Antonio Celesti   University of Messina, Italy
Walter Cerroni   DEIS University of Bologna, Italy
Lydia Chen   IBM, Zurich Research Laboratory, Zurich, Switzerland
Stefano Chessa   Università di Pisa, Italy
Raymond Choo   University of South Australia, Adelaide, Australia
Stuart Clayman   University College London, UK
Panagiotis Demestichas   University of Piraeus Research Center, Greece
Spyros Denazis   University of Patras, Greece
Jose de Souza   UFC, Brazil
Giuseppe Di Modica   University of Catania, Italy
Filip de Turck   Ghent University – IBBT, Belgium
Stefano Giordano   Università di Pisa, Italy
Shiyan Hu   MTU, USA
Prem Prakash Jayaraman   RMIT, Australia
Gregory Katsaros   Intel, Santa Clara, CA, USA
Chang Liu   CSIRO, Australia
Karan Mitra   Lulea Institute of Technology, Sweden
Amir Molzam Sharifloo   University of Duisburg-Essen, Germany
Surya Nepal   CSIRO, Australia
Charith Perera   Open University, UK
Dana Petcu   Institute e-Austria Timisoara, Romania
Omer Rana   Cardiff University, UK
Rajiv Ranjan   CSIRO, Australia
Roberto Riggio   CREATE-NET, Italy
Susana Sargento   Institute of Telecommunications, University of Aveiro,
                                     Portugal

Ellis Solaiman	Newcastle University, UK
Daniel Sun	Data61, Australia
Dhaval Thakker	Bradford University, UK
Massimo Villari	University of Messina, Italy
Chris Woods	Huawei Ireland
Yang Xiang	Deakin University, Australia

Contents

IISSC: Smart Challenges and Needs

Conference on Cloud Networking for IoT (CN4IoT)

IISSC: Smart City Services

Comparison of City Performances Through Statistical Linked Data Exploration

Claudia Diamantini, Domenico Potena, and Emanuele Storti[✉]

Dipartimento di Ingegneria dell'Informazione, Universita Politecnica delle Marche,
via Brecce Bianche, 60131 Ancona, Italy
{c.diamantini,d.potena,e.storti}@univpm.it

Abstract. The capability to perform comparisons of city performances can be an important guide for stakeholders to detect strengths and weaknesses and to set up strategies for future urban development. Today, the rise of the Open Data culture in public administrations is leading to a larger availability of statistical datasets in machine-readable formats, e.g. the RDF Data Cube. Although these allow easier data access and consumption, appropriate evaluation mechanisms are still needed to perform proper comparisons, together with an explicit representation of how statistical indicators are calculated. In this work, we discuss an approach for analysis and comparison of statistical Linked Data which is based on the formal and mathematical representation of performance indicators. Relying on this knowledge model, a set of logic-based services are able to support novel typologies of comparison of different resources.

Keywords: Statistical datasets · Performance indicators · Logic reasoning · Smart cities

1 Introduction

Performance monitoring is becoming a more and more important tool in planning and assessing efficiency and effectiveness of services and infrastructures in urban contexts. This increasing attention is witnessed also by projects (e.g., CITYKeys[1]), standards (e.g., ISO 37120:2014, ISO/TS 37151:2015) and initiatives at international level (e.g., Green Digital Charter[2], European Smart City Index) which push forward the definition of shared frameworks for performance measurement at city level. Statistical data are capable of more effectively guiding municipal administrations in the decision making process and foster civic participation. They can also impact on the capability to attract private investments, which may be stimulated by opportunities that are made explicit by quantitative evidences and comparisons between different municipalities. Also thanks to the rise of the Open Data culture in public administrations, today statistical datasets are more frequently available and accessible in machine-readable formats. This

---

[1] http://citykeys-project.eu/.
[2] http://www.greendigitalcharter.eu/.

© ICST Institute for Computer Sciences, Social Informatics and Telecommunications Engineering 2018
A. Longo et al. (Eds.): IISSC 2017/CN4IoT 2017, LNICST 189, pp. 3–12, 2018.
https://doi.org/10.1007/978-3-319-67636-4_1

enables the possibility to adapt to cities methods and solutions exploited for decades in enterprise contexts to assess the achievement of business objectives.

A recent trend in this respect is to publish statistical data according to the RDF Data Cube vocabulary[3], a W3C standard for the representation of statistical datasets in the web. This format follows the Linked Data approach and conceptually resorts to the multidimensional model [1] adopted in enterprise contexts for Data Warehouses, as observed values (e.g., level of $CO2$) are organized along a group of dimensions (e.g., time and place, as the measure is taken daily and each value refers to a specific monitoring station in the city), together with associated metadata. The publication of performance datasets according to the Linked Data approach allows to reduce heterogeneity, as measures from different datasets may be aligned with the same definition of indicator. However, besides it is a concrete step towards an easier access and interoperability among different datasets, appropriate mechanisms to evaluate and compare performances are yet to come. One of the main reasons is related to the lack of a shared, explicit and unambiguous way to define indicators. Indeed, no meaningful comparisons of performance can be made without the awareness of how indicators are calculated. To make an example, if we were interested in comparing the ratios of delayed trips in two public transportation systems, we would require to understand how such ratios are actually computed, e.g. if the first summed up trips made by trams and bus, while the second considered only the latter, the risk would be to derive wrong consequences and take uneffective decisions.

With the purpose to address the above mentioned issues, in this paper we propose a logic-based approach to enable the comparison of datasets published by different municipalities as Linked Open Data. The approach is based on the formal, ontological representation of indicators together with their calculation formulas. Measures are then declaratively mapped to these definitions in order to express their semantics. In this way, the ontology serves as a reference library of indicators that can be incrementally extended. Finally, a set of services, built on the top of the model and exploiting reasoning functions, offers functionalities to determine if two datasets are comparable, and to what extent. The rest of this work is organised as follows: next Section briefly presents a case study that will be used throughout the paper. In Sect. 3 we discuss an ontology to formally represent statistical indicators with their calculation formulas, and we introduce the representation of statistical data according to the RDF Data Cube vocabulary. These models and languages are exploited in Sect. 4 to provide a set of services aimed to support analysis and comparisons of Linked datasets. Finally, in Sect. 5 we provide conclusions and outline future work.

2   Case Study: Bike Sharing Services

Alternative, more sustainable and energy-efficient forms of urban mobility are among the major goals of many smart cities initiatives, both at national and

---

[3] https://www.w3.org/TR/vocab-data-cube/.

international level. Several cities have already started to share data about transport services with a larger audience as open data. In the following, we introduce a case study focusing on bike sharing services provided by two municipalities, City$_A$ and City$_B$. The example is a simplified version of actual datasets published by a set of US municipalities including New York[4], Chattanooga[5] and many others. In details, let us suppose that each municipality provides a library of datasets, as follows:

- City$_A$ measures the *total distance* (in miles) of bike rides, aggregated with respect to user type (residents/tourists) and time, and the *population* through dimension time.
- City$_B$ measures the *total distance* of bike rides for residents and the *total distance* of rides for tourists aggregated with respect to time; it also measures the *population* with respect to time.

3   Data and Knowledge Layer

In this Section we discuss the models and languages that are used in this work to represent performance indicators (Subsect. 3.1) and datasets (Subsect. 3.2) according to the Linked Data approach.

3.1   Modeling of Performance Indicators

Reference libraries of indicators, e.g. VRM or SCOR [2], have been used as a reference for a long time, especially for performance management in the enterprise domain. More recently, the interest in the systematisation and organisation of the huge amount of existing PIs is witnessed by many collections of indicators proposed by public bodies or specific projects (e.g., [3] in the context of smart cities). Most of them, however, are not machine-readable and lack formal semantics. Several work in the Literature tried to fill this gap, proposing ontologies for declarative definition of indicators (e.g., [4,5]), even though in most cases they do not include an explicit representation of formulas capable to describe how to calculate composite indicators from others. On the other hand, the representation of mathematical expressions in computer systems has been investigated for a variety of tasks like information sharing and automatic calculation. The most notable and recent examples are MathML and OpenMath [6], mainly targeted to represent formulas in the web.

In the context of this work, indicators and their formulas are formally represented in KPIOnto, an ontology conceptually relying on the multidimensional model and originally conceived as a knowledge base for a performance monitoring framework for highly distributed enterprise environments [7]. As reported in Fig. 1, within the classes defined in KPIOnto[6] for the purpose of this work we focus on the following:

---

[4] https://www.citibikenyc.com/system-data.
[5] https://data.chattlibrary.org/.
[6] Full ontology specification is available online at http://w3id.org/kpionto.

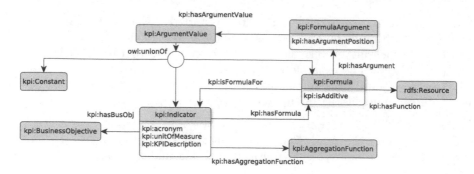

Fig. 1. KPIOnto: main classes and properties.

- **Indicator**, that represents a quantitative metric (or measure) together with a set of properties, e.g. one or more compatible dimensions, a formula, a unit of measurement, a business objective and an aggregation function.
- **Formula**, that formally represents an indicator as a function of other indicators. An indicator can indeed be either atomic or compound, built by combining several other indicators through a mathematical expression. Operators are represented as defined by OpenMath [6], an extensible XML-based standard for representing the semantics of mathematical objects. On the other hand, operands can be defined as indicators, constants or, recursively, as other formulas.

As regards the case study, we define indicators *Distance* and *TotalPopulation* for City$_A$, *Distance_Tourists* and *Distance_Citizens* for City$_B$.

3.2 Representation of Statistical Datasets

Several standards for representation of statistical data on the web have been adopted in the past with the purpose to improve their interpretation and interoperability, e.g. SDMX (Statistical data and metadata exchange) [8] and DDI (Data Documentation Initiative)[7] just to mention the most notable examples. In the last years, in order to rely on more flexible and general solutions for publishing statistical datasets on the web, several RDF vocabularies have been proposed in the Literature. To address the limits of early approaches (e.g., the capability to properly represent dimensions, attributes and measures or to group together data values sharing the same structure), the Data Cube vocabulary (QB) [9], was proposed by W3C to publish statistical data on the web as RDF following the Linked Data principles. According to the multidimensional model, the QB language defines the schema of a cube as a set of dimensions, attributes and measures through the corresponding classes qb:DimensionProperty, qb:AttributeProperty and qb:MeasureProperty. Data instances are represented in QB as a set of qb:Observations, that can be optionally grouped in subsets named Slices.

---

[7] http://www.ddialliance.org/.

To make an example about the case study of Sect. 2, the data structure of the first dataset for City$_A$ includes the following components:

- `cityA:Distance`, a qb:MeasureProperty for the total distance;
- `sdmx-dimension:timePeriod`, a qb:DimensionProperty for the time of the observation;
- `cityA:userType`, a qb:DimensionProperty for the user type.

Please note that the prefix *"qb:"* stands for the specification of the Data Cube vocabulary[8], *"sdmx-dimension:"* points to the SDMX vocabulary for standard dimensions[9], while *"cityA:"* is a custom namespace for describing measures, dimensions and members of the dataset for City$_A$. In order to make datasets comparable, the approach we take in this work is to rely on KPIOnto as reference vocabulary to define indicators. As such, instances of MeasureProperty as defined in Data Cube datasets have to be semantically aligned with instances of `kpi:Indicator`, through a RDF property as follows: `cityA:Distance rdfs:isDefinedBy kpi:TotalDistance`. In this way, the semantics of the measure Distance, as used by City$_A$, will be provided by the corresponding concept of TotalDistance in KPIOnto.

For what concerns observations, i.e. data values, we report an example about the measure Distance for City$_A$, for time *December, 5th 2016* (time dimension), and user type *citizen*:

```
cityA:obs001 a qb:Observation;
            sdmx-dimension:timePeriod"2016-12-05"^^xsd:date;
            cityA:userType cityA:resident;
            cityA:Distance 80214;
            qb:dataSet cityA:dataset1.
```

4   Services for Analysis and Comparison of Datasets

In this Section we discuss a set of services that are aimed to support analysis and comparisons of statistical datasets. As depicted in Fig. 2, services are built on top of the Data/knowledge layer, while access to datasets is performed through SPARQL queries over corresponding endpoints. A single endpoint may serve a library of datasets belonging to the same municipality. In the first subsection, we introduce the reasoning framework, which comprises basic logical functions for formula manipulation, on which the others rely, while in Subsect. 4.2 we focus on services for dataset analysis and comparison. Further services are available in the framework and devised to support indicator management, which enable the definition of new indicators and exploration of indicator structures. For lack of space, we refer the interested reader to a previous work of ours discussing in detail these services [7].

---

[8] https://www.w3.org/TR/vocab-data-cube/.
[9] http://purl.org/linked-data/sdmx/2009/dimension.

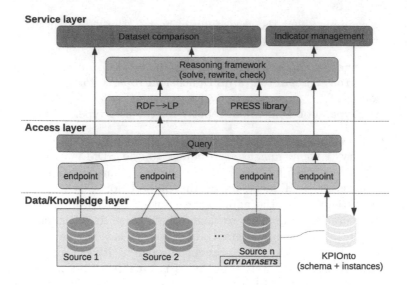

Fig. 2. Architecture of the framework.

In the following, we will refer to the example introduced in Sect. 2. After the definition of the indicators, we assume these mappings have been defined between datasets' measures and KPIOnto indicators:

```
cityA:Distance rdfs:isDefinedBy kpi:Distance.
cityA:Population rdfs:isDefinedBy kpi:TotalPopulation.
cityB:Distance_Residents rdfs:isDefinedBy kpi:Distance_Citizens.
cityB:Distance_Tourists rdfs:isDefinedBy kpi:Distance_Tourists.
cityB:Population rdfs:isDefinedBy kpi:TotalPopulation.
```

Let us suppose also that the formula *kpi:Distance=kpi:Distance_Citizens +
kpi:Distance_Tourists* is defined by the user to state that the indicator can be calculated as the summation of the two types of distances. Moreover, let us suppose that the user is interested to better understand the inclination of the local population in using bike sharing services. For this reason, the user will define a further indicator *AvgDistancePerCitizen*, with formula $\frac{kpi:Distance\_Population}{kpi:TotalPopulation}$, which measures the distance covered on average by residents. As for dimensions, for simplicity we assume that the time dimension is defined as *sdmx-dimension:timePeriod* in all datasets[10].

4.1   Reasoning on Indicator Formulas

A set of logic-based functionalities are defined to enable an easy and transparent management of the indicator formulas defined according to KPIOnto. We refer in particular to Prolog as logic language for its versatility, capability of symbolic manipulation as well as for the wide availability of well-documented reasoners

---

[10] Please note that *owl:sameAs* links can be defined between different definitions of the same dimension for interoperability purposes.

and tools. Indicators formulas are thus translated to Prolog facts, and a set of custom reasoning functions is defined to support common formula manipulations exploited by services discussed in the next subsections, among which:

- `solve_equation(eq,indicator)`, which is capable to solve the equation *eq* with respect to variable *indicator*;
- `get_formulas(ind)`, which returns all possible rewritings of the formula for a given indicator; the predicate is capable to manipulate the whole set of formulas and find alternative rewritings by applying mathematical axioms (e.g., commutativity, associativity, distributivity and properties of equality). This also allows to derive a formula for an atomic indicator, e.g. $Distance\_Citizens = AvgDistancePerCitizen * TotalPopulation$ is inferred by solving the $AvgDistancePerCitizen$ formula w.r.t. the variable $Distance\_Citizens$.
- `derive_all_indicators(measures)`, which returns a list of all the indicators that can be calculated starting from those provided in input. The function exploits `get_formulas` to decompose all the available indicators in any possible way, and each of these rewriting is checked against the list in input. If there is a match, the solution is returned in output, e.g. if in input we have $\{Distance\_Citizens, TotalPopulation\}$, the function returns the list $\{Distance\_Citizens, TotalPopulation, AvgDistancePerCitizen\}$, as the last indicator can be calculated from the others through the formula $\frac{Distance\_Citizens}{TotalPopulation}$.

Such functionalities are built upon PRESS (PRolog Equation Solving System) [37], a library of predicates formalizing algebra in Logic Programming, which are capable to manipulate formulas according to mathematical axioms. We refer interested readers to previous work specifically focused on this reasoning framework [7,10], which includes also computational analyses on efficiency of these logic functions.

4.2 Dataset Comparison and Evaluation

In order to enable performance analyses across multiple datasets, belonging to the same or different libraries (i.e. to different municipalities), a preliminary evaluation must be performed in order to verify whether they are comparable and to what extent. The services discussed in this subsection are hence devised to assess comparability taking into account both measures and dimensions. In detail, we define two datasets comparable at *schema level* if their schemas (i.e. the DataStructure in the Data Cube model) have a non-empty intersection in terms of measures and dimensions. Hereafter, we consider two different cases, namely how to determine the comparable measures of two given datasets and, in turn, how to determine which datasets are comparable with a given indicator.

Evaluation of comparable measures and dimensions. Given two libraries of datasets and their endpoints, the service `get_common_indicators` retrieves available and derivable indicators from each dataset and compares them.

```
1   get_common_indicators(endpoint1,endpoint2):
2       I1= get_all_indicators (endpoint1)
3       I2= get_all_indicators (endpoint2)
4       return I1∩I2
5
6   get_all_indicators (endpoint):
7       measures←get_measures(endpoint)
8       ∀ m ∈ measures:
9           indicators ←get_ind_from_mea(m,endpoint)
10      availableIndicators ←derive_all_indicators(indicators)
11      return availableIndicators
```

In detail, the service `get_all_indicators` firstly retrieves all the MeasureProperties from each library of datasets by executing this SPARQL query to the corresponding endpoint (line 7):

SELECT ?m ?dataset
WHERE {?dataset qb:structure ?s.
      ?s qb:component ?c.
      ?c qb:measure ?m.}

Then, for each measure m the service gets the corresponding KPIOnto indicator (see line 9) through the query:

SELECT ?ind
WHERE {<m> rdfs:isDefinedBy ?ind.}

Finally, the service calls the logic function `derive_all_indicators` (line 5), which is capable to derive all indicators that can be calculated from the available measures through mathematical manipulation. Once compatible measures are found, a similar check is made with respect to dimensions, i.e. firstly the dimensions related to each compatible measure are retrieved, and finally such sets are compared in order to find the common subset.

Let us consider the comparison of libraries $City_A$ and $City_B$. Indicators from the former are $I_A = \{kpi:Distance, kpi:TotalPopulation\}$. On the other hand, $City_B$ includes indicators $\{kpi:Distance\_Citizens, kpi:Distance\_Tourists, kpi:TotalPopulation\}$. By using the logical predicate `derive_all_indicators` on this last set, the reasoner infers that $I_B=\{kpi:Distance\_Citizens, kpi:Distance\_Tourists, kpi:TotalPopulation, kpi:Distance, kpi:AvgDistancePerCitizen\}$. Indeed, the last two indicators can be calculated from $kpi:Distance=kpi:Distance\_Citizens + kpi:Distance\_Tourists$ and $kpi:AvgDistancePerCitizen=\frac{kpi:Distance\_Citizens}{kpi:TotalPopulation}$. As a conclusion, the two libraries share the indicator set $I_A \cap I_B = \{kpi:Distance, kpi:TotalPopulation\}$. Please also note that without the explicit representation of formulas and logic reasoning on their structure, only TotalPopulation would have been obtained. Both indicators are comparable only through dimension $sdmx$-$dimension:timePeriod$. In particular, $kpi:Distance$ is measured by $City_A$ also along the user type dimension. This means that some manipulation (i.e. aggregation) must be performed on $City_A$ values before the indicator can be actually used for comparisons.

Search for datasets measuring a given indicator. Given an indicator, a list of dataset libraries and the corresponding endpoints, the service returns those datasets in which the indicator at hand is available or from which it can be calculated. The approach relies on the exploitation of KPIOnto definitions of indicator formulas, and Logic Programming functions capable to manipulate them. Firstly, for each library the following query is performed to determine if the indicator is explicitly provided by some dataset:

```
SELECT ?m ?dataset
WHERE {?dataset qb:structure ?s.
       ?s qb:component ?c.
       ?c qb:measure ?m.
       ?m rdfs:isDefinedBy <indicator>.}
```

In case the response is negative, the service (1) derives all possible alternative ways to calculate the indicator through the logic function get_formulas. Then (2) it searches into the libraries for combinations of datasets including those measures. Let us suppose to search for the indicator $kpi{:}AvgDistancePerCitizen$ in datasets of City$_A$ and City$_B$. Given that such an indicator is not directly available in any City, the service calls the get_formulas predicate, which returns two solutions, i.e. $s_1 = \frac{kpi{:}Distance\_Citizens}{kpi{:}TotalPopulation}$ and $s_2 = \frac{(kpi{:}Distance - kpi{:}Distance\_Tourists)}{kpi{:}TotalPopulation}$. Please note that this last is a rewriting of s_1, obtained by solving the formula $kpi{:}Distance = kpi{:}Distance\_Citizens + kpi{:}Distance\_Tourists$, with respect to the variable $kpi{:}Distance\_Citizens$. At step 2, each solution is tested against the libraries. Checking a solution means to verify, through queries like the one above, that every operand of the solution is measured by a dataset in the library at hand. As for City$_B$, solution s_1 can be used, as it includes both measure cityB:Distance_Residents (that corresponds to kpi:Distance_Citizens) and cityB:Population (corresponding to kpi:TotalPopulation). As for City$_A$, instead, no solution is valid, as it lacks both kpi:Distance_Citizens (needed by s_1) and kpi:Distance_Tourists (required by s_2):

Library	Formula	Measures
City$_A$	$\frac{kpi{:}Distance\_Citizens}{kpi{:}TotalPopulation}$	× kpi:Distance_Citizens
		✓ kpi:TotalPopulation←cityA:Population
City$_A$	$\frac{kpi{:}Distance - kpi{:}Distance\_Tourists}{kpi{:}TotalPopulation}$	✓ kpi:Distance←cityA:Distance
		× kpi:Distance_Tourists
		✓ kpi:TotalPopulation←cityA:Population
City$_B$	$\frac{kpi{:}Distance\_Citizens}{kpi{:}TotalPopulation}$	✓ kpi:Distance_Citizens←CityB:Distance_Residents
		✓ kpi:TotalPopulation←CityB:Population

The service reports as output, for each solution, the used formula and the available measures, specifying the corresponding mappings between the KPIOnto indicators and the specific MeasureProperty names, according to rdfs:isDefinedBy properties. Output includes also partial solutions (like the first two), in order to make users be aware of which specific measures are missing.

5   Discussion and Future Work

In this work, we discussed a knowledge-based approach to the representation and the comparisons of city performances referring to different urban settings, published as Linked Data and monitored through specific indicators. So far, KPIOnto has been used in a variety of applications, ranging from performance monitoring in the context of collaborative organizations, to serving as a knowledge model to support ontology-based data exploration of indicators [10].

As for RDF Data Cube, we note that some limitations make it not perfectly suited to a variety of real applications, mainly for its lack of proper support for the representation of dimension hierarchies. Some possible extensions have been already proposed in the Literature to overcome such limits (e.g., QB4OLAP [11]), that will be considered in future work. Furthermore, we are investigating to provide a more fine-grained comparison between datasets by means of a more comprehensive notion of comparability taking into account both schema and instance levels of datasets.

References

1. Kimball, R., Ross, M.: The Data Warehouse Toolkit: The Complete Guide to Dimensional Modeling, 2nd edn. Wiley, New York (2002)
2. Supply Chain Council: Supply chain operations reference model. SCC (2008)
3. Bosch, P., Jongeneel, S., Rovers, V., Neumann, H.M., Airaksinen, M., Huovila, A.: Deliverable 1.4. smart city kpis and related methodology. Technical report, CITYKeys (2016)
4. Horkoff, J., Barone, D., Jiang, L., Yu, E., Amyot, D., Borgida, A., Mylopoulos, J.: Strategic business modeling: representation and reasoning. Softw. Syst. Model. **13**(3), 1015–1041 (2014)
5. del Río-Ortega, A., Resinas, M., Cabanillas, C., Ruiz-Cortés, A.: On the definition and design-time analysis of process performance indicators. Inf. Syst. **38**(4), 470–490 (2013)
6. Buswell, S., Caprotti, O., Carlisle, D.P., Dewar, M.C., Gaetano, M., Kohlhase, M.: The open math standard. Technical report, version 2.0, The Open Math Society, 2004 (2004). http://www.openmath.org/standard/om20
7. Diamantini, C., Potena, D., Storti, E.: SemPI: a semantic framework for the collaborative construction and maintenance of a shared dictionary of performance indicators. Future Gener. Comput. Syst. **54**, 352–365 (2015)
8. SDMX: SDMX technical specification. Technical report (2013)
9. Cyganiak, R., Reynolds, D., Tennison, J.: The RDF data cube vocabulary. Technical report, World Wide Web Consortium (2014)
10. Diamantini, C., Potena, D., Storti, E.: Extended drill-down operator: digging into the structure of performance indicators. Concurr. Comput. Pract. Exper. **28**(15), 3948–3968 (2016)
11. Etcheverry, L., Vaisman, A., Zimányi, E.: Modeling and querying data warehouses on the semantic web using QB4OLAP. In: Bellatreche, L., Mohania, M.K. (eds.) DaWaK 2014. LNCS, vol. 8646, pp. 45–56. Springer, Cham (2014). doi:10.1007/978-3-319-10160-6_5

Analyzing Last Mile Delivery Operations in Barcelona's Urban Freight Transport Network

Burcu Kolbay[1]([✉]), Petar Mrazovic[2], and Josep Llus Larriba-Pey[1]

[1] DAMA-UPC Data Management, Universitat Politecnica de Catalunya,
C/Jordi Girona, 1 3 UPC Campus Nord, 08034 Barcelona, Spain
{burcu,larri}@ac.upc.edu
[2] Department of Software and Computer Systems,
Royal Institute of Technology, Stockholm, Sweden
mrazovic@kth.se
http://www.dama.upc.edu/en
http://www.kth.se

Abstract. Barcelona has recently started a new strategy to control and understand Last Mile Delivery, AreaDUM. The strategy is to provide freight delivery vehicle drivers with a mobile app that has to be used every time their vehicle is parked in one of the designated AreaDUM surface parking spaces in the streets of the city. This provides a significant amount of data about the activity of the freight delivery vehicles, their patterns, the occupancy of the spaces, etc.

In this paper, we provide a preliminary set of analytics preceded by the procedures employed for the cleansing of the dataset. During the analysis we show that some data blur the results and using a simple strategy to detect when a vehicle parks repeatedly in close-by parking slots, we are able to obtain different, yet more reliable results. In our paper, we show that this behavior is common among users with 80% prevalence. We conclude that we need to analyse and understand the user behaviors further with the purpose of providing predictive algorithms to find parking lots and smart routing algorithms to minimize traffic.

Keywords: Urban freight · Clustering · Partitioning Around Medoids · User behavior · Smart City · AreaDUM

1 Introduction

Barcelona is considered to be among the smartest cities in the planet. The IESE ranking [1] puts the city in position 33 with a significant amount of projects carried on. It is not necessarily the technology which makes Barcelona smart; the economy, environment, government, mobility, life and people are other indicators which help defining the city as smart.

Barcelona released an urban mobility plan for 2013/2018, where the need for a smart platform was pointed out in order to improve the efficiency, effectiveness and compatibility of freight delivery areas and the distribution of goods to reduce

© ICST Institute for Computer Sciences, Social Informatics and Telecommunications Engineering 2018
A. Longo et al. (Eds.): IISSC 2017/CN4IoT 2017, LNICST 189, pp. 13–22, 2018.
https://doi.org/10.1007/978-3-319-67636-4_2

possible incompatibilities/frictions with other urban uses [2]. Thus, in November 2015, the AreaDUM project was provided by public company *Barcelona Serveis Municipals (B:SM)* to serve the need [3,4].

AreaDUM (Area of Urban Distribution of Goods, Area de Distribucio Urbana de Mercaderies in catalan) intends to develop parking management in such a way that both freight delivery vehicle drivers and the city obtain a benefit. AreaDUM has several components and features:

- Uniquely identifies parking spaces indicated with zig-zag yellow lines in the streets of the city that can only be used by freight vehicles at certain times of the day (usually from 8:00 till 20:00).
- A maximum time to use the AreaDUM spaces (usually 30 min).
- A mobile app that every freight vehicle driver must install in their cellular.
- The enforcement for each vehicle driver to perform a check-in action with the mobile app every time their vehicle is parked in an AreaDUM space.
- It is forbidden to perform consecutive check-ins in the same Delivery Area.
- The analysis of the data collected.

In this paper, and based on the components of AreaDUM, we provide a set of analyses that we discuss in order to understand the user behaviors. The analyses show that the original data has a significant number of check-ins that behave in a special way, i.e. they are done in the same or close by locations to the original one, with different possible reasons. We detect those cases, analyse them and compute clusters of the parking actions, showing that the behaviour of the users is different from that one would expect with the complete dataset. Our conclusions show that there are significant differences among different quarters in the city, calling for further analytics that describe the actual use of the city and allow for a detailed understanding of each AreaDUM parking space and how they are re-dimensioned based on the data obtained.

The rest of the paper is organized as follows. In Sect. 2, we provide an account of the related work. In Sect. 3, we describe the data generated and used. In Sect. 4, we give an overview of the methods used. Then, in Sect. 5, the experiments and results are detailed. Finally, in Sect. 6, we conclude and make remarks about our future work.

2   Related Work

The demand for goods distribution increases proportional to the population, number of households, and development in tourism. There is a lot of research related to the management of urban freight in cities. Those include solutions for pollution, carbon creation, noise, safety, fuel consumption, etc. The main purposes are generally shaped around reducing travel distances (vehicle routing algorithms) and minimizing the number of delivery vehicles in the city [5,6].

Other pieces of work are focused on what restrictions should be applied to vehicle moves in order to control the congestion and pollution level [7]. One of the most common restriction is the time access restrictions for loading/unloading areas [8]. By finding optimal solutions for urban freight management, it is possible to reduce the pollution and traffic congestion, and minimizing fuel use and Carbon emissions. With this purpose, we believe that it is important to understand the vehicle drivers and manage their mobility for their satisfaction. We base our analysis in the observation of the user behaviors for loading/unloading trucks, rather than stablishing punishment policies for the drivers. Providing solutions comes after the problem detection and analysis. This is what we do in this paper, we observe the user behaviors, think about possible reasons of the behaviors and propose solutions in order to keep win-win strategies for the city.

3   Data

The data set used in this study was obtained through a web service which is used to export the data of the AreaDUM application (or SMS) developed by B:SM[1]. The time span of the available AreaDUM data sets ranges from January 1st, 2016 to July 15th, 2016. The sample data set consists of roughly 3.7 million observations described using 14 attributes. Some attributes are not relevant since they include information of the AreaDUM application itself. The most relevant attributes for each check-in, apart from the specific Delivery Area ID, are:

- Configuration ID, which tells us about the days when each Area can be used, the number of parking slots and their size, the amount of time a vehicle can be parked and the use times for similar Delivery Areas.
- Time, which tells us about the time, day of the week and date of the check-in.
- Plate number, which contains a unique encrypted ID for each vehicle.
- User ID, which links the vehicle with a company.
- Vehicle type, which describes the size and type of vehicle: truck, van, etc.
- Activity type, which describes whether the objective is to carry goods, or to perform street work, etc.
- District and Neighborhood ID, which tell us about the larger and smaller administrative geographical area of the AreaDUM parking slot.

After some data cleansing, we ended up with 14 attributes which include: Delivery Area ID, Plate Number, User ID, Vehicle Type, Activity Type, District ID, Neighborhood ID, Coordinate, Weekday, Date, Time.

4   Methods

One of the objectives of the paper is to understand the rough data provided in order to cleanse it if necessary. By exploring it, we noticed that there are a significant number of check-ins by the same vehicle ID, in the same or close by Delivery Areas during one day. This is an abnormal behavior because AreaDUM does not allow making consecutive check-ins in the same Delivery Area. However,

---

[1] The authors want to thank B:SM and, in particular the Innovation team, leaded by Carlos Morillo and Oscar Puigdollers for their support in this paper.

although consecutive check-ins in close by areas are not forbidden, it would be interesting to isolate them.

Thus, we first create a brand new attribute that we name *Circle ID*. The Circle ID will allow us to detect check-ins in close by areas. Thus, we will be able to isolate the abnormal check-ins from those of other vehicles, allowing the cleansing and the study of the those check-ins in an isolated way.

4.1   Creation of a Circle ID Attribute

The Circle ID attribute is needed since we want to group close loading/unloading areas by distance. Because of the square-shaped blocks in Barcelona, loading/unloading areas at the block corners are close to each other, and the maximum distance is 46 m among corners in "Eixample of Barcelona" by design in "Pla Cerda" from the XIX century.

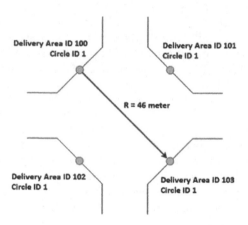

Fig. 1. Square-shaped Block and Location of Loading/Unloading Areas in the "Eixample" of "Pla Cerda"

We think that it does not make any sense for a user to iterate among the corners of a crossing of the "Pla Cerda" grid. It will very seldom happen that a user will go to the opposite corner of a crossing to make a new delivery since the distance is very short. In the case that they do iterate, we need to understand the underlying reason for this.

In Fig. 1, we can see that there 4 loading/unloading areas, and they have their corresponding *Delivery Area ID*s, whereas they have the same *Circle ID*. In order to achieve this, we calculated pair-wised *Haversine* distance among all loading/unloading areas in Barcelona. Haversine is the chosen method to approximate the earth as a sphere, since it works good both for really small and large distances [11].

The distance matrix is created using Haversine formula, where each row and column represents a *Delivery Area ID*. From this distance matrix, we extracted the pairs of Delivery Area IDs with distance less than or equal to 50 m. If the extracted pairs have a common element, we combined these pairs and removed the common one in order to have only unique elements. After the combination process, we check the distance between the first and the last element in the list. If their corresponding distance value in the distance matrix is less than or equal to 100 m, we keep the last element, otherwise we remove it. As a last step, we assigned the same id for the delivery areas which are located in the same group.

4.2   Clustering

The next step is to cluster the behaviour of the vehicles by Neighbourhood. The *Hopkins Statistics* are applied here as a beginning step to see if the data is clusterable. The value of 0.1829171 from Hopkins statistics showed us that we can reject the null hypothesis and conclude that the data set is significantly clusterable [9]. Then, a clustering algorithm was needed in order to group similar neighborhoods by hourly check-ins frequencies in Barcelona. Most of all the clustering techniques (e.g. k-means, Partitioning Around Medoids, CLARA, hierarchical, AGNES, DIANA, fuzzy, model-based, density-based and hybrid clustering) were used for a comparison on the accuracy of results in order to choose the best for our data.

4.3   The Partitioning Around Medoids (PAM) Clustering Algorithm

PAM is a clustering algorithm like k-means in such a way that it breaks the data into smaller groups which are called clusters, and then it tries to minimize the error [10]. The difference is that k-means works with centroids whereas PAM works with medoids[2]. K-means uses centroids as representatives and minimize total squared error. On the other hand, PAM uses the objects in dataset themselves as representatives. We use PAM instead of K-means since K-means is highly sensitive to outliers and it is not suitable for discovering clusters of very different size.

After k representative objects are arbitrarily selected, a *swap* operation is performed for each medoid and for each non-medoid, and it continues until there is no improvement in the quality of clustering. The cost function is the difference in absolute value of error that appears on a swap operation, and it has to be the lowest to be chosen. In a nutshell, the main goal of PAM is minimizing the sum of dissimilarities of the observations to their corresponding representative objects.

5   Experiments and Results

In our data set, attribute Configuration ID holds the rules for parking (i.e. which day, which hour and how many minutes users can use the delivery areas, etc.).

---

[2] A medoid is a representative object of a dataset or a cluster with a data set whose average dissimilarity to all the objects in the cluster is minimal.

Using this attribute, we are able to check if a recorded delivery happened in the right day, right time etc. The *disallowed repeated check-ins* where detected through this attribute.

The rationale that we understand for those repeated check-ins is as follows:

- Some vehicles are used in household or street work. The time required for the work takes longer than the maximum allowance, and the workers keep doing abnormal check-ins.
- There can be some local store owners who have their own vehicles for their own transport of goods. It is possible that they face the problem for finding a parking slot. The reason of this situation is a necessity instead of an occupation purpose.
- The users just use the spaces as free parking for different purposes like having breakfast after a delivery, etc.

Type of Activities for Disallowed Repeated Check-Ins. In our data set, column Activity ID represents the activity type of the delivery. There are 6 different types: Public Work, Carpentry, Installation, Furniture, Transport, and Others. The results presented in this section confirm the types of reasons assumed above for repeated check-ins, as shown in Table 1.

Table 1. The percentage of activity types' disallowed repeated check-ins

Type of activity	Disallowed repeated check-ins
Public work	30.8%
Carpentry	7.0%
Installation	27.2%
Furniture	1.8%
Transport	19.9%
Others	13.3%

The results show that Public Work and Installation have higher percentages of disallowed check-ins than the others. This shows that professionals who spend time in specific locations, need some type of parking space that allows them managing their tempos in a better way. Transport also show quite a high number of disallowed check-ins, which may well be showing the case for local store owners who repeat their check-ins to preserve their parking space.

5.1   The Effect of Disallowed Repeated Check-Ins

In any case, being disallowed or not, the repeated check-ins in close-by Delivery Areas can be removed using the Circle ID explained above.

The new *Circle ID* that we computed created a total of 1484 circle areas, whereas we still have 2038 different delivery areas. The combination of both IDs allowed us for the analysis in the following paragraphs.

In this section, we present the effect of disallowed repeated check-ins removal using *Circle ID*. Table 2 shows the percentage of disallowed repeated check-ins per each district in Barcelona. In other words, these are the percentages of data we lose, in case that we remove the disallowed repeated check-ins occurred in the same circle.

Table 2. The percentage of disallowed repeated check-ins

District name	Percentage of data lost
Ciutat Vella	27.5%
Eixample	27.4%
Sants Montjuic	29.4%
Les Corts	27.6%
Sarria Sant Gervasi	29.2%
Gracia	28.9%
Horta Guinardo	30.4%
Sant Andreu	28.1%
Sant Marti	28.2%

After we see the percentages of disallowed repeated check-ins, it is easy to say that there must be some effects on possible preliminary analyses. We want to see how the clustering results will change in the case that we re-cluster neighborhoods by hourly check-ins frequency.

Neighborhood Clustering: Before vs. After. In our analysis, there are 43 target neighborhoods which are associated with 9 different neighborhoods in Barcelona. We do PAM clustering two times. One for the original data set Before removing disallowed repeated check-ins and one After disallowing repeated check-ins.

For the clustering Before removing the disallowed check-ins, PAM clustering selected two Neighborhood medoids among the other observations in data. After that, PAM assigned each observation to the nearest medoid. These two neighborhoods are the representative objects which minimize the sum of dissimilarities of the observations to their closest representative objects.

Figure 2 shows the clusters obtained by PAM. The plot on the left of Fig. 2 is a 2 dimensional clustering plot which is done by *Principal Component Analysis*. It represents how much of the data variability is explained by a reduced dimension of principal components which are not correlated to each other. The plot on the right of Fig. 2 represents the silhouette widths which shows how the observations

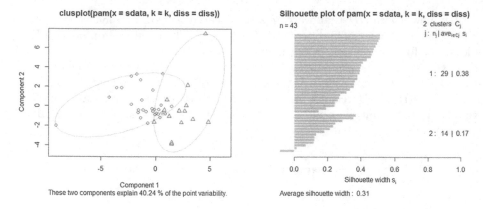

Fig. 2. PAM Clustering Results for the dataset before the disallowed check-ins were removed.

are well clustered. At the bottom of this plot, there is one horizontal line that located on the left side, which represents a misclustered object.

Two clusters are determined by PAM:

- Cluster 1 consists of 29 neighborhoods from 9 districts,
- Cluster 2 consists of 14 neighborhoods from 7 districts.

All neighborhoods from 2 districts (i.e. Gracia and Sant Andreu) are located into Cluster 1, whereas the other districts' neighborhoods are divided into two clusters.

Figure 3 shows the clusters after removing the disallowed repeated check-ins. In this case, the number of clusters increased to 9, and it shows us that variation is significant. On the left side of Fig. 3, there are some silhouette width values of 0, and these clusters have only 1 observation in their clusters. We can basically say that they are both representative objects for themselves. The ones who are

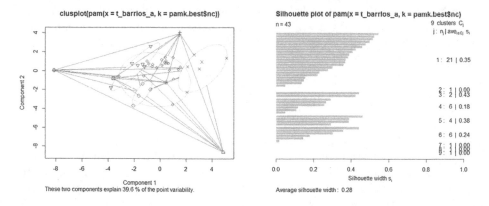

Fig. 3. PAM clustering results for data without disallowed repeated check-ins

located alone in the clusters tell us that these neighborhoods are quite different by hourly check-ins frequency than the others after the removal of disallowed repeated check-ins.

Nine clusters are determined by PAM:

- Cluster 1 consists of 21 neighborhoods from 7 districts,
- Cluster 2 consists of 1 neighborhood,
- Cluster 3 consists of 2 neighborhoods from 2 districts,
- Cluster 4 consists of 6 neighborhoods from 4 districts,
- Cluster 5 consists of 4 neighborhoods from 4 districts,
- Cluster 6 consists of 6 neighborhoods from 3 districts,
- Cluster 7 consists of 1 neighborhood,
- Cluster 8 consists of 1 neighborhood,
- Cluster 9 consists of 1 neighborhood.

Proliferation of Disallowed Repeated Check-Ins. Up until this point, we have detected *disallowed repeated check-ins*, the effect of their removal, and the activity types which cause this situation. We know that 28% of check-ins corresponds to this behavior. The only thing we do not know is that how common it is among the deliverers. Figure 4 shows the results for this. The disallowed check-in practice has grown significantly as time passes, which means that, possibly, social networks or communication among drivers have worked very well.

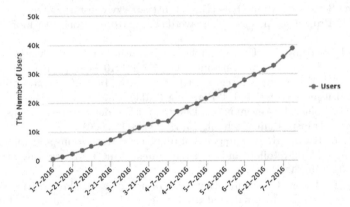

Fig. 4. The proliferation of disallowed repeated check-ins among deliverers

6 Conclusion

Among different components of urban mobility, freight transport is usually considered as the least sustainable. This naturally calls for new technologies, such as mobile data management and analytics, to achieve more efficient freight distribution systems, without the need for large investments or sophisticated sensor technologies. However, in smart and citizen-oriented cities, it is also important to understand the citizens reactions to new technologies. Therefore, in this paper, we focused on deliverers as the main actors in the urban freight transport scheme recently deployed in the city of Barcelona.

We showed that people often look for different ways to bypass the intended use of new technology for their needs, and it can cause undesired effects. In our experimental study, we demonstrated the scope and significance of non-compliance of the parking regulations. For example, after filtering out the disallowed check-ins, we lost 28% of our data, and consequently increased the number of clusters from 2 to 9. Interestingly, we showed that *Public Work* and *Installation* activities which can be related to city governance, are usually associated with larger number of disallowed check-ins. Finally, one of the most important results of our study is the statistical proof that non-compliance of the introduced regulations is not an exception, but a common behavior. For the future work, the city governance needs to solve the issue using different *Configuration ID* for local store owners' vehicles, assigning new parking lots, or categorizing the parking lots into different purposes (e.g. short visit delivery, daily permission etc.).

References

1. New York Edges Out London as the World's "Smartest" City. http://ieseinsight.com/doc.aspx?id=1819&ar=6&idioma=2
2. Ajuntament de Barcelona. http://ajuntament.barcelona.cat/en/
3. Barcelona Serveis de Municipals (B:SM). https://www.bsmsa.cat/es/
4. AreaDUM Project. https://www.areaverda.cat/en/operation-with-mobile-phone/areadum/
5. Hwang, T., Ouyang, Y.: Urban freight truck routing under stochastic congestion and emission considerations. Sustainability 7(6), 6610–6625 (2015)
6. Reisman, A., Chase, M.: Strategies for Reducing the Impacts of Last-Mile Freight in Urban Business Districts. UT Planning (2011)
7. Yannis, G., Golias, J., Antoniou, C.: Effects of urban delivery restrictions on traffic movements. Transp. Plan. Technol. 29(4), 295–311 (2006)
8. Quak, H., de Koster, R.: The impacts of time access restrictions and vehicle weight restrictions on food retailers and the environment. Eur. J. Transp. Infrastruct. Res. (Print) 131–150 (2006)
9. Banerjee, A., Dave, R.N.: Validating clusters using the Hopkins statistic. In: Proceedings of the IEEE International Conference on Fuzzy Systems, vol. 1, pp. 149–153 (2004)
10. Kaufman, L., Rousseeuw, P.J.: Clustering by means of medoids. In: Dodge, Y. (ed.) Statistical Data Analysis Based on L1 Norm, pp. 405–416 (1987)
11. Shumaker, B.P., Sinnott, R.W.: Astronomical computing: 1. Computing under the open sky. 2. Virtues of the haversine. Sky Telesc. 68, 158–159 (1984)

A System for Privacy-Preserving Analysis
of Vehicle Movements

Gianluca Lax[✉], Francesco Buccafurri, Serena Nicolazzo, Antonino Nocera,
and Filippo Ermidio

DIIES, University Mediterranea of Reggio Calabria, Via Graziella,
Località Feo di Vito, 89122 Reggio Calabria, Italy
lax@unirc.it

Abstract. In this paper, we deal with the problem of acquiring statistics on the movements of vehicles in a given environment yet preserving the identity of drivers involved. To do this, we have designed a system based on an embedded board, namely Beaglebone Black, equipped with a Logitech C920 webcam with H.256 hardware encoder. The system uses JavaANPR to acquire snapshots of cars and recognize license plates. Acquired plate numbers are anonymized by the use of hash functions to obtain plate digests, and the use of a salt prevents plate number discovery from its digest (by dictionary or brute force attacks). A recovery algorithm is also run to correct possible errors in plate number recognition. Finally, these anonymized data are used to extract several statistics, such as the time of permanence of a vehicle in the environment.

Keywords: Privacy · Vehicle movements · Beaglebone · JavaANPR

1 Introduction

In the smart city's evolution, embedded systems have played a smaller but no less important role [1,2]. Daily life is full of these systems, we do not see and/or notice them but they exist and they are growing in number: ATMs, washing machines, navigators, credit cards, temperature sensors and so on. Data automatically collected by embedded devices (e.g., sensors) has a great value: typically, such data are processed and transformed into information (knowledge) thanks to which we can make decisions that may or not require human participation.

In this paper, we present a system able to collect data of vehicle movements that can be used for analysis purposes. The system is designed to overcome possible privacy concerns arising from collecting and processing of data linked to one individual (i.e., vehicle driver) by the license plate of the vehicle, a problem very relevant in the literature [3–8]. In particular, we created a license plate recognition system to track vehicles entering or leaving a particular place. Plates are not stored in plaintext: an approach based on salt and hash is adopted to transform plain plate into an apparently random string. However, the approach is such that the same plate will be transformed into the same string each time

© ICST Institute for Computer Sciences, Social Informatics and Telecommunications Engineering 2018
A. Longo et al. (Eds.): IISSC 2017/CN4IoT 2017, LNICST 189, pp. 23–28, 2018.
https://doi.org/10.1007/978-3-319-67636-4_3

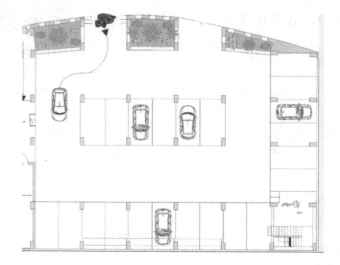

Fig. 1. An example of the system utilization.

the vehicle is tracked. This allows us to enable statistical analysis on stored data yet maintaining anonymity of drivers and vehicles.

The rest of the paper is organized as follows: in the next section, we describe the system architecture, the hardware components and the executed protocols; in Sect. 3, we discuss advantages and limitations of our proposal and draw our conclusions.

2 System Architecture and Implementation

In this section, we describe the architecture of our system and the algorithms used to solve the problem.

In Fig. 1, we sketch a simple example of the use of our system. We consider a closed environment, a parking in the figure, where cars enter and exit periodically and we need to know some statistics about users' habit, for example, the minimum, maximum and average time of permanence of a vehicle in this area. An additional constraint is that the solution has not to reveal any information about any specific vehicle, for privacy reasons. Consequently, solutions based on RFID or similar technologies to recognize a vehicle cannot be adopted.

In the figure, a device placed at the enter/exit of the parking is also shown (it is represented as a simple camera). This device is the system proposed in this paper to solve the problem. Our system is built on the BeagleBone platform [9], a single-board computer equipped with open-source hardware. We used the Beaglebone Black version, a low-cost high-performance ARM device with full support for embedded Linux. It is a perfect device for interfacing to low-level hardware, while providing high-level interface in the form of GUIs and network services. With a price of about 50$ and a clock speed of 1GHz, it is a cheap solution capable of significant data processing tasks. The BeagleBone Black used in

Fig. 2. The BeagleBone and the Logitech C920 webcam.

our proposal is equipped with a high resolution Logitech C920 webcam (Fig. 2), which contains a H.256 hardware encoder to take the workload away from BeagleBone's processor. The Video4Linux2 (typically called V4L2), a framework tightly integrated with the Linux kernel, provides drivers necessary for the webcam. Our BeagleBone runs a software implementing the data processing logic that allows us to obtain privacy preserving logs of vehicle entry and exit. In particular, each time a vehicle enters or leaves the environment, Algorithm 1 is executed.

In the initialization phase, the system randomly generates a 256-bit string, named *salt*, and allocates a persistent memory area, named *log*, in which statistics on vehicles movements are stored (typically, this is a file). When a vehicle enters or leaves the environment, a picture is captured by the webcam and, then, a plate number recognition procedure is run (Line 1). This procedure uses JavaANPR [10], an automatic number plate recognition software, which implements algorithmic and mathematical principles from the field of artificial intelligence, machine vision and neural networks. In case the vehicle is entering the environment, the system computes the hash of the string obtained by concatenating the salt and the binary representation of the plate number (Line 3).

Concerning this operation, we observe that several hash functions can be used in this task: for our purpose, we need that it is not possible to find the salt or p from the knowledge of more hashes. In our implementation, we opted for the SHA-1 algorithm, which is a widely used hash function producing a 160-bit hash value [11]. Indeed, although SHA-1 has been found to suffer from some vulnerabilities that would discourage its use as a cryptographic hash function, in our application such vulnerabilities are not critic. Moreover, its efficiency and effectiveness to verify data integrity, make it a good solution for our necessity.

Then, the algorithm proceeds by storing into the log a tuple containing the type of access of the vehicle (enter of exit), the timestamp of this access, and the result of the hash computation, named p^* (Line 4). This tuple is one of the records that can be elaborated to extract statistics about vehicle accesses. Observe that, no reference to the actual plate number is stored, but only the hash of this number. Moreover, the use of a *salt* [12] in the hash computation protects against dictionary attacks versus a list of password hashes and against pre-computed rainbow table attacks, aiming at guessing the plate number.

Consider now the case in which a vehicle is leaving the environment. In the optimistic case in which the plate number recognition task can be performed

---

Algorithm 1. *Log creation*

Constant   *salt*: a 256-bit string
Constant   log: a persistent memory area
Input   *entry*: a boolean (true in case of vehicle entry, false otherwise)
Variable T: the current timestamp
Variable p: a number plate
Variable p^*: a 64-bit string
Variable P: the set of number plates differing at most 1 digit from p
1: $p =$ plate number recognition
2: **if** *entry* = true **then**
3:      $p^* = \mathcal{H}(salt \parallel p)$
4:      append $\langle entry, T, p^* \rangle$ into LOG
5: **else**
6:      create P from p
7:      **for all** $p \in P$ **do**
8:          $p^* = \mathcal{H}(salt \parallel p)$
9:          **if** p^* is in LOG **then**
10:              append $\langle entry, T, p^* \rangle$ into LOG
11:              **return**
12:          **end if**
13:      **end for**
14:      append $\langle entry, T, -1 \rangle$ into LOG
15: **end if**

---

with no error (i.e., the recognized number p coincides with the actual number of the plate), then it would be sufficient to repeat the operation above and storing into the log the information *exit* instead of *entry*. However, it is possible that some errors occur in plate number recognition. Consequently, we included in the algorithm a procedure to mitigate the consequences derived from this error. Specifically, the first operation done is to compute the set P (Line 6), composed of all plate numbers differing from p at most of 1 digit.

Now, for each element p of the set P, the hash p^* is computed as done above (Line 8) and a search for this value in the logs related to previous vehicle entries is carried out (Line 9). If a match is found, then the tuple containing the information about the exit of the vehicle, the current timestamp, and the result of the hash computation p^* is stored and the algorithm ends (Lines 10 and 11). In words, this operation allows the system to identify the right matching between the vehicle entry and exit (recall that the actual plate number is never recorded – thus, this task is not trivial), even when at most 1 digit of the plate number is wrongly recognized.

Finally, in case no matching is found, the information that an unidentified vehicle (this is coded by using -1 as plate number) is leaving the environment, is stored (Line 14).

At the end of the monitoring period, the log will contain a list of accesses of vehicles to the environment, together with the access timestamp and an *anonymous* reference to the number plate.

This list can be used to infer several statistics about the vehicle accesses, such as the minimum or maximum permanence period of a vehicle in the environment (how to calculate such statistics from this list is a trivial exercise and is not discussed here).

3 Discussion and Conclusion

In this section, we briefly discuss some aspects related to our proposal that have been neglected for space limitations. We designed and implemented a BeagleBone-based system to monitor vehicle entry to and exit from an environment with the purpose of maintaining a privacy-preserving log of these accesses. By this log, it is possible to calculate statistics about the period of presence of a vehicle in this environment (for example, the minimum or maximum permanence). As in a pervasive environment there is no knowledge about vehicles entering the environment, the statistics described above cannot be obtained through a solution different from the one proposed in this paper, if the constraint of not storing any number plate has to be guaranteed. Indeed, the only (usable) identifier is the plate number because the pervasiveness of the scenario inhibits the adoption of a solution based on the use of RFID technology or similar (it is unrealistic to provide any vehicle with an RFID tag).

In our proposal, no plate number is stored in clear, in such a way that any attack on the storage device (by a malware, for example) cannot infer any information about the plate number. Moreover, the use of the SHA-1 algorithm and the salt prevents an attacker to guess the stored plate number. It is worth noting that the well-known (collision and pre-image) vulnerabilities of SHA-1 in our system do not give an attacker any advantage. Indeed, an attack should try a brute force attack on a 256-bit string to guess the salt, and this is currently considered unfeasible.

Another important aspect is that we cannot assume the operation of plate number recognition is carried out with no error. In our proposal, the knowledge about the plate number (or better, its hash) of the vehicles already present in the environment is used to guess the correct plate number in case of recognition error. In our proposal, we limit to 1 the number of errors recoverable (i.e., we guess a plate number only when the recognized plate number differs from the actual one of at most 1 digit). Observe that, this requires to generate and test (recall Lines 6–13 of Algorithm 1) a very limited number of possible plate numbers: this number depends on the country and, for many EU countries, it is about 115. As the computation of SHA-1 is an efficient task [13], the running time of the algorithm is also very limited (much less than 1 s). Concerning this aspect, a preliminary experimental evaluation (which is only summarized here for space constraint) reported that on average 73% plate numbers are recognized with no error, and that in 98% cases the recognition task produced at most 1 digit error (we recall that our algorithm is designed in such a way to tolerate 1-digit errors). This allows us to state that the statistics produced starting from the data collected by our system can be considered quite accurate, as in 98% cases, the matching between entering and leaving cars is correctly carried out.

A possible improvement of this study, which is left as a future work, is a large-scale testing of the system in more *complex* environments, where the presence of highly dynamic accesses and worse conditions (for example, of illumination) may result in a worsening of the plate number recognition task and, consequently, in a general detriment of the system performance. A second improvement regards the relatively naive binary strategy of assigning label unknown to an exiting car not matching any entered car. Specifically, assigning probabilities for which car exits could be a significant improvement especially as these uncertainties could be reduced with multiple returns of the same vehicle. Finally, another improvement is related to the use of different and possibly more effective (than JavaANPR) techniques for plate number recognition, in order to further increase the overall performance of the system.

References

1. Filipponi, L., Vitaletti, A., Landi, G., Memeo, V., Laura, G., Pucci, P.: Smart city: An event driven architecture for monitoring public spaces with heterogeneous sensors. In: 2010 Fourth International Conference on Sensor Technologies and Applications (SENSORCOMM), pp. 281–286. IEEE (2010)
2. Merlino, G., Bruneo, D., Distefano, S., Longo, F., Puliafito, A., Al-Anbuky, A.: A smart city lighting case study on an openstack-powered infrastructure. Sensors **15**(7), 16314–16335 (2015)
3. Hoh, B., Iwuchukwu, T., Jacobson, Q., Work, D., Bayen, A.M., Herring, R., Herrera, J.C., Gruteser, M., Annavaram, M., Ban, J.: Enhancing privacy and accuracy in probe vehicle-based traffic monitoring via virtual trip lines. IEEE Trans. Mob. Comput. **11**(5), 849–864 (2012)
4. Li, H., Dán, G., Nahrstedt, K.: Portunes: privacy-preserving fast authentication for dynamic electric vehicle charging. In: 2014 IEEE International Conference on Smart Grid Communications (SmartGridComm), pp. 920–925. IEEE (2014)
5. Wu, Q., Domingo-Ferrer, J., González-Nicolá, Ú.: Balanced trustworthiness, safety, and privacy in vehicle-to-vehicle communications. IEEE Trans. Veh. Technol. **59**(2), 559–573 (2010)
6. Zhang, T., Delgrossi, L.: Vehicle Safety Communications: Protocols, Security, and Privacy, vol. 103. Wiley, Hoboken (2012)
7. Buccafurri, F., Lax, G., Nicolazzo, S., Nocera, A.: Comparing twitter and facebook user behavior: privacy and other aspects. Comput. Hum. Behav. **52**, 87–95 (2015)
8. Buccafurri, F., Lax, G., Nocera, A., Ursino, D.: Discovering missing me edges across social networks. Inf. Sci. **319**, 18–37 (2015)
9. BeagleBoard: Beagle Board Black Website (2016). http://beagleboard.org/BLACK
10. JavaANPR: Automatic Number Plate Recognition System (2016). http://javaanpr.sourceforge.net
11. Wikipedia: SHA-1 – Wikipedia, The Free Encyclopedia (2016). https://en.wikipedia.org/wiki/SHA-1
12. Wikipedia: Salt (cryptography) – Wikipedia, The Free Encyclopedia (2016). https://en.wikipedia.org/wiki/Salt_(cryptography)
13. Gosselin-Lavigne, M.A., Gonzalez, H., Stakhanova, N., Ghorbani, A.A.: A performance evaluation of hash functions for IP reputation lookup using bloom filters. In: 2015 10th International Conference on Availability, Reliability and Security (ARES), pp. 516–521. IEEE (2015)

Deploying Mobile Middleware for the Monitoring of Elderly People with the Internet of Things: A Case Study

Alessandro Fiore[✉], Adriana Caione, Daniele Zappatore, Gianluca De Mitri, and Luca Mainetti

Department of Innovation Engineering, University of Salento,
Via Monteroni 165, 73100 Lecce, Italy
{alessandro.fiore,adriana.caione,luca.mainetti}@unisalento.it,
{danielemario.zappatore,gianluca.demitri}@studenti.unisalento.it

Abstract. The ageing population and related diseases represent some of the most relevant challenges in the healthcare domain. All that will lead to an increasing demand of innovative solutions in order to guarantee a healthy and safe lifestyle to the elderly. In fact, many researchers are studying the use of Internet of Things (IoT) technologies in the e-health field. In this paper we report a case study where a locale middleware for portable devices has been used to facilitate the development of IoT mobile application in this respect, allowing the communication among different on board sensing technologies. The mobile middleware is built on top of the WoX (Web of Topics) platform and quickly permits the deployment of innovation services thanks to its abstraction and user centric model. A validation test bed involving 31 elderly people living in Lecce (Italy) has been carried out for the monitoring of their activities, mainly those connected to positioning and motility both in indoor and outdoor scenarios. Our approach has demonstrated a practical way to replace obtrusive monitoring technique (typical of caregivers) with unobtrusive ones, in order to obtain proactive intervention strategies for a smart city

Keywords: IoT · WoX · Middleware · Smart environment · Behavior analysis

1 Introduction

In the last years, the increase of aged people with chronic diseases will lead to a growing demand for support digital services. It is estimated that 50% of the population in Europe will be over 60 years old in 2040, while in the USA one in every six citizens will be over 65 years old in 2020 [1]. In addition, people over 75 years usually require continuous monitoring. For this reason, it is necessary to propose new solutions for healthcare that especially guarantee prevention at different levels of intervention and not only treatment of diseases.

So different e-health experiments and projects have started, and the use of the Internet of Things (IoT) paradigm is playing a key role [2]. In fact, IoT integrates all kinds of sensing, identification, communication, networking and information management devices and systems, and seamlessly links all the people and things according to their

© ICST Institute for Computer Sciences, Social Informatics and Telecommunications Engineering 2018
A. Longo et al. (Eds.): IISSC 2017/CN4IoT 2017, LNICST 189, pp. 29–36, 2018.
https://doi.org/10.1007/978-3-319-67636-4_4

interests, so that anybody – at anytime and anywhere – through any device and media, can access any provided information from objects and people to obtain services more efficiently. Currently, the IoT concept is associated with the introduction of an architectural layer that integrates the data provided from many heterogeneous sources [3] (for hardware, software architecture and communication protocol used). This architectural layer is called "IoT middleware" and, besides the integration of data, it is also involved in many other IoT aspects (from networking and communication to security and context management). The union between e-health application and IoT technologies is promising to address the challenges faced by the healthcare sector. For instance, the patients of a healthcare service can be tracked and monitored by using the ubiquitous identification, sensing and communication capacities. Exploiting the global connectivity of the IoT, this information can be collected, managed and analyzed more efficiently. Furthermore, information for healthcare service can be directly provided by patient's mobile devices (smartphones, tablets, wearable devices) through Internet or IoT access (WiFi, 3G, LTE, Bluetooth, ANT, ZigBee, LoRa, etc.), guaranteeing security and authentication policy. In other words, the IoT technologies will enable the transformation of healthcare service from caregiver-centric to patient-centric, make it more efficient, proactive and ubiquitous.

In this paper, we report on how a local model-driven middleware is used to forward incoming information from patient's mobile devices toward an IoT platform in order to monitor the elderly people activities. Furthermore, the benefits of this approach are discussed and compared to other existing systems.

The paper is organized as follows: Sect. 2 briefly reports on the key related work in the area of e-health and IoT. Section 3 provides readers with a brief introduction to the WoX and L-WoX architecture, and the model on which the platform is based. Section 4 demonstrates the middleware working on a real case study in the context of a research project. Finally, Sect. 5 summarizes our key messages and sketches future research directions.

2 Related Work

In the last years, several IoT solutions have been proposed. For lack of space, in this section we limit our attention to IoT middleware applied to e-health services.

Linksmart [4] is a general-purpose middleware and it has already been tested in the e-health field as a tool to allow the easy integration of heterogeneous devices in one solution. The authors illustrate how their solution aims to solve the complexity of a pervasive environment in order to support medical care routine of patients at home. The SAI middleware [5], enabling the development of context-aware applications, is also used for an e-healthcare solution. In fact the middleware is used in a reference application scenario for patient conditions monitoring, alarm detection and policy-based handling. In [6], a solution for tracking the daily life activities, by using mobile devices and cloud computing services, is discussed. The system permits to collect heterogeneous information from sensors located in the house and share them in the cloud. The system monitors the elderly people and generates reminders for scheduled activities along with alerts for critical situations to caregivers and family members, so reducing the health expenditures. In [7], an IoT based architecture for providing healthcare services to elderly and incapacitate individuals is proposed. As the underlying technology for implementing this architecture, 6LoWPAN is used for active communications, and radio frequency identification (RFID) and near-field communications (NFC) are used for passive communications. Another platform based on the IoT is proposed in [8]. This platform resolves different limitations (for example interoperability, security, the streaming quality of service). Its feasibility has been verified by installing an IoT-based health gateway on a desktop computer as reference implementation. A solution for monitoring patients with specific diseases such as diabetes using mobile devices is discussed in [7]. This system provides continuous monitoring and real time services, collecting the information from healthcare and monitoring devices located in the home environment and connected to mobile devices. Always in this area, in [9] is discussed the potential benefits of using m-IoT in non-invasive glucose level sensing and the potential m-IoT based architecture for diabetes management.

The above quoted related work is more focused on the technological aspects and they do not seem to pay a primary attention to the user's needs. Despite them, the advantage of the solution we propose is directly connected to the model-driven approach due to a user centered design. The user, in this case the patients' needs have guided, since the beginning, the design process in order to easily develop unobtrusive scenarios starting from geriatric parameters.

3   WoX and L-WoX Model and Reference Architecture

Web of Topics (WoX) [10, 11] is a model-based middleware for the IoT, specifically aimed at minimizing the language distance between people (end users, developers) and technology, while at the same time abstracting the multifaceted complexity of the considered IoT hardware and communication protocols.

Based on a hierarchical publish/subscribe approach, where every entity within the WoX conceptual framework can also be considered as a broker for other WoX entities, the Web of Topics makes the development of scalable applications easier by hiding the heterogeneity of the underlying IoT communication protocols, thus acting as an intermediate abstraction layer between the Web of Things (WoT) and consumer applications (Fig. 1). In particular, a WoX entity can generically refer to a wide range of both IoT hardware nodes and consumer applications (varying from mere single-user applications to enterprise systems for machine learning and Big Data Analytics), and it can be modeled as a set of {role; topic} couples. WoX delegates to entities the responsibility of interacting with topics, both in terms of capabilities towards a given topic (which is equivalent to providing a service) and needs (which is equivalent to requesting a service). In this context, the role concept is used to express the entity's technological (source/ executor/function) and collaborative (capability/need) dimensions within the considered scenario.

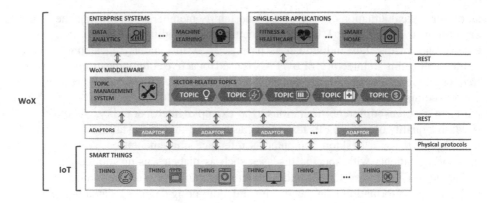

Fig. 1. WoX reference model

The topic concept, which is at the heart of the WoX approach, is used instead as a carrier for meaningful information concerning IoT capabilities exchanged between entities acting as providers and consumers. Furthermore, WoX topics can be grouped into three macro-domains:

- Cloud WoX, which includes all the topics residing in Cloud-based environments;
- Local WoX (L-WoX), which includes all the topics residing on mobile devices;
- Embedded WoX (M-WoX), which includes all the topics residing on embedded systems as, for example, wearable devices, micro-controllers, actuators, weather stations, etc.

Moreover, each topic consists of:

- A feature of interest (e.g., *temperature*, which refers to the temperature measured in a given place).
- A specific URI-identified location associated with the previously mentioned feature of interest (e.g., *italy:apulia:lecce:school:lab:desk1*, which refers to a desk situated in the science laboratory of an ordinary high school in Lecce, Apulia, Italy).
- The current value of such feature (e.g., *64 °C*, referring to the temperature example), which can be updated by any entity capable of providing additional information.

Any concrete or virtual property of the domain that is perceivable, definable, measurable or controllable – from raw sensor data to more abstract concepts, such as mathematical functions or human behaviors – can be used as a feature. Since WoX entities are allowed to decide whether forwarding topic updates to parent entities or not, entities at the edge of the architecture will deal with relatively few, very specific topics, while entities near the core retain a higher level of knowledge through their access to more abstract topics. In particular, the L-WoX middleware, being an extension of the cloud WoX platform, replicates the topic-based, model-driven approach of the Web of Topics on a local level, and manage the lifecycle of topic instances available for any WoX-enabled application running on mobile devices. It also mediates the communication between different on-board sensing technologies (with their heterogeneous, native APIs) and client applications through a set of plugin adaptors used to update specific topics with the incoming data. As a consequence of this approach, topic management responsibilities are effectively distributed among the involved nodes, thus turning mobile devices into aggregators for L-WoX entities. Furthermore, in several circumstances it may also be more efficient to keep low-level topics locally on the device, such as:

- Multiple mobile apps querying or updating the same shared topic;
- Multiple mobile apps referring to different topics, which are updated by the same on-board sensor.

4   Case Study: The H2020 City4Age Project

The City4Age project [12, 13] is a research project co-funded by the European Commission under the H2020 program that utilizes data from smart cities and ad-hoc sensors for the prevention of Mild Cognitive Impairment (MCI) and frailty of aged people. In particular, behavior change detection and 1-to-1 communication for IoT-enhanced intervention are some of the project's key features, following two main areas of strategic importance for the project:

- **Social dimension:** through the involvement of urban communities in conjunction with health services, smart cities can provide an invaluable support to the growing number of families facing Mild Cognitive Impairment (MCI) and frailty of the elderly, especially in these times of demographic imbalance and ageing populations afflicting most of the European countries. Prevention of MCI and frailty-related risks through early detection of dangerous situations and timely interventions will play a pivotal role in guaranteeing, in the least-obtrusive possible way, the well-being of the elderly people, as well as providing a more empathic communication between the social ICT services and the involved people.
- **Technological dimension:** City4Age pursues the creation of a highly-innovative framework of already existing technical components – such as wearable and mobile devices, sensor networks, systems for data analytics and machine learning – in order to collect large amounts of potentially heterogeneous data pertaining individuals that will be used, after several processing phases, to identify large segments of population at risk as well as to closely monitor few individuals, thus promoting more effective observing procedures and proactive interventions. This requires the ability to assign a geriatric meaning to the raw data gathered by the sensors, and to infer knowledge about the monitored subjects and their behaviors over the time.

The Lecce's pilot for the City4Age project, which involves the cooperation of 31 volunteer individuals of proper age and situation, focuses on monitoring their activities, with particular attention paid to those features connected to positioning and motility both in indoor and outdoor scenarios, and demonstrates a practical way to replace obtrusive monitoring techniques (typical of caregivers) with unobtrusive ones (typical of the IoT context), while at the same time achieving a high level of proactive intervention strategies for a smart city.

For the Lecce's pilot, an IoT Android application, enabling the communication among different on board sensing technologies (accelerometers, GPS, etc.) and paired sensors (SensorTag, smart plug, BLE - Bluetooth Low Energy - beacons, etc.), has been developed on top of a local middleware (L-WoX), which is part of the Web of Topics platform and allows a fast deployment of innovative services thanks to its abstraction and user-centric model. The main objective of the developed architecture is to turn the smartphone into a gateway between the environment and the rest of the WoX platform, collecting motility and positioning events related to a person that is moving inside a BLE-monitored location.

In the considered case study (as exemplified in Fig. 2, which describes the overall architecture of the WoX ecosystem), the user updates a specific topic moving close to a beacon (e.g., the *MOVING_START* or *MOVING_STOP* topics), which sends to the user's smartphone a BLE message (referring to the correct feature of the topic) telling any WoX-compliant listener its current position (e.g., the *room-id*). The L-WoX service installed on the smartphone is then able to detect the BLE beacon and forward the local topic information to any local mobile app subscribed to the considered topic. Furthermore, the mobile app can update (through 4G connection) the corresponding global topic located in the Cloud, where the WoX module redirects the data to several repositories for temporary event persistence, according to their macro-category. Then, a specifically designed Data Aggregation Module, which continuously listens for WoX Topic updates, extracts and aggregates the sensors' data on a daily basis in order to generate a set of high-level measures (e.g., *TM*, which refers to the *total amount of time spent moving* by the monitored subject) indicating how the user is performing according to certain criteria.

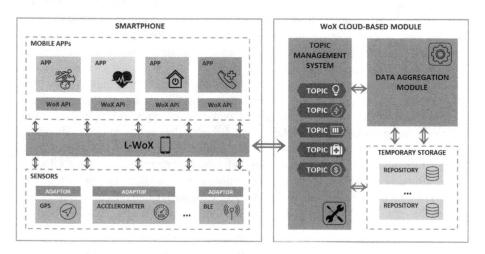

Fig. 2. WoX ecosystem for the Lecce's pilot

It is worth noticing that the model-driven approach characterizing the Web of Topics paradigm is inherently well suited for the intervention strategies laid down within the framework of the City4Age initiative. These set of strategies and procedures are in turn based on a hierarchy defined according to the following concepts:

- Geriatric Factors (GEF), such as *Motility*.
- Geriatric Sub-factors (GES), such as *Moving*.
- Measures, such as the previously mentioned *TM* aggregated measure.
- Gathering Method, which can refer to a wide range of sensors and devices, such as BLE beacons or built-in GPS sensors.

The Data Aggregation Module finally loads the resulting measures in the City4Age repository for further processing, where a central engine is used to detect and predict behavioral patterns. The early detection of risks related to a specific health condition can help geriatricians and caregivers to enact appropriate interventions that can slow down the progression of the condition itself, with beneficial effects on both the patients' quality of life and treatment costs. In fact, late diagnoses are known to decrease the chances of recovery, while at the same time increasing the costs of medical treatments. Furthermore, as a result of their behavioral pattern analysis, the monitored subjects can receive timely interventions – in a healthcare sector where medical protocols are less precisely established and prevention is usually left to the families and carried out via direct human contact – aimed at improving or avoiding behaviors known for their potentially detrimental effects on their health. The final aim of the test bed is to establish an empathic and persuasive relationship with the individual through a tailored, one-to-one communication, capable of convincing the subject to modify his/her behavior in a positive way, in order to prevent further decay.

5 Conclusion

In this paper, we proposed a mobile middleware able to monitor elderly people in their daily activities. Our solution allows important benefits: (i) compared to other solutions and the related work, it permits to progressive deliver unobtrusive techniques for elderly supervising in the e-health field; and (ii), more in general, it can be easily extended in order to develop innovative services in the smart city context for active and healthy ageing starting from defined geriatrics factors. Furthermore, the WoX middleware is able to transparently collect sensor data coming from heterogeneous devices and forward them to the remote reasoning server, in order to trigger appropriate alarms, generate notifications, and activate interventions.

As part of future activities, the project will start its testing phases and this will lead to apply risk detection algorithms on real data related to elderly behaviors. Furthermore, the WoX platform could be enhanced with a complex reasoning in order to handle the communications arising from various sources, and conflicting data that need to be normalized.

Acknowledgments. This work partially fulfills the research objectives of the City4Age project (Elderly-friendly City services for active and healthy ageing) that has received funding from the European Union's Horizon 2020 research and innovation program under the grant agreement No 68973, topic PHC-21-2015.

References

1. Corchado, J.M., Bajo, J., Abraham, A.: GerAmi: improving healthcare delivery in geriatric residences. IEEE Intell. Syst. **23**(2), 19–25 (2008)
2. Miorandi, D., Sicari, S., De Pellegrini, F., Chlamtac, I.: Internet of Things: vision, applications and research challenges. Ad Hoc Networks **10**(7), 1497–1516 (2012)
3. Celesti, A., Fazio, M., Giacobbe, M., Puliafito, A., Villari, M.: Characterizing cloud federation in IoT. In: AINA Workshops, pp. 93–98 (2016)
4. Jahn, M., Pramudianto, F., Al-Akkad, A.-A.: Hydra middleware for developing pervasive systems: a case study in the eHealth domain. In: International Workshop on Distributed Computing in Ambient Environments, Paderborn, Germany, 15–18 September 2009
5. Paganelli, F., Parlanti, D., Giuli, D.: A service-oriented framework for distributed heterogeneous data and system integration for continuous care networks. In: CCNC 2010 7th IEEE (2010)
6. Fahim, M., Fatima, I., Lee, S., Lee, Y.-K.: Daily life activity tracking application for smart homes using android smartphone. In: IEEE 14th International Conference on Advanced Communication Technology (ICACT), pp. 241–245 (2012)
7. Shahamabadi, M.S., Ali, B.B.M., Varahram, V., Jara, A.J.: Anetwork mobility solution based on 6LoWPAN hospital wireless sensor network (NEMO-HWSN). In: Proceeding 7th International Conference Innovation Mobile Internet Services Ubiquitous Comput. (IMIS), July 2013, pp. 433–438 (2013)
8. Zhang, X.M., Zhang, N.: An open, secure and flexible platform based on Internet of Things and cloud computing for ambient aiding living and telemedicine. In: Proceeding of International Conference Computer and Management (CAMAN), May 2011, pp. 1–4 (2011)
9. Villarreal, V., Fontecha, J., Hervás, R., Bravo, J.: Mobile and ubiquitous architecture for the medical control of chronic diseases through the use of intelligent devices: using the architecture for patients with diabetes. Future Gener. Comput. Syst. **34**, 161–175 (2014)
10. Mainetti, L., Manco, L., Patrono, L., Sergi, I., Vergallo, R.: Web of topics: an IoT-aware model-driven designing approach. In: WF-IoT 2015, IEEE World Forum on Internet of Things. Milan, Italy, 14–16 December 2015, pp. 46-51. IEEE, Piscataway, NJ, USA (2015). doi:10.1109/WF-IoT.2015.7389025, ISBN 978-150900365-5
11. Mainetti, L., Manco, L., Patrono, L., Secco, A., Sergi, I., Vergallo, R.: An ambient assisted living system for elderly assistance applications. In: PIMRC 2016, 27th Annual IEEE International Symposium on Personal, Indoor and Mobile Radio Communications, Valencia, Spain, 4–7 September 2016, pp. 2480-2485. IEEE, Piscataway, NJ, USA (2016). ISBN 978-1-5090-3253-2
12. Paolini, P., Di Blas, N., Copelli, S., Mercalli, F.: City4Age: Smart cities for health prevention. In: IEEE International Smart Cities Conference (ISC2), 12–15 September 2016, Trento (2016)
13. Mainetti, L., Patrono, L., Rametta, P.: Capturing behavioral changes of elderly people through unobtruisive sensing technologies. In: 24th International Conference on Software, Telecommunications and Computer Networks (SoftCOM), 22–24 September 2016, Split (2016)

Detection Systems for Improving the Citizen Security and Comfort from Urban and Vehicular Surveillance Technologies: An Overview

Karim Hammoudi[1,2](✉), Halim Benhabiles[3], Mahmoud Melkemi[1,2], and Fadi Dornaika[4,5]

[1] Université de Haute-Alsace,
IRIMAS, LMIA EA 3993, 68100 Mulhouse, France
karim.hammoudi@uha.fr
[2] Université de Strasbourg, Strasbourg, France
[3] ISEN-Lille, Yncréa Hauts-de-France, Lille, France
[4] Department of CS & AI, University of the Basque Country,
20018 San Sebastiàn, Spain
[5] IKERBASQUE, Basque Foundation for Science, 48011 Bilbao, Spain

Abstract. This paper presents emerging detection systems for improving the citizen security and comfort in vehicular and urban contexts. To this end, we firstly provide an overview of existing detection systems dealing with innovative citizen security and comfort functionalities based on vision technologies. Secondly, we expose two vision-based detection prototypes we developed for proposing services more specifically addressed to security agencies and to car drivers.

Keywords: Smart urban mobility · Citizen security and comfort · Urban monitoring · Embedded vision systems · Surveillance technologies

1 Introduction and Motivation

This paper presents an overview of detection systems for improving the citizen security and comfort in vehicular and urban contexts. More precisely, many surveillance sensors already equip urban infrastructures for security applications. However, their exploitations for the development of non-supervised security systems as well as for proposing comfort-related services remains relatively underused. In this paper, we present various emerging surveillance technologies as well as detection systems that are exploited in the literature for enhancing the security and the comfort of citizens. Additionally, we present experiments and results directly related to our designed detection and communication architectures and approaches which aim to support advanced police aid services as well as advanced driver assistance service.

© ICST Institute for Computer Sciences, Social Informatics and Telecommunications Engineering 2018
A. Longo et al. (Eds.): IISSC 2017/CN4IoT 2017, LNICST 189, pp. 37–45, 2018.
https://doi.org/10.1007/978-3-319-67636-4_5

2   Related Surveillance, Detection and Communication Systems

This section presents some existing system architectures supporting urban and vehicular security and comfort developments (e.g.; surveillance services) through vision-based detection, computation and communication technologies.

2.1   Black Box Systems for Vehicles

Car black boxes are new trend products for car and motorcycle drivers. A black box for car is a camera with a storage system that is installed onto the windshield. Similar black box can be installed onto the helmets for motorcyclists (e.g.; dash cam). The acquisition device permits to collect videos of road environments corresponding to the vehicle displacements but can also be used to register videos inside the car. A black box often includes a looped recording functionality which save its video if an incident occurs. Additionally, the system can be equipped with a GPS sensor allowing to store different types of information related to the vehicle driving (e.g.; speed, direction, steering angles). For motorcyclists, it can be difficult to find low-cost systems, easy to install on helmets and integrating black box functionalities.

The collected video data are then exploited for clarifying the situations to the insurance companies in case of accidents. This can be done within the frame of insurance telematics which stands for the use of telecommunication technologies directly proposed by the insurance companies in order to remotely manage their customers. For more information about telematics insurance, we refer the reader to [6] which describes its advantages and drawbacks.

In this context, several works have been recently proposed which attempt to exploit black box systems in different innovative manners.

For instance, Prasad et al. [17] proposed to incorporate an automatic processing module into the black box system allowing an objective accident analysis. The module allows also to immediately send a short alert message to a predefined phone number in case of detected accident. To this end, they proposed their own black box prototype composed of 12 sensors regulated by a Raspberry Pi and an Arduino device.

Lee and Yoo [12] proposed to exploit the internal camera of the black box in order to monitor the driver tiredness through analysis of observed eye states (e.g.; open or closed).

Park [16] proposed a forensic analysis technique of the car black box. His work is motivated by the increasing number of insurance frauds caused by the deletion of data from the black box by the car driver following an accident. Indeed, in this latter case, the driver attempts to conceal his error. To fix this issue, the author proposed an investigation tool to restore deleted information while checking their originality and integrity. Similarly, Yi et al. [25] proposed a module to check recorded data integrity.

2.2   Vision-Based On-Board Systems Integrated to Vehicles

The next generation of vehicle is equipped with integrated vision-based systems (on-board systems). Some vision-based on-board systems of vehicles are dedicated to the analysis of outdoor scenes (road traffic) and include parking assistance systems [20], collision avoidance radar systems [24], traffic flow monitoring systems [14], traffic sign recognition systems [5] and can also be used as a car black box systems. Moreover, other vision-based on-board systems of vehicles are dedicated to the analysis of indoor scenes. Notably, they are oriented in direction of the driver for analyzing his behavior and triggering security-related alerts (e.g.; driver drowsiness detection systems [19], driver mirror-checking action detection system [13]). Additionally to the behavior analysis for security aspects, recent works have been undertaken for remotely controlling car functionality or comfort options through hand gesture recognition [23]. For instance, the driver can switch on/off the radio, the air conditional or answer a phone call by employing pre-determined hand gestures.

2.3   Vision Systems of Existing Urban Infrastructures

Many urban infrastructures (building, parking, street poles) are already equipped with digital cameras for the surveillance of the road traffic (drivers, pedestrians). These cameras permit to acquire a huge amount of video at strategic locations and with various orientations. Foremost, these videos are exploited by public agencies for security reasons. In many cases, the acquired images are observed by a human operator. This makes the analysis tasks more or less fastidious and uncertain. For this reason, various vision algorithms have been proposed in the literature that exploit these existing raised cameras for automatically performing certain analysis tasks such as abnormal behavior detection [21, 27] or monitoring the road traffic [4]. In France, such systems are employed in certain cases for automatically sending fines to drivers having done a detected infringement. This functionality is called "vidéo-verbalisation".

2.4   Vehicular Ad-Hoc Networks and Cloud Computing Systems

Vehicular Ad-Hoc Networks (VANETs) support the spontaneous creation of a wireless network for data exchange between mobile infrastructures [18]. They permit to carry out inter-vehicle communications. They also permit to communicate with urban infrastructures (e.g.; Road Side Units). VANETs can then be employed for exchanging video information between vehicular systems as well as with online platforms. Since vision-based on-board systems of vehicles can have limited computational resources, online platforms such as Cloud Computing services can be used for processing collected videos to extract relevant information [3].

In resume, such communication and processing technologies can then be used in conjunction with connected car black boxes or vision-based on-board systems of vehicles (mobile sensors) and/or with wireless cameras of urban infrastructures (static sensors) for constituting a wide-scale camera-based surveillance systems and cooperative detection systems aiming to enhance citizen security and comfort services [11]. In this sense, the next section presents our related designed and implemented detection and communication prototypes which have been undertaken for supporting advanced police aid services as well as advanced car parking assistance services.

3   Our Designed and Experimented Detection and Communication Systems

As previously mentioned, our first designed and implemented detection and communication system aims to develop advanced police aid services. The targeted services are focused on the improvement of the security for citizen. In particular, development complexities of these services lied in the statement of strategies for processing video acquired by on-board vehicular system and in the elaboration of a simulated communication architecture for exchanging on the processed data. Also, a complexity lied in combining these technologies of varied natures. Besides, our second designed and implemented experimental detection and communication architecture aims to develop a parking assistance system for drivers. The targeted service is focused on the improvement of the comfort for citizen. In particular, development complexities of this service lied in the elaboration of a car occupancy detection method from images acquired by a camera pole. These architectures are presented in more detail in next subsections.

3.1   Advanced Vision-Based Police Aid Systems

Police and security agencies need services for automatically recognizing searched individuals. In this sense, the studied architecture proposes to exploit vision-based on-board systems integrated to vehicles (such as those presented in Subsect. 2.1 and 2.2) for cooperatively enhancing the field of searches. More precisely, we assume at short term that a set of service vehicles (taxis, buses, police cars) will integrate connected camera systems. The flow of collected images tagged with associated GPS locations will be transferred on-the-fly to online computational machines such as cloud computing systems. Then, face detection systems already known for their efficiencies [22] will be applied in order to extract face sub-images of observed individuals for each collected image. These sub-images will be then rescaled and matched with identity photos of searched individuals obtained from reference databases of the police. Since the query sub-images are associated with their GPS locations, the matched sub-images will then provide the approximate location of the searched individual at a particular time and consequently will facilitate the security investigations.

In the same way, vehicle license plates detection systems already known for their efficiencies [26] will be applied onto the flow of collected images in order to extract the license plate characters of vehicles; notably by using Optical Character Recognition Systems (OCRs) [15]. The extracted characters of vehicle license

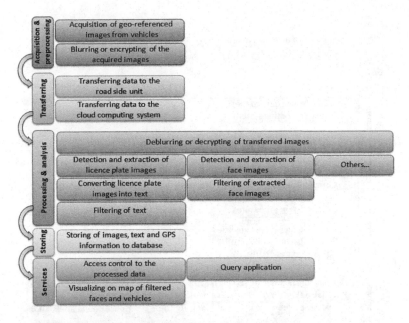

Fig. 1. Global Data-flow diagram to develop varied vehicle-based services with vision-based systems.

plates are then matched with those of stolen vehicles obtained from reference database of the police. Similarly to the previous application, GPS locations associated to the license plate characters extracted on-the-fly will permit then to immediately determine the approximate location of searched vehicles in case of matching between license plate characters.

Figure 1 illustrates a data-flow diagram shared by our two presented systems. This data-flow diagram exposes a generalized bottom-up representation of the employed major stages that can help to the development of other high-level services from vision-based feature detection systems. Moreover, an architecture (based on technologies presented in Subsect. 2.4) we designed for supporting the experiments of the two presented systems is described in more details in [9].

3.2   Advanced Vision-Based Parking Occupancy Detection

The traffic flows are more and more important in urban environments. This makes the finding of available parking slots particularly difficult during daily driving. For this reason, we developed a parking slot occupancy detection system that can exploit camera systems of existing urban infrastructures such as described in Subsect. 2.3 and we assume that the camera is imaging a car parking. More specifically, an image of an empty parking is captured from a camera pole. This image (reference) will be used for detecting changes by comparison with the flow of images acquired in real-time from the same camera pole. Then, a human operator will manually delineate visible footprints of parking slots in

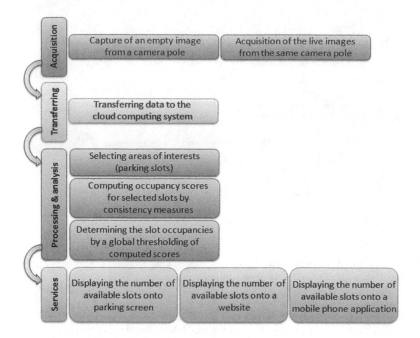

Fig. 2. Data-flow diagram of a parking occupancy detection service developed for camera pole of parkings.

the reference image in order to initialize the system. Once done, the reference image as well as the acquired live images are transferred to a remote machine for computing a dissimilarity score between reference slots and live images of slots. Next to this stage, a global thresholding of computed scores is applied to determine the occupancy status of selected parking slots. By this way, we can determine the number of available parking slots and transmit this information to drivers located into a surrounding perimeter. This can be done by displaying this information on dispatched parking screens, on a dedicated website or via a dedicated application for mobile phone. Figure 2 illustrates a data-flow diagram of these major stages.

Besides, two strategies were experimented for automatically measuring in real-time the consistency of parking slot images and taking a slot occupancy decision. The first one was based on a Canny edge detector (e.g.; see [1]) and considered the rate of contour points detected into each slots. The second one was based on robust image-based metrics such as Sum of Absolute Differences (SAD), Sum of Squared Differences (SSD), Zero-mean Sum of Squared Differences (ZSSD) (e.g.; [2]) and exploited a dynamical thresholding mechanism. Both experimented strategies was based on a global threshold. Figure 3 gives an overview of the developed detection system as well as occupancy results automatically computed in real-time. Details on the computational mechanisms of this system are described in [7,8,10].

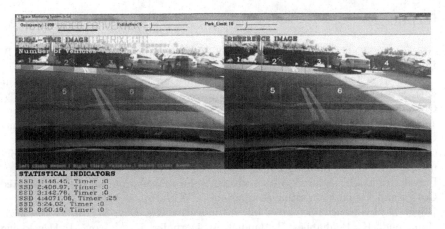

Fig. 3. System developed for the automatic detection of available parking slots in real-time [7,8,10]. Slots colorized in green and red represents detected vacant and occupied slots, respectively (color figure online).

4   Contributions and Conclusion

This paper proposes an overview of detection systems for improving the citizen security and comfort from urban and vehicular surveillance technologies. Indeed, a large variety of surveillance, detection and communication technologies are presented through the description of diverse use cases with black box systems for vehicles, vision-based on-boards systems integrated to vehicles, camera systems of existing urban infrastructures as well as with Vehicular Ad-Hoc Networks and Cloud Computing Systems.

Moreover, two vision-based detection prototypes we developed are described in more details and covers both security and comfort aspects. The developed security system exploits efficient vision-based detectors already intensively exploited in the literature. A complexity of the services lie in the combined action of heterogeneous systems (mobile and static systems, vision-based systems, communication and computation systems) for cooperatively supporting these services. The service descriptions stress a generalized data-flow diagram of the different stages assigned to each system. The developed car parking assistance system deals with analysis from static cameras. The description is focused on the elaboration of the proposed parking slot occupancy detection system. By this way, we hope that the highlighted detection systems as well as technological possibilities will foster the enhancement of new security and comfort services for the citizens.

References

1. Bradski, G., Kaehler, A.: Learning OpenCV: Computer Vision with the OpenCV Library. O'Reilly Media Inc., USA (2008)
2. Chen, J.-H., Chen, C.-S., Chen, Y.-S.: Fast algorithm for robust template matching with M-estimators. IEEE Trans. Signal Process. **51**(1), 230–243 (2003)
3. Chen, N., Chen, Y., You, Y., Ling, H., Liang, P., Zimmermann, R.: Dynamic urban surveillance video stream processing using fog computing. In: IEEE International Conference on Multimedia Big Data (BigMM), pp. 105–112 (2016)
4. Chen, Z., Ellis, T., Velastin, S.A.: Vision-based traffic surveys in urban environments. J. Electron. Imaging **25**(5), 051206–051221 (2016)
5. Fleyeh, H.: Traffic sign recognition without color information. In: IEEE Sponsored Colour and Visual Computing Symposium (CVCS), pp. 1–6 (2015)
6. Goyal, M.: Insurance telematics. Int. J. Innovative Res. Dev. **57**(10), 72–76 (2014)
7. Hammoudi, K., Benhabiles, H., Jandial, A., Dornaika, F., Mouzna, J.: Developing a vision-based adaptive parking space management system. Int. J. Sens. Wirel. Commun. Control **6**, 192–200 (2016)
8. Hammoudi, K., Benhabiles, H., Jandial, A., Dornaika, F., Mouzna, J.: Self-driven and direct spatio-temporal mechanisms for the vision-based parking slot surveillance. In: IEEE Science and Information Conference (SAI Computing), pp. 1327–1329 (2016)
9. Hammoudi, K., Benhabiles, H., Kasraoui, M., Ajam, N., Dornaika, F., Radhakrishnan, K., Bandi, K., Cai, Q., Liu, S.: Developing vision-based and cooperative vehicular embedded systems for enhancing road monitoring services. Procedia Comput. Sci. **52**, 389–395 (2015)
10. Hammoudi, K., Benhabiles, H., Melkemi, M., Dornaika, F.: Analyse et gestion de l'occupation de places de stationnement par vision artificielle. In: French-speaking Workshop "Gestion et Analyse des donnes Spatiales et Temporelles" (GAST) of the Conference "Extraction et Gestion des Connaissances" (EGC), pp. 91–98 (2017)
11. Joshi, J., Jain, K., Agarwal, Y.: Cvms : cloud based vehicle monitoring system in vanets. In: IEEE sponsored International Conference on Connected Vehicles and Expo (ICCVE), pp. 106–111 (2015)
12. Lee, J., Yoo, H.: Real-time monitoring system using RGB-infrared in a vehicle black box. Microwave Opt. Technol. Lett. **57**(10), 2452–2455 (2015)
13. Li, N., Busso, C.: Detecting drivers' mirror-checking actions and its application to maneuver and secondary task recognition. IEEE Trans. Intell. Transp. Syst. **17**(4), 980–992 (2016)
14. Magrini, M., Moroni, D., Palazzese, G., Pieri, G., Leone, G., Salvetti, O.: Computer vision on embedded sensors for traffic flow monitoring. In: IEEE International Conference on Intelligent Transportation Systems (ITSC), pp. 161–166 (2015)
15. Nguwi, Y., Lim, W.: Number plate recognition in noisy image. In: IEEE Cosponsored International Congress on Image and Signal Processing (CISP), pp. 476–480 (2015)
16. Park, D.-W.: Forensic analysis technique of car black box. Int. J. Softw. Eng. Appl. **8**(11), 1–10 (2014)
17. Prasad, M., Arundathi, S., Anil, N., Harshikha, H., Kariyappa, B.: Automobile black box system for accident analysis. In: IEEE Co-sponsored International Conference on Advances in Electronics, Computers and Communications (ICAECC), pp. 1–5 (2014)

18. Saini, M., Alelaiwi, A., Saddik, A.E.: How close are we to realizing a pragmatic vanet solution? a meta-survey. ACM Comput. Surv. **489**(2), 29:1–29:40 (2015)
19. Selvakumar, K., Jerome, J., Rajamani, K., Shankar, N.: Real-time vision based driver drowsiness detection using partial least squares analysis. J. Sig. Process. Syst. **85**(2), 263–274 (2015)
20. Song, Y., Liao, C.: Analysis and review of state-of-the-art automatic parking assist system. In: IEEE International Conference on Vehicular Electronics and Safety (ICVES), pp. 1–6 (2016)
21. Sun, M., Zhang, D., Qian, L., Shen, Y.: Crowd abnormal behavior detection based on label distribution learning. In: IEEE Sponsored International Conference on Intelligent Computation Technology and Automation (ICICTA), pp. 345–348 (2015)
22. Viola, P., Jones, M.: Robust real-time face detection. Int. J. Comput. Vis. **57**(2), 137–154 (2004)
23. Wang, K., Kärkkäinen, L.: Free hand gesture control of automotive user interface. US Patent 9239624 B2 (2016)
24. Wang, X., Tang, J., Niu, J., Zhao, X.: Vision-based two-step brake detection method for vehicle collision avoidance. Neurocomputing **173**, 450–461 (2016)
25. Yi, K., Kim, K.-M., Cho, Y.J.: A car black box video data integrity assurance scheme using cyclic data block chaining. J. KIISE **41**(11), 982–991 (2014)
26. Yu, S., Li, B., Zhang, Q., Liu, C., Meng, M.Q.-H.: A novel license plate location method based on wavelet transform and emd analysis. Pattern Recogn. **48**(1), 114–125 (2015)
27. Zhu, S., Hu, J., Shi, Z.: Local abnormal behavior detection based on optical flow and spatio-temporal gradient. Multimedia Tools Appl. **75**(15), 9445–9459 (2015)

IISSC: Smart City Infrastructures

A Public-Private Partnerships Model Based on OneM2M and OSGi Enabling Smart City Solutions and Innovative Ageing Services

Paolo Lillo[✉], Luca Mainetti, and Luigi Patrono

Department of Innovation Engineering, University of Salento, Lecce, Italy
{paolo.lillo, luca.mainetti, luigi.patrono}@unisalento.it

Abstract. The smart cities promise to offer innovative services to citizens in order to improve the level of life quality but currently, the integration among different ecosystems of data are still lacking. It is noteworthy that data, produced and consumed by public and private institutions, and citizens, may be a precious resource if abstraction and effectiveness are guaranteed in the interface mechanism between data-producers and data-consumers. This work proposes a coupling model, based on standards, technologies, and methodologies, able to make easy and effective the distribution, access, and use of data between services providers and citizens. The system architecture has been designed and developed by using the OSGi technology exploiting a support supplied by Docker, a platform able to ensure greater freedom in the modularization of software platforms oriented to micro-services. Furthermore, for higher levels, an approach based on the OneM2M standard has been adopted in order to obtain a middle layer useful to large-scale coordination of aspects related to the gathering, discovery, security and distribution of data and services. An use case has been defined and summarized in order to clearly show potential benefits of the proposed system for all stakeholders.

Keywords: Smart cities · oneM2M · OSGi · Docker · Micro-services

1 Introduction

A very challenging issue related to smart cities is related to the integration of heterogeneous data and services in order to guarantee an efficient and effective support in the daily activities of citizen, especially for the elderly people.

Currently, who provides a service for a smart-city often makes available more or less 'raw' and 'open' data, stored on more or less 'raw' supports (e.g., CSV files or relational databases). Furthermore, the access to such data by the consumer requires the knowledge of logical and semantic aspects, the implementation of articulated polling mechanisms in order to detect data updates, the implementation of filtering, aggregation and reasoning processes of accessed data due to application needs. Other times, the service is provided in a fully enclosed manner, through the development of the complete cycle of collection, formatting, data storage and distribution through a proprietary front-end. On the contrary, a 'harmonious' development of services to citizens would certainly

© ICST Institute for Computer Sciences, Social Informatics and Telecommunications Engineering 2018
A. Longo et al. (Eds.): IISSC 2017/CN4IoT 2017, LNICST 189, pp. 49–57, 2018.
https://doi.org/10.1007/978-3-319-67636-4_6

be facilitated by the availability of open, semantic data, accessible by third parties on-demand through the adoption of a modularized system supporting the full decoupling of the components related to the production and the consumption of data.

In such a context, some public and private operators would provide a service of gathering and delivery of raw/semantic data, assigning to the system the task of managing issues about marshalling, reasoning and delivery of data to other public and private operators, in the role of consumers, on their preferred channels; adaptation and supplying operate symmetrically with respect to the core system by providing respectively data abstraction and data concretization.

The interaction between systems and external agents must be designed by minimizing the coupling between components (manufacturer, system, consumer) and respecting the principles of the "reactive manifesto" [1].

The efforts of the oneM2M Global Initiative [2, 3], an international project involving eight leading standard ICT bodies (ARIB, ATIS, CCSA, ETSI, TIA, TSDSI, TTA, TTC) are oriented in the direction of the development of specifications able to simplify and harmonize the integration of systems on issues related to the IoT and the M2M communication. This happens in a highly fragmented context, full of methodologies based on a plethora of protocols and proprietary solutions that make very difficult the discovery and the access to data and common services by applications. A lot of works in the scientific literature are converging on the oneM2M specifications, strengthening infrastructural [4, 5] or semantic [6] aspects, but to the best of our knowledge, issues related to the decoupled and reactive interaction between applications and system have not been resolved yet.

The goal of this work is to stimulate the development of applications and services by public and private 'third parties', making easier the access, in 'asynchronous' and 'reactive' mode, involving various channels (e.g., REST, streams, brokers, etc.), not only to the raw data but exploiting abstractions based on semantics and reasoning.

This paper proposes a modularized architectural model composed of the following levels: (i) platform (Docker), (ii) middleware orchestration (OneM2M), and (iii) micro-services (OSGi) [7, 8]. Furthermore, the proposed model is therefore applied in a project aimed at behavioral monitoring of elderly by means of data gathered using IoT technologies whose name is City4Age [9].

The rest of the paper is organized as follows. Section 2 describes the proposed system architecture. Details about middleware orchestration by adopting OneM2M standard are reported in Sect. 3, while an micro-services implementation of the proposed system, based on OSGi, is described in Sect. 4. Section 5 reports a short discussion of a use case the uses the proposed system. Concluding remarks are drawn in Sect. 6.

2   Proposed System Architecture

The proposed architecture aims at decoupling producer and consumer of data through the introduction of the concept of Data Producer/Consumer Channels (respectively DP Channels and DC Channels) among which the system acts as a "smart coupler". Figure 1 shows the Level 1 DFD (Data Flow Diagram) with a high level of abstraction, highlighting the components participating in the process of production, gathering, parsing, processing, adaptation, delivery and consumption of information.

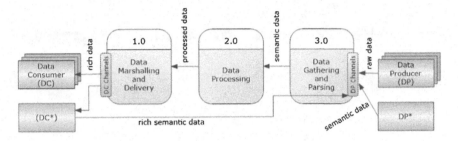

Fig. 1. Level 1 DFD: overall architecture

The specific DP Channel supplied by the producer may be of different type from that required by the consumer.

Producers and consumers are connected to the system through multi-channel adapters able to support the various levels of intelligence, technology and performance of related agents. For example, a DP (DP* in Fig. 1) can provide a stream of semantic data, ready to feed the knowledge base (embedded in the process 2.0 in Fig. 1, named "Data Processing") with a minimum adaptation effort. Another provider can provide access to its own data in "pull" mode by equipping the system with credentials in order to access its DBMS (Data Base Management System) via a public URL. Another can provide raw data by uploading a CSV file in "push" mode using a REST API supplied by the system or alternatively in "pull" mode, providing a URI of the CSV file which updates can be periodically monitored by the system.

On the other hand, the Data Consumer (DC), aiming at offering services to citizens (but also - as in the case of the consumer DC* in Fig. 1 - the implementation of further reasoning processes or enrichment of the information), has the freedom to access the data by choosing the preferred mode via DC Channels related to specific RESTful API, push notifications, stream, brokering protocols (e.g., MQTT, AMQP, XMPP).

The proposed architecture has the objective to 'normalize' the access mechanism to the system, providing external agents with standardized, modern and responsive ways to gather and provide data, then giving responsibility to the system about most of activities related to issues about coupling, processing and distribution.

2.1 Data Processing and Challenges

The proposed system implements a mechanism of data adaptation from the producer to the consumer foreseeing, at the same time, a model able to guarantee data processing through the use of semantic and linguistic tools.

At a higher level of detail, Fig. 2 shows in a Level 2 DFD a possible development of the Data Processing, steering it towards a highly declarative approach that supports high levels of system automation.

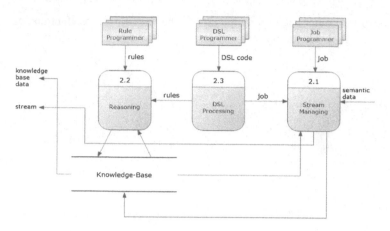

Fig. 2. Level 2 DFD: Details of the Data Processing block

In practice there are well-established solutions for the aspects of the representation and the semantic reasoning: the implementation of the Reasoning block (Process 2.2) can therefore be reasonably reduced to an activity of integration, in the proposed system, of well-known OWL (Ontology Web Language) technologies and open-sources java tools such as OWL API [10, 11]; the conclusions inferred from reasoning will be available to business logic in the form of events.

Conversely, the implementation of the DSL Processing block (Process 2.3) proposes an interesting challenge on the ability to use 'ad hoc' grammars (and related compilers/interpreters) in order to support, declaratively and as close as possible to the varius application domains, the interaction between agents and system about issues of (i) negotiation of the requested/offered services and (ii) submission of 'jobs' to be executed in the system. A very interesting approach to the question is provided by the Xtext framework [12].

Note that the process 2.3 does not add paradigmatic elements (rules and job) but incorporates them by introducing a further abstraction.

3   Middleware Orchestration

The interconnection and exchange of data and services among heterogeneous and distributed systems are inevitable and it would behoove to use the standards in a manner as shared as possible, exposing the functionalities to the agents in the most accessible way.

OneM2M achieves its targets of decoupling and integration by means of a model based on the concept of "resource" and related CRUD + N functionalities (Create, Retrieve, Update, Delete and Notify) accessible both through blocking-requests as through synchronous/asynchronous non-blocking-requests.

The oneM2M specification defines a network topology based on the following node types: Infrastructure Node (IN), Middle Node (MN), Application Service Node (ASN), Application Dedicated Node (ADN), and Non-oneM2M Node (NoDN).

Inside a network of a specific organization, services are exposed by one or more Common Service Entities (CSE) to the Application entities via "Mca Reference points"; the interaction between services deployed on distinct internal nodes (Asn, MN) is managed by the "Mcc Reference points" while, the Infrastructure Nodes, by means of Mcc' Reference Points, mediate the interaction between distinct Service Providers, enabling the distribution of services shared on a large-scale.

The communication mechanism is abstracted and conveyed using a protocol layer below implemented via HTTP (Hyper Text Transfer Protocol)/COAP (Constrained Application Protocol)/MQTT (MQ Telemetry Transport).

This paper introduces inside the architecture of OneM2M, through its own paradigm, some entities, resources and CSE (Common Service Entity) aimed to a flexible and responsive coupling between DP and DC, assisting the developers in implementing reactive programming models.

Figure 3 shows as new Common Service Functions (CSF) are included within the CSE (Common Service Entity) related to the system architecture proposed in this paper.

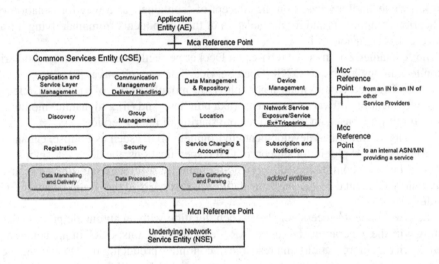

Fig. 3. New common service functions

According to its own type, each node maybe contain specific entity types among those represented in Fig. 3. The proposed architecture fully is able to satisfy the requirements of modularity and scalability enabling integration of different structures (Providers) through IN nodes that provide the interaction among the infrastructural services via "Reference Points" of type Mcc'.

The interaction between the new CSF and their interaction with the outside world is mediated by the exchange of a new set of oneM2M Resources [3], introduced in order to support, in a oneM2M context, the functional paradigm introduced by the system proposed in this work. Only some of the most significant Resources are reported:

- DPChannel: description of the data-channel proposed to the system.
- DPChannelRequest: request to create a referenced DPChannel.

- DPChannelResponse: outcome of a DPChannelRequest and detail of the access parameters to the related DPChannel.
- DCChannel: description of the data-channel requested to the system.
- DCChannelRequest: request to access a referenced DCChannel.
- DCChannelResponse: outcome of a DCChannelRequest and detail of the access parameters to the related DCChannel.

4   OSGi Micro-Services Implementation

The goal of decoupling is to be achieved not only in terms of the implementation aspects but also in terms of the independence of design/development teams, leaving them free to design, implement, test and install system components and services, eliminating or minimizing the interference with other teams and operators but always respecting a shared application model.

With those expectations, a PaaS (Platform as a Service) model based on Docker [11], well known technology based on the concept of 'container' as a way for isolation of application components and for the isolation of the components from underlying infrastructure, has been adopted.

The 'containerization' system based on Docker perfectly matches with a modularization technology known as OSGi (Open Service Gateway initiative) [7].

The OSGi specifications make it possible (i) the modularization of packaging, release and deployment of software components (aka bundles), and (ii) a 'dynamic' modularization at run-time based on local and remote sharing of micro-services.

By using an integrated development environment (IDE) such as Eclipse, enhanced with BndTools [14] plugin for support of OSGi specifications, the design/development team can build its continuous-delivery environment by splitting itself into subgroups, individually dedicated to the implementation of several modular components (OSGi bundles).

The development process concludes each iteration with an automatic process that, starting with the generation of a single JAR file (which contains: OSGi implementation, microservices, configurations and resources), continues producing the Docker 'image' (the container) of the entire application component (including all dependencies required for its execution) and finally ends with the deployment of the container in a Docker environment.

Once installed, the container is fully integrated with the system by registering its offered services and by 'hooking' its requested services through the local registration service and the discovery mechanisms provided by implementations of the Remote Services specifications defined in the enterprise section of OSGi specifications [8].

As reported in [15], a rather natural approach to the interworking between oneM2M and OSGi is the implementation of the oneM2M Resources by means of OSGi services by exposing a hierarchy of Java interfaces with root-interface as reported, below, mapping its methods on the attributes [15], in the Table 9.6.1.3.1-1, *resourceType, resourceID, resourceName, parentID, creationTime, lastModifiedTime, labels,* universal to all resource types:

```
public interface oneM2MResource {
    public int getResourceType();
    public String getrResourceID();
    public void setResourceName(String resourceName);
    public String getParentID();
    public Date getCreateionTime();
    public Date getLastModifiedTime();
    public String[] getLabels();
}
```

5   Use Case Discussion: City4Age Project

With the aim to validate the system proposed in this work we applied the model to the intervention mechanism of the City4Age project [16] in the context of the pilot in the Lecce Municipality.

"City4Age - Elderly-friendly city services for active and healthy ageing", a project co-funded by the Horizon 2020 Programme of the European Commission, supports smart cities to empower social/health services facing MCI and frailty of the elderly population. In particular, the City4Age project aims to utilize digital technologies at home and in the city to monitor behaviors of elderly people with the goal of properly intervene on them in order to delay the onset and progression of MCI and frailty.

As a result of their behavioral patterns analysis, participants will receive interventions aimed at improving behaviors known to affect risk of onset or worsening of MCI and frailty. There are two types of interventions: (i) informative intervention characterized by general information related to the same city, and (ii) specific intervention related to personal risks.

Furthermore, the Municipality of Lecce offers to citizenship, as open-data [17], information accessible mainly through CSV text files. Emulating the work of a municipal employee responsible for the publication of information on cultural events offered by the same city, we provided a structured CSV format for that purpose.

The proposed system, instantiated for City4Age case study, has been set to prepare a DPChannel resource ('resource' in terms of oneM2M paradigm) sending a description of the provided data-source (DPChannel resource) through: (i) an URI, pointing the CSV file, (ii) a semantic description of fields (the comma-separated values) and (iii) a semantic description of the channel.

The system responded by creating a DPChannel resource (with a referencing ID in the DPChannel response) and automatically set up a polling mechanism with access to the CSV file every 30 s (default) and consequent updating of a data base.

Acting in the role of operators for City4Age, we therefore asked the system to create a second DPChannel provided in the form of a REST API to be invoked for the push (from the outside) of a set of data related to recognition of a behavior of an older person (e.g. excessive physical inactivity); also in this case we have accompanied the request with the following description: (i) a semantic description of the input parameters and (ii) a semantic description of the channel.

Then the system has been ordered to create two DCChannel resources: the first to receive the continuous stream of behavioral data and the second to perform, via REST API, filtered requests relating to scheduled cultural events.

Finally, we have implemented and ran an application (outside but connected to the system) that collects data from the stream (containing, among others, the elderly and the data type of the detected behavior), via REST queries the system on appropriate events to chance and sends the elder's phone a PUSH notification via Amazon SNS containing the suggested advice.

The adopted validation approach has shown the effectiveness of the proposed architecture allowing external agents to seamlessly integrate with the system maintaining a high degree of decoupling.

6   Conclusions

With the aim of facilitating interaction between producers and consumers of data for the development of services for the smart-city this article has proposed a modular architecture based on technologies (OSGi and Docker) and standard (oneM2M) aimed to support the development of reactive applications based on micro-services. The proposed model has been applied to the intervention mechanism of a case study (i.e., City4Age project) focused on services for elderly people showing potential benefits, in term of effectiveness, of the approach based on the decoupling between the system and the specific requirements of access by producers and consumers of data.

Acknowledgment. The City4Age project has received funding from European Union's Horizon 2020 research and innovation programme under grant agreement No. 689731.

References

1. http://www.reactivemanifesto.org/
2. http://www.onem2m.org/
3. oneM2M-TS-0001 "Functional Architecture", August 2016. http://www.onem2m.org/technical/published-documents
4. Swetina, J., Lu, G., Jacobs, P., Ennesser, F., Song, J.: Toward a standardized common M2M service layer platform: introduction to oneM2M. IEEE Wireless Commun. **21**(3), 20–26 (2014)
5. Glaab, M., Fuhrmann, W., Wietzke, J., Ghita, B.: Toward enhanced data exchange capabilities for the oneM2M service platform. IEEE Commun. Mag. **53**(12), 42–50 (2015)
6. Kanti Datta, S., Gyrard, A., Bonnet, C., Boudaoud, K.: oneM2M architecture based user centric IoT application development. In: 3rd International Conference on Future Internet of Things and Cloud, 24–26 August 2015
7. The OSGi Alliance. https://www.osgi.org/
8. OSGi Release 6. https://www.osgi.org/developer/downloads/release-6/
9. Paolini, P., Di Blas, N., Copelli, S., Mercalli, F.: City4Age: Smart cities for health prevention. In: IEEE International Smart Cities Conference (ISC2), 12–15 September 2016, Trento (Italy) (2016)

10. http://owlapi.sourceforge.net/
11. Horridge, M., Bechhofer, S.: The OWL API: a Java API for OWL Ontologies. Semant. Web J. **2**(1), 11–21 (2011). Special Issue on Semantic Web Tools and Systems
12. http://www.eclipse.org/Xtext/
13. https://www.docker.com/
14. bndtools.org/
15. HUAWEI: Interworking between oneM2M and OSGi. ftp://ftp.onem2m.org/Meetings/ARC/ 20160516_ARC23_Seoul/ARC-2016-026-Possible_Solution_of_Interworking_between_ oneM2M_and_OSGi.ppt
16. Mainetti, L., Patrono, L., Rametta, P.: Capturing behavioral changes of elderly people through unobtruisive sensing technologies. In: 24th International Conference on Software, Telecommunications and Computer Networks (SoftCOM), 22–24 September 2016, Split (Croatia) (2016)
17. OpenData Lecce Municipality. http://dati.comune.lecce.it/

eIDAS Public Digital Identity Systems: Beyond Online Authentication to Support Urban Security

Francesco Buccafurri, Gianluca Lax$^{(\boxtimes)}$, Serena Nicolazzo,
and Antonino Nocera

DIIES, University Mediterranea of Reggio Calabria, Via Graziella,
Località Feo di Vito, 89122 Reggio Calabria, Italy
lax@unirc.it

Abstract. The European regulation eIDAS introduces in EU States interoperable public digital identity systems whose native application is secure authentication on online services. In this paper, we try to offer an enhanced view of the potential benefits that such systems can have in our physical environments. Indeed, cities have seen a dramatic increase in the number of violent acts and crimes. The possibility of monitoring people access to physical critical places is certainly an important issue because this gives the possibility to deny the access to dangerous people, to find the offender of a crime, and, in general, to track suspicions activities. In this paper, we show how to exploit an eIDAS-compliant public digital identity system to meet the above requirements, thus offering a concrete solution with high level of interoperability.

Keywords: Urban security · Public digital identity · eIDAS · SPID · Critical environments · Physical access control

1 Introduction

The problem of identity management [1] is related to many applications, among which physical access control of people and identity auditing and monitoring, are particularly important in the context of urban security [2–4]. Consider a physical place where the access of individuals is controlled, for example a museum or an airport. In the case of a museum, we need that only people with a valid ticket can access: however, it should be useful to log their identities in order to enable accountability activities. In contrast, the access to an airport gate should be granted to users with a valid ticket, only after having verified their identity does not belong to some black list.

Recently, Regulation (EU) No 910/2014 eIDAS (electronic IDentification Authentication and Signature) [5] has been issued with the objective of removing existing barriers to the cross-border use of electronic identification means used in the Member States for authentication. As this Regulation does not aim to intervene with regard to electronic identity management systems and related

© ICST Institute for Computer Sciences, Social Informatics and Telecommunications Engineering 2018
A. Longo et al. (Eds.): IISSC 2017/CN4IoT 2017, LNICST 189, pp. 58–65, 2018.
https://doi.org/10.1007/978-3-319-67636-4_7

infrastructures established in Member States, each Member State can design its own secure electronic identification and authentication system, which will be accepted in all EU countries if is complaint with eIDAS: For example, the Public Digital Identity System (SPID) [6] is the Italian identity management system complaint with eIDAS.

The Italian system SPID is an open system thanks to which public and private entities, provided that they are accredited by the Agency for Digital Italy, can offer services of electronic identification for citizens and businesses. The providers of such services have to ensure a suitable procedure for the initial identification and have to implement the authentication of citizens to service providers, which are public or private organizations, provided that they adhere to SPID. SPID is based on the technical specifications widely accepted in Europe and already adopted by experimental projects as Stork and Stork2 (Secure Identity Across Borders Linked) [7,8]. Italy has also already notified the Commission the institution of SPID. Thus, according to eIDAS, since July 2016, SPID is recognized and accepted by all other EU Member States.

In this paper, we try to offer an enhanced view of the potential benefits that such systems can have in our physical environments. In particular, we propose a system to monitor people access to physical places exploiting an eIDAS-compliant public digital identity system. To be concrete, we contextualize our proposal in the Italian framework, thus exploiting the system SPID. Our system has the scope of identifying users and is able to decide whether granting them the access to a monitored area, also logging such accesses. The topic here studied is an emerging research challenge which is attracting a great deal of attention (e.g., [9–15]). The main contribution of our proposal with respect to the state of the art relies on the fact that our solution is based on the use of an authentication tool (i.e., SPID in our solution instantiation), which is simple to use, considered secure, accepted in all EU countries, and expected to be used by the most part of the population in the next years. Consequently, our solution can be considered cheap, effective, and secure w.r.t. the state of the art.

In the next section, we describe how SPID is exploited for users identification. The architecture and protocol of the system are presented in Sect. 3. Finally, we draw final discussion and conclusion in Sect. 4.

2   The SPID Framework

In this section, we present the Public Digital Identity System (SPID) framework [6] and the technical details necessary to understand our proposal. SPID is a SAML-based [16] open system allowing public and private accredited entities to offer services of electronic identification for citizens and businesses. SPID enables users to make use of digital identity managers to allow the immediate verification of their identity for suppliers of services.

Besides users to identify, the stakeholders of SPID are Identity Providers, which create and manage SPID identities and Service Providers, public or private organizations providing a service to authorized users. Moreover, we have

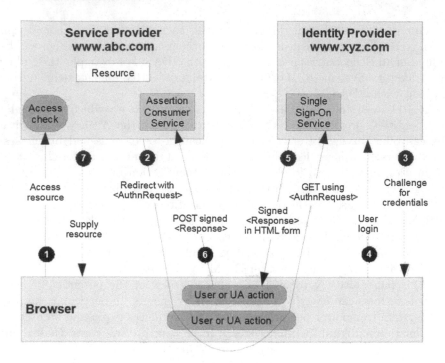

Fig. 1. Authentication by SPID.

a Trusted Third Party (TTP), which guarantees the standard levels of security required by SPID and certifies the involved entities (in Italy, it is "The Agency for Digital Italy").

To obtain a SPID identity, a user must be registered to one Identity Provider, which is responsible of the verification of the user identity before issuing the SPID ID and the security credentials.

A SPID user who needs to access a service sends a request to the Service Provider that gives this service (this is typically done by a Web browser). Then, the Service Provider replies with an **Authentication Request** to be forwarded to the Identity Provider managing the SPID identity of the user.

When the Identity Provider receives such an **Authentication Request**, verifies that it is valid and performs a challenge-response authentication with the user. In case of successful user authentication, the Identity Provider prepares the **Assertion**, a message containing the statement of user authentication for the Service Provider.

Now, Identity Provider returns to the user the message **Response** containing the **Assertion**, which is forwarded to the Service Provider (typically via HTTP POST Binding).

All the steps carried out in a SPID-based authentication are represented in Fig. 1.

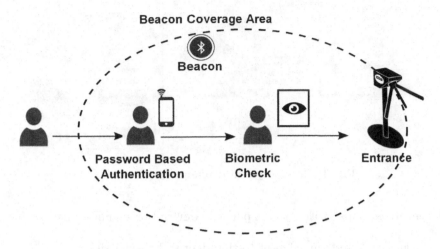

Fig. 2. The physical infrastructure underlying our approach.

Concerning the authentication, SPID supports three different levels: L1 based on only password, L2 using both password and one time password (it is sent to the user by a channel different from the browser), and L3 requiring the use of a smart card in addition to password.

In our proposal, we include a level L4, in which both password and biometric information[1] are exploited.

The SPID identification level to be used depends on the context and the security needs: for example, in case only accountability of user accesses is required (as for a museum), level L1 could be sufficient; in case the access to a zone should be granted to only selected users (as for an airport), then the use of L4 is required.

3 System Architecture and Implementation

In this section, we describe the architecture of our system and provide some details about the technologies and hardware used.

Without lost of generality, we refer to an airport as application scenario, in which the entrance to a secured zone (e.g., the gates area), has to be granted only to authorized users. Figure 2 sketches a representation of the physical infrastructure considered in our approach.

In our solution, we assume that:

1. The SPID identity of authorized users is available to the system;

---

[1] The currently standardized biometrics used for this type of identification system are facial recognition, fingerprint recognition, and iris recognition. Biometric identification is adopted in many countries: for example, in USA, beginning on April 1, 2016, the electronic passport contains relevant biometric information [17].

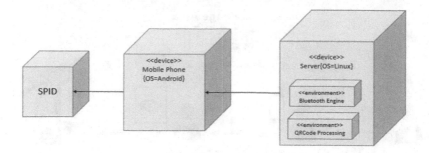

Fig. 3. The deployment diagram of our system.

2. Users are equipped with a smart portable device (for example, a smartphone or a tablet);
3. The device of users can connect to the Identity Provider site.

Our solution integrates the SPID service to authorize the accesses to secured areas. To describe the approach in a very synthetic way, we can say that the authorization procedure starts when a user approaches the entrance of a secured zone, such as an airport turnstile. Here, an access point of the system is placed and the user is prompted to perform the SPID authentication via his personal device. The result of this procedure is used by the system to decide if the user is authorized to access the secured area, depending on his SPID identity.

The system implementing our proposal, whose deployment diagram is illustrated in Fig. 3, is composed of two main subsystems:

– User Interface Subsystem (UI, for short), which implements all the features to allow the user interaction with the system. It is a single module implemented through an application running on the mobile device of the user.
– Physical-Service Provider Subsystem (PSP, for short), which performs all verifications to monitor the entrance to secured zone. It consists of three main modules, namely: PreAuth Module, IDScanner Module, and Processing Module.

The first module involved in the protocol is the PreAuth Module, which inquiries users devices approaching the secured zone entrances to initiate the SPID authentication. It is implemented by using Bluetooth beacons placed on airport turnstiles to initialize the communication with UI subsystem. The design choice of using Bluetooth beacons is due to the extremely simple integration in existing infrastructures. Indeed, this kind of device belongs to a class of low energy bluetooth hardware transmitters [18,19], often battery powered, able to broadcast messages and perform basic interactions with smart devices in close proximity. Typically, Bluetooth beacons are used to issue location-based actions on devices and have been already adopted in environments where check-in is needed.

In proximity of the monitored zone, the user device receives via Bluetooth the authentication request from the PreAuth Module and is prompted to execute

---

Algorithm 1. Workflow of our approach

Notation U: user entering a secured zone
Notation UI: user interface on mobile device
Notation PM: PreAuth Module on Bluetooth Beacon
Notation IDM: IDScanner Module on QR Code Scanner
Notation $ProsM$: Processing Module on Central Server
 1: U approaches a monitored entrance
 2: PM inquiries UI to initiate the SPID authentication
 3: UI generates a QR Code for this Authentication Request
 4: U inserts his credential for SPID authentication via UI
 5: U approaches the entrance and shows the QR Code to IDM
 6: U performs biometric authentication
 7: IDM verifies the assertion and forwards it to $ProsM$
 8: $ProsM$ grants/denies access

---

the SPID authentication, which is executed by connecting to the site of the
Identity Provider of the user. Moreover, this module randomly generates a QR
Code [20], which is associated with this `Authentication Request` and shown
on the mobile device of the user.

As for authentication, we assume that L4 authentication is required (this
is typical for an airport): thus, both password and biometric information are
exploited in two different steps. In this first step, user is required to insert the
password.

Observe that because this first step may require more time, it can starts
when the user is quite distant from the access point (depending on the Beacon
coverage area).

When the user arrives in the access point, the second step of the authentication is done: the user shows the QR Code to the IDScanner Module.

This module is a smart 2D bar code scanner placed right in the turnstile:
because QR Code scanning requires high proximity, this solution is particularly
suitable in our scenario to avoid de-synchronization between user physical access
and identity verification.

In this step, the biometric authentication is performed and the result of this
authentication, which contains the `Assertion`, is returned to the Processing
Module. This module is deployed in a central server and receives all the access
requests coming from the different PreAuth Module. It enforces access policies
by driving the opening of turnstiles: in our example, it verifies that this SPID
identity is of an authorized user.

The algorithm describing the whole approach is reported in Algorithm 1.

4   Conclusion

In this paper, we designed and implemented a system based on SPID to monitor physical access of individuals to controlled areas. The exploitation of our
proposal gives two main advantages with respect to a standard management of
accesses (i.e., when a human operator is in charge of verifying user's identity):
the first advantage is to speed up this process, the second one is to make user's
identification more robust to human errors.

Moreover, filtering mechanisms can be enabled (e.g., only adults may access), or the use of attribute providers can be involved to remove the need of showing an electronic ticket (the ticket is associated with the identity).

Concerning pervasiveness, we observe that, even though our implementation makes use of SPID, our approach supports any identity management system complaint with eIDAS. This is an important aspect because there are many cases in which individuals may have heterogeneous nationalities.

As for accountability, it is easily obtained by suitably storing all information need (for example, besides the identity, also the timestamp of the access).

The last observation is related to the technologies that can be exploited. In our example, we showed the use of Beacon and QR Code. However, they can be replaced by other similar technologies, such as Wi-Fi or NFC, or by long-range UHF RFID systems.

References

1. Buccafurri, F., Lax, G., Nocera, A., Ursino, D.: Discovering missing me edges across social networks. Inform. Sci. **319**, 18–37 (2015)
2. Jara, A.J., Genoud, D., Bocchi, Y.: Big data in smart cities: from poisson to human dynamics. In: 2014 28th International Conference on Advanced Information Networking and Applications Workshops, AINA 2014 Workshops, Victoria, BC, Canada, 13–16 May 2014, pp. 785–790 (2014)
3. Anttiroiko, A., Valkama, P., Bailey, S.J.: Smart cities in the new service economy: building platforms for smart services. AI Soc. **29**(3), 323–334 (2014)
4. Buccafurri, F., Lax, G., Nicolazzo, S., Nocera, A.: Comparing twitter and facebook user behavior: privacy and other aspects. Comput. Hum. Behav. **52**, 87–95 (2015)
5. European Union: Regulation EU No 910/2014 of the European Parliament and of the Council, 23 July 2014. http://eur-lex.europa.eu/legal-content/EN/TXT/HTML/?uri=CELEX%3A32014R0910&from=EN
6. European Union: Regulation EU No 910/2014 of the European Parliament and of the Council, 23 July 2014. http://ec.europa.eu/growth/tools-databases/tris/en/index.cfm/search/?trisaction=search.detail&year=2014&num=295&dLang=EN
7. Leitold, H.: Challenges of eID interoperability: the STORK project. In: Fischer-Hübner, S., Duquenoy, P., Hansen, M., Leenes, R., Zhang, G. (eds.) Privacy and Identity 2010. IFIP AICT, vol. 352, pp. 144–150. Springer, Heidelberg (2011). doi:10.1007/978-3-642-20769-3_12
8. Cuijpers, C., Schroers, J.: eidas as guideline for the development of a pan European eid framework in futureid. In: Open Identity Summit 2014. vol. 237, pp. 23–38. Gesellschaft für Informatik (2014)
9. Edwards, A., Hughes, G., Lord, N.: Urban security in Europe: translating a concept in public criminology. Europ. J. Criminol. **10**(3), 260–283 (2013)
10. Zhang, R., Shi, J., Zhang, Y., Zhang, C.: Verifiable privacy-preserving aggregation in people-centric urban sensing systems. IEEE J. Sel. Areas Commun. **31**(9), 268–278 (2013)
11. Krontiris, I., Freiling, F.C., Dimitriou, T.: Location privacy in urban sensing networks: research challenges and directions (security and privacy in emerging wireless networks). IEEE Wirel. Commun. **17**(5) (2010)

12. Niu, B., Zhu, X., Chi, H., Li, H.: Privacy and authentication protocol for mobile RFID systems. Wireless Pers. Commun. **77**(3), 1713–1731 (2014)
13. Forget, A., Chiasson, S., Biddle, R.: Towards supporting a diverse ecosystem of authentication schemes. In: Symposium on Usable Privacy and Security (Soups) (2014)
14. Doss, R., Sundaresan, S., Zhou, W.: A practical quadratic residues based scheme for authentication and privacy in mobile RFID systems. Ad Hoc Netw. **11**(1), 383–396 (2013)
15. Habibi, M.H., Aref, M.R.: Security and privacy analysis of song-mitchell RFID authentication protocol. Wireless Pers. Commun. **69**(4), 1583–1596 (2013)
16. Wikipedia: Security Assertion Markup Language – Wikipedia, The Free Encyclopedia (2016). https://en.wikipedia.org/w/index.php?title=Security_Assertion_Markup_Language&oldid=747644307
17. Security, H.J.H.: Visa Waiver Program Improvement and Terrorist Travel Prevention (2016). https://www.congress.gov/bill/114th-congress/house-bill/158/text
18. Miller, B.A., Bisdikian, C.: Bluetooth Revealed: The Insider's Guide to an Open Specification for Global Wireless Communication. Prentice Hall PTR, New Jersey (2001)
19. Bluetooth, S.: Bluetooth Specification (2017). https://www.bluetooth.com/specifications/bluetooth-core-specification
20. Soon, T.J.: Qr code. Synth. J. **2008**, 59–78 (2008)

Knowledge Management Perception in Industrial Enterprises Within the CEE Region

Ivan Szilva, Dagmar Caganova, Manan Bawa, Lubica Pechanova[✉],
and Natalia Hornakova

Faculty of Material Science and Technology, Slovak University of Technology,
Institute of Industrial Engineering and Management, J. Bottu 25, 91724 Trnava, Slovakia
{Ivan.szilva,Dagmar.caganova,Manan.bawa,Lubica.pechanova,
Natalia.hornakova}@stuba.sk

Abstract. Smart Cities work with many data collected from various sources. The data are useless unless people know how to process them effectively. The aim of the submitted paper is to find out what the attitudes of the employees working in industrial enterprises in the CEE region are towards the Knowledge Management and it also focuses on finding the means of possible improvements of the Knowledge Management implementation. In the first part, definition and importance of the knowledge is explained for better understanding of the dealing issue. The second part describes our questionnaire survey with sample of 650 respondents. Selected survey results are presented and interpreted in the following section. Main research findings and recommendations can be found in the fourth part. The last part summarizes all previous parts of the article. From the survey results can be concluded that there is a significant relationship between knowledge management performance and the ease of use of knowledge management tools.

Keywords: Knowledge · Knowledge management · Perception · Industrial enterprise · Blue collars

1 Introduction

People use technology in their everyday life. Constant progress in science bring new possibilities for improving way of living. City is a permanent human settlement with boundaries. Smart Cities are results of combination of people, technology and processes that try to effectively solve problems which are developing daily. Data are needed for searching solutions. The large amount of data needs to be processed for further use, changing to information. In the final level, the information change to knowledge which make possible for human to resolve given issues.

In a rapidly changing work environment, organizations face challenges of how to manage their knowledge assets efficiently in order to generate market value and to gain competitive advantage. The focus for knowledge influences almost all parts of the organization such as its strategy, products, processes and ways of the workflow organisation. Thus, knowing what to manage as a knowledge is a critical issue. While having this in mind, it is necessary to distinguish between information and knowledge, between

© ICST Institute for Computer Sciences, Social Informatics and Telecommunications Engineering 2018
A. Longo et al. (Eds.): IISSC 2017/CN4IoT 2017, LNICST 189, pp. 66–75, 2018.
https://doi.org/10.1007/978-3-319-67636-4_8

information management (IT) and knowledge management (KM). Information can be anything that can be digitised, while knowledge is the capacity to act effectively. This is why our research focused on the perception of knowledge management within organisations in CEE region. When knowing how KM is perceived by management, but the blue collars as well one can approach more efficient ways of applying KM methods and tools to the enterprise processes.

What knowledge should one be managing? This question might seem trivial, but in fact it is quite hard to answer. A trite answer is, "Everything!" But of course if you attempted to capture and collate everything, you would be swamped, information overload would soon set in, and you would not be able to distinguish high-value, reliable, and useful information and knowledge from low-value, dubious knowledge [1].

The knowledge that you need to manage is that which is critical to your company—that which adds value to your products or to your services. Here are some examples:

- Knowledge of a particular job, such as how to fix a fault in a piece of critical manufacturing equipment.
- Knowledge of who knows what in a company, who solved a similar problem last time.
- Knowledge of who is best to perform a particular job or task, who has the latest training or best qualifications in a particular subject.
- Knowledge of corporate history—has this process been tried before, what was the outcome?
- Knowledge of a particular customer account and knowledge of similar customers.
- Knowledge of how to put together a team that can work on a project, who has worked successfully together in the past, what skills were needed on similar projects [1].

In order to manage something you must be able to recognize it. Knowledge does not exist in isolation though. It is not something that can be picked up or locked in a company vault. An important notion here is that knowledge involves the recognition or the understanding of patterns. This involves the creation of mental models, exemplars, or archetypes. When a pattern exists between the information, the pattern has the potential to represent knowledge [2].

However, the patterns representing knowledge must have a context. Data, information, and knowledge can be considered, not as discrete entities, but as existing along a continuum, as illustrated in Fig. 1 [1].

In the field of cognitive sciences, and even more so in epistemology, great deal of research and work has been done to attempt to identify and define knowledge. Unfortunately, in management, we do not know what managerial knowledge really is and even though we have a vague feeling for it, there are few definitions of knowledge within a "managerial" context.

Kim suggested that knowledge is a combination of "know-how" and "know-why." [3] Other authors, including Nonaka, identify different types of knowledge, i.e., tacit and explicit knowledge [4].

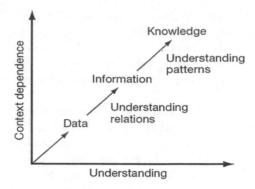

Fig. 1. Relationship of context to understanding [1].

Explicit knowledge, on the one hand, refers to the formal, systematic language, the rules and procedures that an organization follows. This kind of knowledge can be transferred and therefore can be a subject of education and socialization. Knowledge-based Systems also work with explicit knowledge.

Properties of explicit knowledge are following:

- Ability to disseminate, to reproduce, to access and re-apply throughout the organization.
- Ability to teach, to train.
- Ability to organize, to systematize, to translate a vision into a mission statement, into operational guidelines.
- Transfer knowledge via products, services, and documented processes [5].

Tacit knowledge, on the other hand, is mainly based on lived experiences and therefore is difficult to identify and to transfer. Deeply rooted in action, commitment and involvement in a specific context, it refers to personal qualities such as cognitive and technical elements inherent to the individual [6].

Tacit knowledge properties are following:

- Ability to adapt, to deal with new and exceptional situations.
- Expertise, know-how, know-why, and care-why.
- Ability to collaborate, to share a vision, to transmit a culture.
- Coaching and mentoring to transfer experiential knowledge on a one-to-one, face-to-face basis [5].

The term "knowledge management" is relatively new. Its emergence as a management concept is the result of the recognition of "knowledge" as an intangible yet very valuable corporate asset which needs systematic attention and careful managing in order to get the maximum value from it [7].

According to the Awad, Ghaziri, knowledge management (KM) is a newly emerging interdisciplinary business model that has knowledge within the framework of an organization as its focus. It is rooted in many disciplines, including business, economics, psychology, and information management. It is the ultimate competitive advantage for today's firm. Knowledge management involves people, technology, and processes in overlapping parts (Fig. 2) [8].

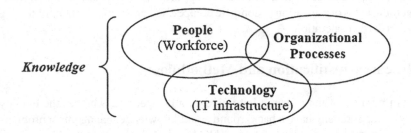

Fig. 2. Overlapping Human, Organizational and Technological factors of KM (own elaboration based on Awad, 2007) [8]

In a simple form, knowledge management means the process of collecting, organizing, classifying and disseminating information throughout an organization. In a wider sense it can be understood as the philosophy and technique of recognizing, increasing and exploiting the organization's intangible assets [9].

Ruggles and Holtshouse identified the following key attributes of knowledge management:

- Generating new knowledge.
- Accessing valuable knowledge from outside sources.
- Using accessible knowledge in decision making.
- Embedding knowledge in processes, products and/or services.
- Representing knowledge in documents, databases, and software.
- Facilitating knowledge growth through culture and incentives.
- Transferring existing knowledge into other parts of the organization.
- Measuring the value of knowledge assets and/or impact of knowledge management [10].

The points mentioned above suggest that the key difference between management and knowledge management is that knowledge management moves management to higher level of effectivity by collecting data from internal and external sources for decision making, applying them to processes, products and services, transfer existing knowledge throughout the whole organization focusing on knowledge growth through culture and incentives. Final step is measurement of the value of knowledge assets and the impact of knowledge management on the enterprise.

For the organization, knowledge management:

- Helps drive strategy.
- Solves problems quickly.
- Diffuses best practices.
- Improves knowledge embedded in products and services.
- Cross-fertilizes ideas and increases opportunities for innovation.
- Enables organizations to better stay ahead of the competition.
- Builds organizational memory [5].

From the previous facts can be concluded that the knowledge management has positive influence on various areas of the enterprise, including strategy creation, problem solving, ideas, knowledge and innovation opportunities improvement. Knowledge management helps organization to compete competition and build memory of the organization for further operation.

2 Research Justification and Methodology

The main purpose of the research is to give us a perspective, whether the employees working in the company have a background about knowledge management problematic and if so, how do they perceive the KM and KM tools. Whether they think it's important to use knowledge management tools, and what is their attitude to using such kind of tools.

We will also test whether they think it's important for them and the company to have a methodology that keeps and spreads the knowledge within the company.

Main reason however is to find the "weakest link" in the industrial enterprise when it comes to knowledge management tools usage. Find whether employees are unable or unwilling to use the opportunities given by knowledge management implementation. These factors need to be identified closely in order to undertake corrective actions that could make them understand and use the possibilities given by knowledge management systems.

Because of the variety of attitudes and possible answers many of the questions in the survey, using the Likert scale and evaluating the questions quantitatively we did not find satisfactory. Therefore we decided to build up the questionnaire to be subsequently evaluated qualitatively. This kind of approach is often more time consuming, but the data obtained is much more meaningful.

2.1 Research Sample

The final survey was carried on in Slovakia and in Czech Republic. We mainly targeted medium (50–249 employees) and large (250 + employees) enterprises, since small enterprises (0–49 employees) are not likely to have knowledge management systems, nor are likely to have the interest to invest in these systems.

The companies participating in the questionnaire were chosen at random, while they had to fulfill two basic requirements:

- To be an industrial enterprise/have an assembly in-house/
- To have at least 50 employees

Companies were from all the regions of Slovakia and two regions of Czech Republic.

The survey was divided into 16 questions out of which 12 were only with one possible answer and 4 had multiple answers possible. In addition 8 of the questions had an opened option available, where the participant could propose his own answer.

Correctly filled surveys were obtained from 144 companies where 650 employees participated. The employees were chosen at random across all the departments and positions to get the most objective idea about the knowledge management perception within the industrial companies and to identify the hindrances to KM.

3   Selected Survey Results

As mentioned in the previous paragraph, the survey consisted of 16 questions. These were divided into three main groups:

- General questions (age, position, etc.)
- Attitudes towards Knowledge Management
- Weak links in the KM and KM tools

We mainly focused on getting more information about the problems employees face while getting confronted with everyday use of knowledge management tools. Diminishment of these issues could lead to higher efficiency of KM tools.

To retain this article in a reasonable length we choose four most interesting findings from the questionnaire. Some of these questions offered a possibility of multiple choices, that is why the total number of responses may exceed the total number of participants.

30% said that poor knowledge sharing is the main issue related to knowledge retention. 28% said it was reinventing the wheel. 22% said it was the loss of a crucial employee leaving with his experience. 11% said it was the lack of various information. On the other hand 9% said it was information overload.

46% of the employees stated that knowledge creation should come "from the top". 20% said that it was everyone's job to contribute to new knowledge formation. 14% did not have an opinion or did not know. The same amount (14%) said it was the job of R&D Department. Only 6% have chosen other option.

40% said that convincing employees to share their knowledge is going to be the biggest issue while implementing KM. 30% said it would be the lack of KM tools usage by employees. 15% said that knowledge grows faster as it can be captured. 11% said that management is going to be hard to convince about KM implementation. 4% picked other.

26% of the respondents claimed that the integration of KM tools into day to day work is a burden. 25% of them said that lack of training is a common issue. 19% found insufficient communication as a problem. 17% claimed that there is short amount of time to learn. 9% found KM system too complicated. 4% reported other issues.

3.1   Survey Results Interpretation

As one may see from Fig. 3, even in the companies with working KM system the biggest challenge that employees face is the poor knowledge sharing within the organization. This is closely followed by "reinvention of the wheel" which however is usually caused by the poor knowledge sharing. Question number 9, that has not been mentioned in this article showed, that 82% of the employees struggle to get relevant documents or information within the company from several hours up to several days. According to the survey, this often makes them listless and that could be the main cause of the reinvention of the wheel.

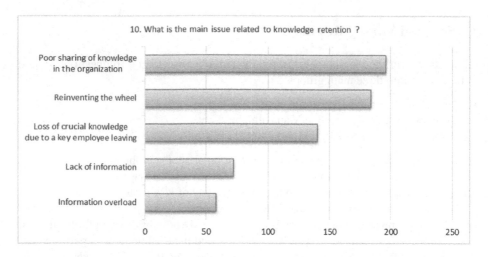

Fig. 3. Distribution of employee opinions about issues leading to knowledge retention

Figure 4 suggests that almost half of the employees participating in the survey believe that knowledge creation is solely the job of the top management. These opinions are imperative to be changed by continuous information throughout the entire company structure, to make employees aware that knowledge creation is to be done from bottom to top and not vice versa. In this question, the employees have often chosen the opportunity to write their own suggestion. Often an idea about having "knowledge owners" occurred. Those would be employees specifically responsible about a tacit knowledge regarding a certain part of the manufacture and production.

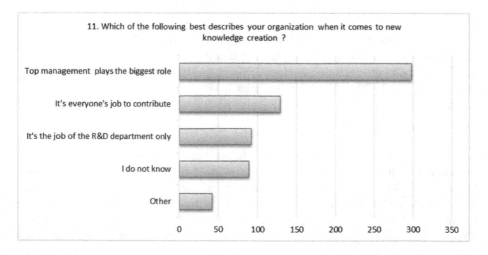

Fig. 4. Distribution of employee opinions regarding the knowledge creation within the company.

Figure 5 shows two biggest issues when it comes to KM tools implementation. The first one is convincing the employees to add their tacit or explicit knowledge to the KM system and the other one is making other people using these information. This is why the main target for the KM tools should be its ease of use and simplicity in contribution. Tools that would meet these requirements would ensure that the access to the relevant data for the employees would be reduced from several hours and days to several dozen of minutes.

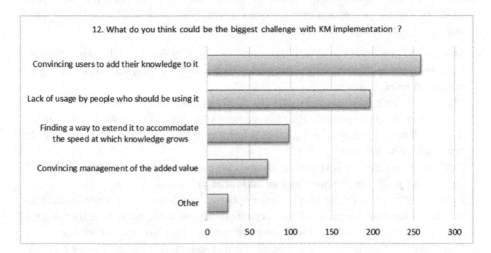

Fig. 5. Distribution of employee opinions about the biggest challenges in KM implementation.

Figure 6 shows the most common problems of the employees that are using KM tools in their daily work. Most often they claim that the tools are complicated and they do not reflect the common practices at the workplace. This might be solved by having the above mentioned "knowledge owner" that employees may refer to with their

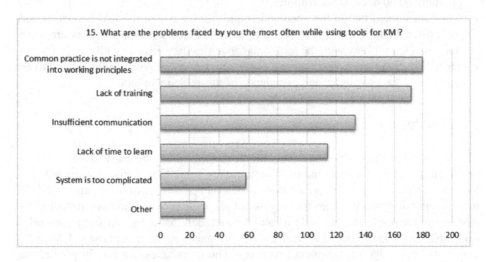

Fig. 6. Distribution of most common problems faced by the employees while using KM tools.

questions or concerns when the knowledge tools would not be clear or they would need an explanation or suggest an improvement.

4   Main Research Findings and Recommendations

Following are the major findings of the study, carried out in Slovakia and the Czech Republic to find the perception of employees working in various industrial enterprises regarding the Knowledge Management:

- Most of the employees in industrial companies have high school diploma followed by employees with university education. Only a tiny fraction has lower or higher education level achieved.
- Majority of the employees are males 31–53 years old.
- The awareness about Knowledge Management systems and tools within the companies could be worked on, since almost 1/3 of the employees did not know about the processes to be followed.
- Getting to the relevant KM tools consumes unreasonably long, that effects the efficiency and quality of the manufacture and other processes.
- Employees meet with seemingly two opposing problems. They experience poor sharing of the knowledge within the organization, but at the same time they experience an information overload with information that often are not too relevant.
- Employees often believe that top management is responsible for knowledge creation. This might mean that the management does not send a proper signal to the employees to contribute to and use various tools of knowledge management.
- Two biggest issues that came out from the survey when it comes to usage and creation of knowledge is that it's either hard to convince people to record they knowledge and on the other hand it's also not easy to convince employees to use guidelines created.
- Employees believe that a well-functioning KM could benefit to less error rates in production and decrease downtimes.
- Often mentioned fact in the open-ended questions was that the KM processes and tools often do not reflect the common practices in their workspaces. They are often not possible to follow with the tools and capacities they dispose with.
- Most of the employees feel that one of the most essential type of information to be captured is the knowledge and experience of the skilled workers.

5   Conclusion

This research has been carried on mainly for the purpose of finding out, what the attitudes of the employees working in industrial enterprises in the CEE region are towards the Knowledge Management. It also focused on means of possible improvements of the KM implementation when it comes to daily use of the tools provided to the employees by KM. From the results of the study it can be concluded that there is a significant relationship between knowledge management performance and the ease of use of KM tools, clarity of knowledge management processes. These variables can jointly predict the knowledge management efficiency and performance. It can also be concluded from the results, that the knowledge management can become an effective and strategic instrument for achieving organizational objectives. Organizational learning however must depend on every employee contributing and that message needs to be clearly delivered from the top management to the rest of the employees.

Acknowledgement. The paper is a part of the project H2020 project RISE-SK with title Research and Innovation Sustainability for Europe which was approved as an institutional project with foreign participation.

References

1. Watson, I.: Applying Knowledge Management. Morgan Kaufmann Publishers, San Francisco (2003)
2. Haslinda, A., Sarinah, A.: A review of knowledge management models. The Journal of International Social Research **2**(9), 187–198 (2009)
3. Kim, D.: The link between individual and organizational learning. Sloan Management Review (1993)
4. Nonaka, I., Takeuchi, H.: The Knowledge-Creating Company: How Japanese Companies Create the Dynamics of Innovation. Oxford University Press, New York (1995)
5. Dalkir, K.: Knowledge Management in Theory and Practice. The MIT Press, Massachusetts (2011)
6. Baets, W.: Knowledge Management and Management Learning: Extending the Horizons of Knowledge-Based Management. Springer, Marseille (2005). doi:10.1007/b136233
7. Davenport, T.H., Prusak, L.: Working Knowledge: How organizations manage what they know. Harvard Business School Press, Boston (2000)
8. Awad, E.M., Ghaziri, H.M.: Knowledge Management. Dorling Kindersley (India) Pvt. Ltd., New Delhi (2008)
9. Mothe, J., Foray, D.: Knowledge Management in the Innovation Process. Kluwer Academic Publisher, Massachusetts (2001)
10. Ruggles, R., Holtshouse, D.: The knowledge advantage. Capstone Publishers, New Hampshire (1999)
11. Goodall, B.: The Penguin Dictionary of Human Geography. Penguin, London (1987)

Cold Chain and Shelf Life Prediction of Refrigerated Fish – From Farm to Table

Mira Trebar[(⊠)]

Faculty of Computer and Information Science, University of Ljubljana,
Večna pot 113, 1000 Ljubljana, Slovenia
mira.trebar@fri.uni-lj.si

Abstract. Fresh perishables are normally stored and distributed with a proper cold chain control in the supply chain from farm to retail. Usually, the consumers break the cold chain after the point of sale. The question is whether consumers are aware of requirements during the transport to and storage at home. The handling conditions and temperature changes can significantly decrease the shelf life and cause faster spoilage of food. The study presents two examples of shelf life prediction. The first one is based on temperature measurements of fish covered with ice in a Styrofoam box with supported information of environment temperatures in the cold store, uncooled car and refrigerator. In the second, measurements from first phase of storage on temperatures (0 °C–4 °C) were used with assumption of fish stored later on higher temperatures without ice. The results show important shortening of shelf life after the point of sale.

Keywords: Cold chain · Shelf life · Prediction · Fish supply chain

1 Introduction

Mainly, shelf life studies of seafood were performed by using kinetic models for growth of spoilage bacteria in various conditions. Higher temperatures increase rates of growth which is the reason for the use of cold chain monitoring in the supply chain. Consumers prefer buying fresh fish which is high quality food product that is labeled with capture date information [1]. The survey presented the conclusion that it is very important to give consumers the information on sensory and microbiological shelf life. Many shelf life prediction tools run simulations to provide that information in possible and expected scenarios based on real cold chain data [2]. Chemical methods were used to specify the shelf life at different storage temperatures. The study provided the information that the exposition time of fish at the point of sale (PoS) and in consumers' household is critical.

New technologies, time temperature integrators (TTI) were used to provide predictive modeling of seabream shelf life in the dynamic temperature conditions [3]. Tests were validated by experimental measurements of microbiological spoilage results. Radio frequency identification (RFID) can be successfully used in cold chain monitoring to provide temperatures of environment conditions and also products in the package [4]. The information could be used at the point of sale to calculate dynamic

© ICST Institute for Computer Sciences, Social Informatics and Telecommunications Engineering 2018
A. Longo et al. (Eds.): IISSC 2017/CN4IoT 2017, LNICST 189, pp. 76–83, 2018.
https://doi.org/10.1007/978-3-319-67636-4_9

shelf life and presented to consumer on mobile devices. The development of sensors combining biochemical and microbial spoilage is getting a significant value in food supply chain [5]. The smart quality sensor was tested to measure quality and predict its progress in fresh cod under commercial ice storage conditions.

Unfortunately, the important phase of consumers handling fish is still not adequately evaluated and the information of remained shelf life before the preparation of fish isn't exactly specified and presented. Lately, consumers are well informed about the use of a slogan "From Farm to Fork" in connection to the place of origin and food traceability. All that is regulated by international and regional legislation and standards to provide the food quality and safety supported with shelf life information to consumers. The industrial relevance of selection and use of the optimal TTI smart label for monitoring food products allows reliable estimations of the remaining shelf life leading to improved management of the cold chain from production to the point of consumption [6].

Usually, consumers have the general information of food handling conditions during the storage. They also know the domestic refrigerator temperatures and home storage time of chilled food. The awareness of all that and their behavior at home have a great impact on food safety. A study was considering the above mentioned facts to couple them with a general rule that could be incorporated in shelf life studies [7] and safety risk assessment.

The focus of the presented cold chain study is the importance of integration of temperature monitoring during supply chain processes and modelling the transport and home conditions of consumers. Predicted shelf life results can be presented on mobile devices with recommendations of further storage and use of perishable food products. Implementations of various fixed and mobile sensor systems are available in cold stores and logistic processes and temperature measurements are collected and stored by supply chain partners. The last and most important step of sharing and making data public to perform detailed analysis is missing. The results could give all partners the approval of their work and provide confidence about the food quality and provenance to consumers.

This paper is organized as follows. Section 2 gives a description of cold chain divided in two phases. The first one is part of the controlled supply chain up to the point of sale and the second one continues during the consumers handling of product. In Sect. 3, the corresponding case study of temperature measurements with shelf life prediction results is presented. In the end, conclusions are made in Sect. 4.

2   Cold Chain

Cold chain (CC) systems are required in the food supply chain (SC) to monitor the handling conditions of products during processing, packaging, transport and storage phases to the point of sale. Various wireless sensors, other sensor and identification devices are connected to the internet and used to collect environment temperatures on regular basis [8]. Lately, they are well known as Internet of Things (IoT) and used in the supply chain.

Mostly, for perishable food real time data is provided in a form of temperature and sometimes humidity measurements from warehouses during the storage period and from trucks during short or long transport phases. Companies can use the data for their own management (automated reporting, improvements and alarms). Rarely, partners in the supply chain exchange that data and use it for determination of rejection problems at the delivery of food.

At the point of sale, consumers are not aware of the information collected or exchanged in the supply chain. They don't know whether there was something wrong with the product available for sale and can only believe what they are told. Usually, they are not aware of the importance of required conditions after purchase, including transport and storage at home. In case of highly perishable food products for which the cold chain was broken by different storage conditions it is very important to evaluate and consider changed shelf life information.

2.1 CC: From Farm to Sale

The supply chain of fresh and especially perishable food is well controlled in each phase. Figure 1 shows an example of measurements collected during transport (sensors are placed in the truck or van), warehousing with fixed temperature systems and at the point of sale in the retail. The final collection of cold chain measurements can be presented at the end after the exchange of data between all partners is performed.

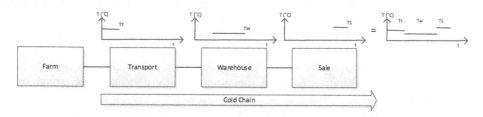

Fig. 1. Cold chain monitoring – temperatures are measured separately in each phase of the supply chain from the farm to the retail or other locations of sale (T_T – transport temperatures; T_W – warehouse temperatures; T_S – retail temperatures).

Figure 2 shows another option of measuring temperatures of product in the entire supply chain using the latest technology, smart RFID data loggers with temperature sensors, that are reusable and can be read at any time by mobile readers and presented to all partners in SC and consumers on mobile device.

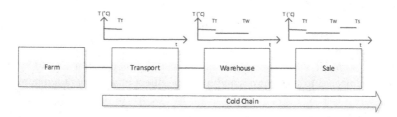

Fig. 2. Cold chain monitoring – temperatures are measured successively in all phases of the supply chain from the farm to the retail or other locations of sale.

2.2   CC: From Sale to Table

Cold chain is always broken at the point of sale. Consumers must have confidence in the product quality based on supply chain conditions. Afterwards, the product is transported in unsupervised environment to home for shorter period of time and will be then consumed shortly after the transport or stored in the fridge (Fig. 3). The cold chain monitoring can be then specified by the estimated temperature of 7 °C or 8 °C.

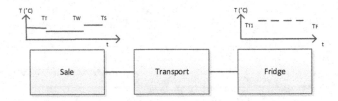

Fig. 3. Cold chain assumptions – temperatures are not measured after the sale. They could be estimated for the specific storage condition.

3   Shelf Life

The definition of shelf life is connected to recommendations of food producers and food industry about the maximum time for which food and their products can be stored under recommended conditions in the supply chain [9]. It is about the quality, health and freshness which are presented to the consumer at the point of sale. It is important to distinguish between high quality and edible shelf life when providing quality food products for higher prices.

Usually, the "expiry date" or "use before" are appointed and fixed in the processing phase to be printed on the label with recommended storage temperatures and attached to the package. The consumer has only the information for how long and how he should store the product before the use. Basically, the shelf life of food specified as a constant time interval as expiry date with specific conditions that will guarantee safety of products.

For example, the high quality shelf life of fish is 8 to 10 days when covered with ice and stored on temperatures between 0 °C and 4 °C. It is supposed that this was true in the supply chain that started at fish farm when fish was caught, packed and transported to the retail before was available for sale to the consumer.

3.1   Case Study

The aim of the presented study is shelf life prediction based on real data from temperature monitoring in fish cold chain during the storage process performed by company and data modeling of the transport and home conditions of consumers. The high quality shelf life evaluation will be presented to provide the actual information to the consumer. Fish was packed in the Styrofoam box and covered with melted ice. The cold chain was performed using RFID data loggers [4] with temperature sensor in the period of two days (from 16.7.2015, 14:15 to 18.7.2015, 11:15). Figure 4 shows environmental and fish temperatures measured during three phases of supply chain, starting in cold store (CS) with temperatures around 0 °C, continuing in transport (TR) in the car with high temperatures up to 30 °C and finally in the home refrigerator (R) with temperatures between 5 °C and 8 °C.

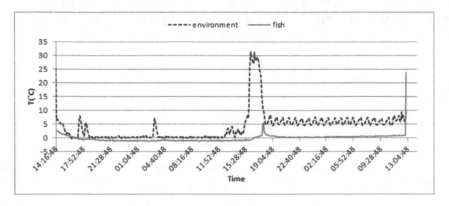

Fig. 4. Cold chain monitoring – environment and fish temperatures were measured in three phases including cold store (CS = 25 h), transport (TR = 2 h), refrigerator (R = 18 h).

3.2   Shelf Life Prediction

The proposed shelf life prediction model uses low level digital algorithm to translate periodic temperature measurements into remaining shelf life [10]. The calculation is based on the definition of start shelf life of X days at the temperature T. For each temperature measurement that is higher or lower than T, exists a different shelf life. For the corresponding time interval x (sampling interval) the product had been spent on temperature T. Therefore, an array of pairs T_i and X_i (Table 1) is defined for that product to get the best shelf life modelling. Additionally, the total shelf life at standard temperature is defined as X_s.

Table 1. -High quality shelf life for seabass related to storage time and temperature.

T (°C)	X	T (°C)	X	T (°C)	X	T (°C)	X
0	8	8	2.7	16	1.1	24	0.75
1	6.5	9	2.35	17	1	25	0.73
2	5	10	2	18	0.92	26	0.71
3	4	11	1.75	19	0.89	27	0.69
4	3.5	12	1.5	20	0.85	28	0.67
5	3.35	13	1.4	21	0.83	29	0.62
6	3.15	14	1.3	22	0.8	30	0.6
7	3	15	1.2	23	0.78	31	0.57

The algorithm that performs calculations of updated remaining shelf life X_r is defined as follows:

1. Determine temperature T_i that is closest to the measured temperature T.
2. For temperature T_i look up the suitable value X_i shown in Table 1.
3. Calculate the ratio x/X_i for value X_i (fraction of the total shelf life since the last temperature measurement).
4. Multiply the ratio by total shelf life X_s to get incremental shelf life consumption in days defined as $X_{is} = x * (X_s/X_i)$.
5. Subtract the incremental shelf life from current estimate of remaining shelf life at standard temperature to get X_r.
6. Update $X_r = X_r - X_{is}$.

Shelf life prediction is presented for three scenarios to show the importance and the impact of cold chain in fish supply chain. The total shelf life X_s equals 8 days at storage temperatures between T = 0 °C and T = 4 °C. Table 2 presents high quality shelf life calculations (QSL-remain) at the end of the performed test and separately QSL that was consumed for the first phase in cold store (QSL$_C$-CS) and for the second phase in transport and refrigerator (QSL$_C$-TR&R).

Table 2. Quality shelf life (QSL-remain) calculations of seabass stored in Styrofoam box in days/hours (d/h).

Test	QSL$_C$-CS (d/h)	QSL$_C$-TR&R (d/h)	QSL-remain (d/h)
Fish (Fig. 4)	2/0	0/20	5/4
Environment (Fig. 4)	2/6	2/10	3/8
Fish: CS(0 °C) + TR(28 °C) + R(7 °C)	2/0	2/16	3/8
Fish: CS(0 °C) + TR(10 °C) + R(7 °C)	2/0	2/2	3/22

First two tests show QSL results based on real fish and environmental temperature measurements shown in Fig. 4. The QSL-remain differs for approximately two days which indicates that environment temperatures aren't adequate information according to the cold chain conditions of fish in the Styrofoam box.

Next two tests included estimated temperatures of fish stored in the Styrofoam box without ice. In the first one, the prediction results for temperatures in CS (0 °C), TR (28 °C) and R (7 °C) are the same for the QSL-remain of environmental measurements, but they are different for QSL$_C$-CS and QSL$_C$-TR&R according to alterations between real measurements and estimations. For lower estimates of temperatures during transport phase (TR = 10 °C) is the QSL-remain improved for 16 h. This indicates how is minimized the remained shelf life for 14 h in only two hours on 18 °C higher temperatures.

The impact of temperatures and time in the period of consumers transport and the storage of fish before the consumption is very important. Considering the assumption that supply chain handling conditions correspond to standardized regulations (fish package includes melted ice to sustain the required humidity and temperature T = 0 °C) and the remained shelf life is available at the point of sale, the consumers can be convinced about the fish quality. Usually, they are not aware of the fact how they affect the faster spoilage of fish afterwards. For each labeled fish, displayed for sale [11], are as a part of mandatory information included storage conditions (temperature) and one of the following information available as expiry date, best before date or use by date. In addition, food operators provide the voluntary information like date of catch/harvest, nutrition declarations and other information.

Table 3 provides calculations of remained shelf life to conform to the quality the consumer anticipates for the food he consumes. It provides and additional information to be included together with the verification of place of origin and other traceability information in mobile applications. Shelf life calculations are based on the information that will be received at the time of purchase concerning storage conditions of fish (T = 0 °C), total shelf life equals 8 days, and QSL_{SC}-remain was 5 days.

Table 3. The impact of time and temperatures on shelf life calculations during transport and storage phases at consumers home.

TR (Time, T) (h, °C)	QSL_C-TR (d/h)	R (T = 7 °C) (d)	QSL_C-R (d/h)	QSL-remain (d/h)
1: 0, 10, 20, 30	0/1, 0/4, 0/10, 0/14	1	2/16	2/7, 2/4, 1/22, 1/18
		2	5/8	–0/9, –0/12, –0/18, –0/22
2: 0, 10, 20, 30	0/2, 0/10, 0/23, 1/8	1	2/16	2/6, 1/22, 1/9, 1/0
3: 0, 10, 20, 30	0/3, 1/5, 2/20, 4/0	1	2/16	2/5, 1/3, –0/12, –1/16

In Table 3 are described three tests depending on time of transport (TR Time = 1, 2, 3 h) with four examples of possible temperatures (T = 0, 10, 20, 30 °C) during that time linked to fish in environmental conditions. Storage of fish in refrigerator (T = 7 °C and R Time = 1, 2 days) is included in each test.

The analysis of presented results show high importance of shortest possible time during transport and lowest temperatures. In three hours on temperature T = 30 °C the consumed QSL equals four days. In case of QSL-remain calculations for R = 2 days are shown negative values which indicate the expiry date of product. The QSL-remain is highly related with both parameters (T, Time) and should be considered by consumers which means that environment temperatures aren't adequate for cold chain conditions of fish.

4   Conclusion

The cold chain monitoring of fish supply chain was used to provide the shelf life predictions in the first phase from fish farm to the point of sale. These results should be presented to consumer because they do not have the impact on them but should be informed about the QSL_remain. Additionally, the next very important phase of consumers' involvement in cold chain from point of sale to the final preparation of food is analyzed with various options of time and temperatures scenarios to be used for remained shelf life calculations. The results can be used to give recommendations of how fish should be stored and for how long they can keep the quality and freshness of fish after the purchase.

Acknowledgments. This work has been supported by Slovenian research agency under ARRS Program P2-0359 Pervasive computing and in collaboration with Fonda.si which provided the data.

References

1. Ostli, J., Esaiassen, M., Garitta, L., Nostvold, B., Hough, G.: How fresh is fish? Perceptions and experience when buying and consuming fresh cod fillets. Food Qual. Prefer. **27**, 26–34 (2013)
2. Gogou, E., Katsaros, G., Derens, E., Alvarez, G., Taoukis, P.S.: Cold chain database development and application as a tool for the cold chain management and food quality evaluation. Int. J. Refrig **52**, 109–121 (2015)
3. Tsironi, T., Stamatiou, A., Giannoglou, M., Velliou, E., Taoukis, P.S.: Predictive modelling and selection of time temperature integrators for monitoring the shelf life of modified atmosphere packed gilthead seabream fillets. LWT Food Sci. Technol. **44**, 1156–1163 (2011)
4. Trebar, M., Lotrič, M., Fonda, I., Pleteršek, A., Kovačič, K.: RFID data loggers in fish supply chain traceability. Int. J. Antennas Propag. **2013**, 1–9 (2013)
5. Garcia, R.M., Cabo, L.M., Herrera, R.J., Ramilo-Fernandez, G., Alonso, A.A., Balsa-Canto, E.: Smart sensor to predict retail fresh fish quality under ice storage. J. Food Eng. **197**, 87–97 (2017)
6. Giannoglou, M., Touli, A., Platakou, E., Tsironi, T., Taoukis, P.S.: Predictive modeling and selection of TTI smart labels for monitoring the quality and shelf-life of frozen food. Innov. Food Sci. Emerg. Technol. **26**, 294–301 (2014)
7. Roccato, A., Uyttendaele, M., Membre, J.M: Analysis of domestic refrigerator temperatures and home storage time distributions for shelf-life studies and food safety risk assessment. Food Res. Int. (2017). doi:10.1017/j.foodres.2017.02.017
8. Heising, J.K., Boekel, M.A.J.S., Dekker, M.: Simulations on the prediction of cod (Gadus morhua) freshness from an intelligent packaging sensor concept. Food Pack. Shelf Life **3**, 47–55 (2015)
9. Limbo, S., Sinelli, N., Riva, M.: Freshness decay and shelf life predictive modelling of European sea bass (Dicentrarchus labrax) applying chemical methods and electronic nose. LWT Food Sci. Technol. **42**, 977–984 (2009)
10. Roberts, W., Cox, J.L.: Proposal for standardized core functionality in digital time-temperature monitoring SAL devices. A White Paper by the temperature Tracking Work Group of the SAL Consortium (2003)
11. A Pocket Guide to the EUs new fish and aquaculture consumer labels, Publications Office of the European Union (2014). https://ec.europa.eu/fisheries/sites/fisheries/files/docs/body/eu-new-fish-and-aquaculture-consumer-labels-pocket-guide_en.pdf. ISBN 978-92-79-43893-6. doi:10.2771/86800

A HCE-Based Authentication Approach for Multi-platform Mobile Devices

Luigi Manco(✉), Luca Mainetti, Luigi Patrono, Roberto Vergallo, and Alessandro Fiore

Department of Innovation Engineering, University of Salento, Lecce, Italy
{luigi.manco,luca.mainetti,luigi.patrono,roberto.vergallo,
alessandro.fiore}@unisalento.it

Abstract. Mobile devices are able to gather more and more functionalities useful to control people's daily life facilities. They offer computational power and different kinds of sensors and communication interfaces, enabling users to monitor and interact with the environment by a single integrated tool. Near Field Communication (NFC) represents a suitable technology in the interaction between digital world and real world. Most NFC-enabled mobile devices exploit the smart card features as a whole: e.g., they can be used as contactless payment and authentication systems. Nevertheless at present heterogeneity in mobile and IoT technologies does not permit to fully express potentialities of mobile devices as authentication systems, since most of the proposed solutions are strictly related to specific technological platforms. Basing on smart payment card approach, Europay, MasterCard e VISA (EMV) protocols and Host Card Emulation (HCE) technology, the current work proposes a distributed architecture for using NFC-enabled mobile devices as possession factor in Multifactor Authentication (MFA) systems. The innovative idea of the proposal relies on its independence with respect to the specific software and hardware technologies. The architecture is able to distribute tokens to registered mobile devices for univocally identifying user identity, tracing its actions in the meanwhile. As proof of concept, a real case has been implemented: an Android/iOS mobile application to control a car central locking system by NFC.

Keywords: Smart cities · Smart building · NFC · Mobile · HCE · Cloud

1 Introduction

In smart cities, advanced systems as sensing technologies and smart IoT devices, are addressed to improve and automate processes within a city [1], trying to enhance and ease citizens daily life: several real cases show that IoT technologies support added-value services for the administration of the city and for the citizens [2]. On the other hand, smart cities call for newer technical solutions and best-practice guidelines. In this regard, the presented paper analyses an innovative solution by which smartphones can be used as authentication system instead of common physical key: the smartphones can replace smart card, badges, tokens, and other long-standing, but often uncomfortable, methods of identification and security, providing to users a single mean of

© ICST Institute for Computer Sciences, Social Informatics and Telecommunications Engineering 2018
A. Longo et al. (Eds.): IISSC 2017/CN4IoT 2017, LNICST 189, pp. 84–92, 2018.
https://doi.org/10.1007/978-3-319-67636-4_10

authentication, their own smartphones. Such solution has several applications in smart cities: one need only think to the buildings with access control systems based on badge. Another example is related to car sharing: the proposed solution offers a simple way to implement the car locking system that can recognise the user by means of only his smartphone, tracking also his movements during the use of the car.

Nowadays, the smartphone is clearly the collector of people's virtual social network. Nevertheless, research and industry offer exciting possibilities with respect to interaction between smartphones and the real world, mainly related to home automation and the Internet of Things (IoT) scenarios, thanks to the embedded sensors and the communication interfaces. In this sense, the smartphone is taking on the features of several daily life objects, acting as proxy for the interactions between people and environment.

Modern security systems adopt the so-called Multifactor Authentication (MFA) paradigm: authentication and security are guaranteed combining more than one method of authentication from independent categories of credentials to verify the user's identity in its mission-critical transactions. An authentication factor is a category of credential used for identity verification. The three most common categories are often described as something the user knows (the knowledge factor), something the user has (the possession factor), and something the user is (the inherence factor). Typical instances of the aforementioned factors are, namely, the password, the security token, and the biometric verification.

During the last years, several work in scientific and technical literature have focused on using mobile devices as tools for providing authentication factor facilities in MFA systems, namely [3–6].

In a mobile MFA system, NFC is the way forward: NFC Card emulation mode is well suited for mobile identification-based scenarios as possession factor [7–9]. Furthermore, NFC Card emulation mode is compatible with pre-existing smartcard-based authentication systems, at present widely distributed.

However, the widespread use of proprietary technologies in the mobile sector makes it difficult to use smartphones as universal tool for interacting with physical world. Specifically, NFC interface is not freely exploitable: iOS applications cannot leverage software tools, such as SDK APIs, to control NFC interface, and there is no way to use NFC in Apple devices, except by means of Apple Pay wallet. Moreover, NCF suffers for well-known security issues, but both industrial and research studies identified solutions for facing them [10–13]. So, there is the dire need of a solution that enables users to take advantage of such IoT technology independently from the specific smartphone platform, in order to enable the implementation of the virtual world typical scenarios in real life. As an example, Table 1 compares four recognised industrial solutions for second factor authentication system by means of mobile devices. It is worth noting that only one of them uses NFC technology and it is compatible only with Android devices. Moreover, none of them is compatible with pre-existing authentication systems.

The presented study tries to overcome the problem of using smartphones as authentication means and credential category in a mobile MFA system independently from their specific operative system and software/hardware restrictions, maintaining all the necessary security requirements. The core idea is to use the recent Host Card Emulation (HCE) technology, through which the cloud generates and distributes virtual smart card

Table 1. Industrial solutions for mobile possession factor

Product	HW	Modality	Compatibility		
			iOS	Android	Pre-existing infrastructures
SPG	BLE	Nearby	Y	N	N
Lockitron	BLE+WiFi	Nearby	Y	Y	N
Key2Share	NFC	Proximity	N	Y	N
Unikey	BLE	Nearby	Y	Y	N

to mobile devices, enabling the smartphone to use NFC card emulation mode to communicate with smart devices and identify itself emulating the virtual card received by the HCE cloud. Such approach also permits to authenticate the user throughout the NFC transactions by means of a software solution, while leveraging cryptographic processes traditionally used by hardware-based secure elements without the need for a physical secure element.

The goal of the study is to create a system that permits to a mobile application to communicate with a smart device via NFC interface, transmitting to it user data useful for its authentication by the system. As specified in the paper introduction, the main obstacle is related with iOS platforms, since for such system NFC interface control is exclusively delegated to Apple Pay wallet. On the other hand, Android OS makes available specific APIs able to totally control smartphone NFC transceiver. So, the challenge is to implement in the smart device a software component able to read and accurately interpret the instructions received from the smartphone, regardless of which is the smartphone OS between the two considered. Shortly, the original contribution of the paper relies on the fact that the created system is platform-agnostic: the designed architecture enables both Android and Apple devices to be used as authentication factor, bypassing the limit imposed by Apple devices.

Finally, the proposed architecture has been validated by means of a proof-of-concept: a prototype able to control the car locking system by means of the user smartphone as second authentication factor.

The rest of the paper is organized as follows. Section 2 describes the design of the system architecture. Here the authors analyse the software and hardware architecture model and the information flowing through it. Section 3 presents the proof-of-concept validating the architecture.

2   System Architecture

2.1   Architecture Model

The proposed system architecture consists of three main components, as clearly shown by the UML deployment diagram reported in Fig. 1: (i) a mobile application for iOS/Android able to communicate via the smartphones NFC interface, (ii) a smart device equipped with NFC transceiver, and (iii) a cloud architecture based on Host Card Emulation (HCE) approach for sharing and synchronizing of virtual smart cards among subscribed smartphones.

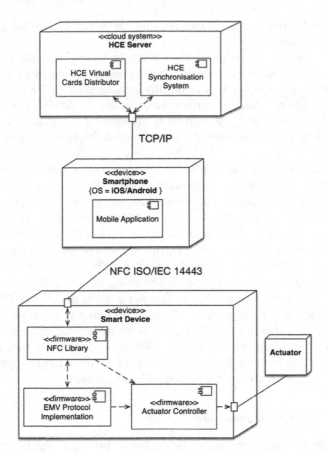

Fig. 1. Architecture deployment diagram: the mobile device authenticate itself to the Smart Device using the token provided by the HCE server and passing it through a communication channel compliant with NFC standard. The Smart Device hosts a custom implementation of EMV standard.

The main idea is based on the use of HCE technology, through which the cloud generates and distributes virtual smart card, also known as token, to mobile devices. The NFC card emulation mode allows the smartphone to emulate contactless card by means of such tokens. Another common secure system commonly used for card-emulation mode in NFC contactless transactions is the Secure Element, a chip embedded directly into the device's hardware, or in a SIM/UICC card provided by network operators, in which can be found the secure tokens and execution environment. Differently from this last, HCE moves the secure components to the cloud and avoids any hardware restriction.

As shown in Fig. 1, in the presented architecture a mobile application receives and manages the virtual card from a HCE server. More specifically, within iOS platforms such application is exclusively represented by Apple Pay wallet, while for Android platforms it can be a dedicated application also. Through the NFC card emulation mode, such mobile application can communicate with the Smart Device using the HCE-generated virtual smart card.

In order to perform the communication with the smartphone, the Smart Device grounds on three main software modules. The first one is the interface for the communications with the smartphone. It is physically implemented on the device though a dedicated driver library aimed to interface the smart device with its own NCF antenna and to reorganise the data received from the smartphone. On the other side, there is the interface for controlling the actuator, the second module implemented within the smart device.

The third module is completely dedicated to overcome the iOS restrictions relating to the use of NFC. It is a custom implementation of EMV standard, an open-standard set of specifications for smart card payments, also known as chip cards, and payment terminals for reading them. The EMV specifics are based on various standards, such as ISO/IEC 7816 for contact cards payment and ISO/IEC 14443 for contactless cards ones. Relating to the present study, the Smart Device in the architecture embeds the implementation of the ISO/IEC 14443 standard, since it is the protocol involved in the Apple Pay wallet contactless payment processes. Therefore, in such architecture the Smart Device acts as a sort of Electronic Funds Transfer at Point of Sale (EFTPOS), which receives a payment request from the wallet and performs some resulting actions. By means of such module, the Smart Device uses payment information received from smartphone to authenticate the Apple Pay wallet users. Differently with respect to a standard EFTPOS, in this case the module does not initialize a payment process for an authenticated user, but it invokes the Actuator Controller module.

2.2 Architecture Information Flow

The Fig. 2 depicts a high-level abstraction schema that shows the information flow through the presented architecture.

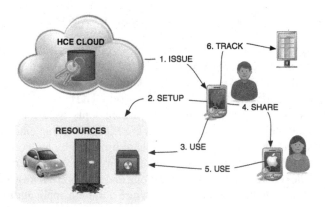

Fig. 2. Information flow describing the steps in using mobile devices as authentication factor.

The user loads his own personal information in the smartphone by means of the ad-hoc Android mobile application or the Apple Pay wallet, depending on the considered operative system. In the latter case, such information have to be strictly related to a physical smart card, since the mobile application are dealing with a mobile wallet. What matters is that, ones loaded into the smartphone, such information are transmitted to the HCE platform and they do not rely anymore on the smartphone, coherently with the required security standards.

The HCE cloud platform stores the personal information for the registered users and it generates a linked virtual smart cards, so that mapping the user/smartphone pair to the virtual smart cards exploitable for NFC communication. Next, the HCE platform provides the smartphone with the generated virtual smart card.

Once obtained the virtual smart card, the smartphone can establish a communication channel with the smart device by the NFC card emulation mode. During a first phase, the smartphone sets up the smart device to get it trusting the virtual smart card information. Subsequent smartphone/smart device communication streams are aimed to activate the bound actuator.

Furthermore, the virtual smart card can be shared among users, so that sharing the access to the physical resources and the cloud architecture can keep trace of the whole actions performed by user, by means of a synchronizing service.

3   Proof of Concept

The presented study proposes a HCE-compliant cloud architecture that permits to convert the Android and iOS smartphones into a strong user authentication means. In order to validate the architecture, a mobile application system for controlling the electric door locking mechanisms in building and automotive areas by means of the smartphone has been realised.

According as the considered operative system, Android or iOS, the prototype is composed by two different mobile applications and two HCE cloud platforms. Accordingly, the smart device embeds the firmware able to treat differently the NFC requests coming from the two OSs.

In iOS devices, as stated in the previous sections, it was necessary to use Apple Pay wallet in order to establish NFC communications with the smart device. It uses a proprietary HCE cloud platform, compliant with the described architecture.

Instead, for Android devices, an ad-hoc HCE platform and a mobile application have been created. The application aimed to send to HCE platform the user credentials and to communicate with the smart device via NFC. The HCE platform was able to receive the user credentials sent by the smartphone and to reply sending to it an access token suitable for being used during the NFC card emulation mode communications.

The smart device has been composed by an Arduino Mega board equipped with a compatible NFC expansion shield. Also, it was connected to the actuator, namely the locking motor, by means of two relays, as shown in Fig. 3.

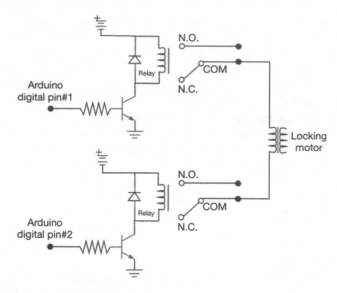

Fig. 3. Electric scheme of the connection block between the Arduino board and the locking motor

Coherently with the workflow depicted in the Fig. 2, the user authenticates itself to smart device, communicating with it by NFC card emulation mode. The smart device verifies the user identity basing on the data set during a preparation phase and, in case of success, it activates the two relays. They are disposed and connected to the circuit so

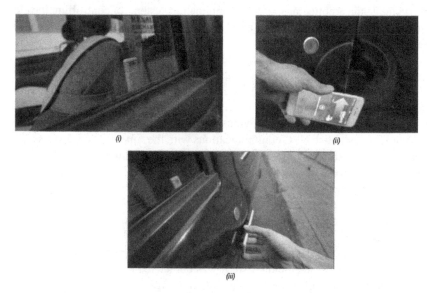

Fig. 4. Implementation of the prototype in a real case: the car locking system is not blocked (i). When the smartphone is moved closer the NFC antenna embedded in the car door (ii), the blocking system gets locked (iii)

as to be activated in a complementary manner, accordingly with the Arduino board directives: the Arduino board can activate one by one the relays according to the state of the locking motor, imposing a clockwise or a counter clockwise rotatory motion to it. In this way, two consecutive proximity communication steps between the smartphone and the smart device force two complementary motor directions, hence closing and opening the door, and vice versa.

Finally, the prototype has been implemented in a real case: the smart device was assembled in a car door and connected to the locking motor. Figure 4 shows the prototype at work by means of an iOS smartphone: when the smartphone is moved closer to the NFC antenna embedded in the car door, the locking motor is activated and the car locking system blocks or unblocks the corresponding door.

4 Conclusions and Future Work

The presented work introduced a software and hardware solution able to implement a multifactor authentication system in which possession factor is represented by the user NFC-compliant smartphone. The security token useful for the second factor in the authentication system is handed out to user mobile device by a HCE-based cloud software component. Mobile device communicate such token for authenticating the user via NFC card emulation mode, so that emulating a real smartcard.

The described strategy is compatible with both Android and iOS mobile platforms, bypassing the iOS restrictions in using NFC features. It can be also seamless integrated in pre-existing smartcard-based authentication systems, thanks to the adoption of the card emulation mode.

The model validation has included the implementation of a prototype able to control the car locking system by means of the user smartphone as second authentication factor. The experimentation showed the proper functioning of the developed solution.

The future work concern the improvement of the features for the developed HCE system by adopting the newest techniques on the cloud topic.

References

1. Hancke, G.P., de Carvalho e Silva, B.: The role of advanced sensing in smart cities. Sensors **13**(1), 393–425 (2013). Multidisciplinary Digital Publishing Institute, Switzerland
2. Zanella, A., Bui, N., Castellani, A., Vangelista, L., Zorzi, M.: Internet of Things for smart cities. IEEE Internet Things J. **1**(1), 22–32 (2014)
3. Aloul, F., Zahidi, S., El-Hajj, W.: Two factor authentication using mobile phones. In: 2009 IEEE/ACS International Conference on Computer Systems and Applications, pp. 641–644 (2009)
4. Smith, M., Tassone, J., Holmes, D.: Method and system for providing identity, authentication, and access services. US 9076273 B2, 07 July 2015
5. Mandalapu, A., Raj, L.D.: An NFC featured three level authentication system for tenable transaction and abridgment of ATM card blocking intricacies. In: 2015 International Conference and Workshop on Computing and Communication (IEMCON), pp. 1–6 (2015)

6. Chen, W., Hancke, G.P., Mayes, K.E., Lien, Y., Chiu, J.-H.: NFC mobile transactions and authentication based on GSM network. In: 2010 Second International Workshop on Near Field Communication, pp. 83–89 (2010)
7. Adukkathayar, A., Krishnan, G.S., Chinchole, R.: Secure multifactor authentication payment system using NFC. In: 2015 10th International Conference on Computer Science & Education (ICCSE), pp. 349–354 (2015)
8. Ivey, R.G.F., Braun, K.A., Blashill, J.: System and method for two factor user authentication using a smartphone and NFC token and for the automatic generation as well as storing and inputting of logins for websites and web applications. 14/600391, 20 January 2015
9. Subpratatsavee, P., Sriboon, W., Issavasopon, W.: Automated car parking authentication system using NFC and public key cryptography based on android phone. Appl. Mech. Mater. **752–753**, 1006–1009 (2015)
10. Armando, A., Merlo, A., Verderame, L.: Trusted host-based card emulation. In: 2015 International Conference on High Performance Computing & Simulation (HPCS), pp. 221–228 (2015)
11. Cavdar, D., Tomur, E.: A practical NFC relay attack on mobile devices using card emulation mode. In: 38th International Convention on Information and Communication Technology, Electronics and Microelectronics (MIPRO), pp. 1308–1312 (2015)
12. Oh, S., Doo, T., Ko, T., Kwak, J., Hong, M.: Countermeasure of NFC relay attack with jamming. In: 12th International Conference & Expo on Emerging Technologies for a Smarter World (CEWIT), pp. 1–4 (2015)
13. Urien, P.: New direction for open NFC trusted mobile applications: the MOBISIM project. In: IEEE Conference on Communications and Network Security (CNS), pp. 711–712 (2015)

IISSC: Smart Challenges and Needs

Smart Anamnesis for Gyn-Obs: Issues and Opportunities

Lucia Vaira[✉] and Mario A. Bochicchio

Set-Lab, Department of Engineering for Innovation, University of Salento, Lecce, Italy
{lucia.vaira,mario.bochicchio}@unisalento.it

Abstract. Completeness and accuracy of data is probably a persistent and intrusive problem in any process related to data capture. This is especially true in the clinical field, where omitting significant information can have considerable implications for diagnosis and treatment in general. History taking from patients represents a crucial phase for physicians in order to evaluate the patient's wellness status and to perform correct diagnoses. As a routine procedure, it is a time-consuming and not so appealing obligation. In this paper we present a smart approach to anamnesis in order to gain as much data as possible and to have high quality information by avoiding any misunderstandings or errors. The approach is mainly based on the possibility to capture data directly at the source increasing the overall effectiveness of physician's time and of the visit itself. Its feasibility has been evaluated in the context of a complex clinical domain: maternal and fetal assessment during pregnancy.

Keywords: Medical history taking · Data incompleteness · Data quality · Data capture · Maternal and fetal assessment

1 Introduction and Background

The medical history taking is the most common task performed by physicians. That is why Engel and Morgan defined it "the most powerful, sensitive and versatile instrument available to the physician" [1].

Scientific discoveries and technological innovations have deeply changed the way to perform diagnoses and to treat diseases. But neither scientific nor technological advances in medicine have changed the fact that a "good" history taking contributes significantly to problem detection, diagnostic accuracy and patient health outcomes. By the medical history, physicians acquire 60–80% of the information that is relevant for a diagnosis [2] and the history alone can lead to the final diagnosis in 76% [3].

History taking and communication skills programs have become cornerstones in medical education over the past 30 years and are implemented in most US, Canadian, German and UK medical schools [4]. However, history taking cannot be represented by specific and universal rules since it is highly contextual, depending on situation, patient and physician, cultural characteristics and other similar factors.

The medical history does not involve only the current situation of the patient. Very important are similarly the past medical history, the drug history, the family history (in

© ICST Institute for Computer Sciences, Social Informatics and Telecommunications Engineering 2018
A. Longo et al. (Eds.): IISSC 2017/CN4IoT 2017, LNICST 189, pp. 95–104, 2018.
https://doi.org/10.1007/978-3-319-67636-4_11

order to find out if there are any genetic conditions within the family) and the social history, including all the patient's background: smoking, alcohol, habits, etc.

Having access to all these information is not a trivial task.

Physicians need to remember many questions relating to the management of each condition and omitting an important question can actually compromise the diagnosis. For example, studies show that 50% of psychosocial and psychiatric problems are missed during medical consultations [5] and that 54% of patient problems and 45% of patient concerns are neither elicited by the clinician nor disclosed by the patient [6].

Computer-assisted history taking systems (CAHTS in the following) are tools that aim to aid physicians in gathering data from patients to inform a diagnosis, a treatment plan or both [7].

Although CAHTS were first described in the 1960s [8], there is still uncertainty about the impact of these methods on medical history data collection, clinical care and patient outcomes, hence they often remain underused in routine clinical practice [9].

Bowling in [10] describes that the various CAHTS typologies depend on three inter-related factors:

- the information technology used to collect the information (e.g. personal computer, personal digital assistant, Internet, telephone, etc.);
- the administration mode (e.g. administered by an interviewer or self-administered);
- the presentation channel (e.g. auditory, oral or visual).

The author presented the different and serious effects that the administration mode for example can have on data quality. Indeed, a very important aspect to take into account when dealing with the medical history taking, is represented by the social desirability bias [11]: a factor defined as the effect of disturbance that comes into play when the patient, responding to an interview, has a chance to give answers which may be deemed to be "more socially acceptable" than others in order to look more "normal" as possible.

If patients use an electronic device for a CAHTS, they are less likely to falsify data when compared with those using pen-and-paper, as demonstrated by 4 randomized controlled trials [12–15].

In particular, self-administered computer-assisted interviewing is perceived favorably by patients because computer systems cannot be judgmental towards sensitive behavioral data. Therefore, CAHTS are particularly useful in eliciting potentially sensitive information (e.g. alcohol consumption, psychiatric care, sexual health and gynecological health).

In this paper we discuss the issues and opportunities for the adoption of a smart approach to anamnesis in the context of maternal health and wellbeing as well as fetal growth monitoring. The approach is in line with the current evolution of smart hospitals for smart cities and it is mainly based on the possibility to to gain as much data as possible directly at the source in order to have high quality information and to increase the overall effectiveness of physician's time and of the visit itself.

2 Motivation

Perinatal period is a very delicate stage of life for both mother and families. Maternal and fetal constant monitoring during the whole pregnancy is a critical aspect since it may detect early alarm signals for a wide range of pathologies in order to promptly treat potential complications and to avoid unnecessary obstetric interventions at the time of delivery.

Physicians refer to standard reference charts to evaluate the fetal growth development but such reference values are characterized by a series of limitations making difficult to use them as a standard for diagnoses, such as data obsolescence, methods heterogeneity, lack of data, hospital-based samples, exclusion criteria, missing of several important factors to take into account (lifestyle, familial aspects, physiological and pathological variables, etc.) that may lead to inaccurate diagnoses of fetuses as small (SGA) or large (LGA) for gestational age.

The lack of data is the major limitation. Considering that every year in the world there are about 160 millions of newborns, the huge amount of data potentially involved in the analysis of fetal growth and maternal wellness should provide a comprehensive analysis able to avoid false-positives and false-negatives diagnoses and to prevent undue anxiety in families which typically leads to unnecessary and expensive further investigation.

Unfortunately, a global strategy which addresses the lack of data issue does not exist. Data are still missing and this can be due to several reasons which are not only of technical nature [16]:

- the local nature of traditional data collections, managed by bureaucratic units;
- the legitimate conflict of interest among physicians (practicing defensive medicine), patients (interested in health protection) and Health Administrations (focused on cost reduction);
- the lack of adoption of proper data harvesting strategies and techniques.

Defining new approaches to data collection in order to analyze, visualize and share information that could be useful in decision-making processes and hence to take advantage from the big amount of accumulating clinical data in order to extract useful knowledge and understand patterns and trends within the data.

Mothers and families are very sensitive to all aspects concerning the fetal wellbeing and are hence highly motivated to change their lifestyle and their approach to healthcare. This means that, although physicians may be reluctant to use electronic devices for data gathering that could require extra time, patients have a clear and valid reason to spend additional time to address their own problems and so there is no need to educate them on how the adoption of a new approach to data collection would improve the entire system.

3   Our Approach

In the era of Internet of Things (IoT), smart devices can help to transform clinical practice and hence to improve the delivery of care. As specified in [17], in order to collect data from all possible sources directly from the field, new data harvesting techniques can be adopted:

1. form-based input on Web pages and mobile App;
2. new generation mobile devices, which typically are packed with sensors (e.g. GPS, gyroscopes, accelerometers, touch-sensitive surfaces, microphones and cameras) or have physical interfaces that allow the connection of external modules (e.g. blood pressure cuffs, blood glucose monitoring) or wearable sensors (e.g. heartbeat and contraction monitoring) linked to smartphone to harvest and monitor data;
3. direct connection to medical equipment (e.g. medical imaging machines, medical ventilators, medical monitors, etc.) with automatic DICOM metadata decoding and/ or signal processing techniques;
4. automatic data extraction from medical documents, both printed and digital, provided to patients after medical test or extracted from large digital archives;
5. data-scraping techniques able to emulate a human agent interacting with the user interface of a non-interoperable software in order to insert/extract relevant data from electronic documents (web pages, electronic forms, etc.), for specific purposes or for massive ingestion;
6. smart digital devices (e.g. for weight and height measurement, speech-to-text software, etc.) provided to physicians to simplify data collection at the clinic visit.

For sake of simplicity, in the rest of the paper we will refer to these techniques with the name of channels.

In the gynecological and obstetrical sector, channel 1 (form-based input adoption) is more appropriate for patients which in general have a strong motivation to spend their time to describe in detail and to precisely address their own problems. This is a time-intensive channel and for this reason it is rarely adopted by physicians. Furthermore, physicians do not trust very much the ways their patients may collect data via electronic devices since patients' participation can cause an overflow of irrelevant or trivial information, due to the fact that patients are typically unable to assign to data the appropriate significance (i.e. its medical meaning). Physicians typically handle medical information on paper and hence avail themselves of collaboration of clinicians to transcribe hand-written worksheets.

Channel 1 has been deeply exploited as a sort of "self-reported interview pre-visit": the patient fills out a questionnaire a few days before the visit by using a personal computer, a smartphone or a tablet.

Such questionnaire is composed by two main parts: a profile section which includes:

- personal data (e.g. name, date and place of birth, age, maternal and paternal ethnicity, place of residence, educational background, job, contact information like email and phone, etc.);

- medical data (e.g. potential pathologies and infections which can be developed during pregnancy, before pregnancy or can be due to genetic conditions within the family);
- biometric data (e.g. weight, height, etc.);
- lifestyle data (smoking, nutrition, physical activity, alcohol consumption, hobby, allergies, intolerances, etc.). A screenshot of the profile section is showed in Fig. 1.

Fig. 1. Web-based questionnaire filled out by patients before visits

The second part of the questionnaire includes the actual anamnesis:

- menstrual history: the first important historical information that obstetricians usually gather is the Last Menstrual Period (LMP). Beyond the date of the first day of the LMP, patient has to insert cycle length in days and normality. Information on prior contraception and fertility treatment are also important to add in order to determine the utility of the LMP to predict the Estimated Date of Delivery (EDD);
- obstetric history: past pregnancy history is an important predictor of pregnancy risk in multiparous women. Patients has to indicate the dates of deliveries, types of deliveries (vaginal or cesarean), indication and type of uterine incision if a cesarean delivery was performed, birth weight and gestational age of previous infants, complications of previous pregnancies, and current state of health of previous children;
- psychosocial evaluation: a description of the workplace and the woman's job responsibilities should be elicited to rule out any significant exposure to toxins or ergonomic stressors that could have a negative impact on the pregnancy. Pre-existent problems of anxiety and hypertension should be also elicited;
- medical and surgical history: patients are asked specifically about common medical conditions as well as uncommon conditions that are known to have serious effects on pregnancy. Common problems include for example diabetes, chronic hypertension, asthma, cardiac diseases, etc. Less common but equally important issues include lupus, thyroid disorders, chronic hepatitis, tuberculosis, bleeding disorders, chronic

renal disease, cancer, etc. A surgical history with emphasis on abdominal procedures or orthopedic procedures involving the pelvis is also taken into consideration.

Once filled out, the questionnaire is available for consultancy to the Secretariat of the hospital or of the medical office in order to create the patient report. This interface allows to suggest in real-time to physicians which part of the anamnesis has to be completed and which values are "borderline". The quality of inserted data is guaranteed by means of data validation checks. In this way, gathering such data does not need to add to physicians' time and, in principle, permits more time for the patient to discuss their actual health problem rather than routine aspects of medical history with physicians.

Channel 2 (new generation mobile devices adoption) is based on the possibility to exploits the benefits that can be achieved by adopting wearable sensing devices for health monitoring which allow to sync data with the smartphone. New generation mobile devices are typically packed with sensors which allow to harvest data. There are many devices already on the market for fitness and wellness that use consumer-facing applications which can be easily incorporated into clinical practice in order to help both patients and physicians monitor vital signs and symptom.

During the third trimester of pregnancy, mothers can wear on the belly a small and flexible device in order to continuously monitor the baby kicks by uploading automatically the information to smartphones. Other kinds of sensors can allow to detect and record the baby's heartbeat and to measure the frequency and duration of contractions in order to provide an early indication of baby's and mother's health.

The direct involvement of mothers allows to constantly monitor their baby's fetal activities and alert their caregivers when something seems out of the norm.

In case of high-risks pregnancy, this channel allows to provide physicians an observation over time of heart rate variations in order to develop a sort of heartbeat history during pregnancy.

Channels 3, 4, 5 and 6 allow a direct and automatic data transfer eliminating hence the need for human entry. Direct data capture improves data ingestion and reduces potential sources of errors leading hence to a greater accuracy.

Channel 3 (direct connection to medical equipment) allows data collection directly at the source, i.e. at the output of the medical equipment used for the assessment of fetal biometric parameters, such as the traditional Ultrasound machine. In this case, the adopted standard for the distribution and viewing of medical images is the DICOM (Digital Imaging and Communications in Medicine) standard, which allows obtaining discrete values directly from its headers.

The direct connection with the ultrasound machine allows to gather data (acquired pictures and biometric measures) during the visit and to manage and integrate them in the patient history at the time of visit with no need for human entry.

In our case, channel 4 (automatic data extraction from medical documents) is based on the adoption of the Optical Character Recognition (OCR) technique, which allows to analyze and extract textual data typically included in the ultrasound pictures which are usually accompanied by measures (biometric parameters with the corresponding values), derived data (gestational age measured in weeks and days) and other info (ultrasound machine model, exam date, etc.).

This channel is used in strict connection with the previous one, since it allows to automatically assemble several parameters starting from the pictures acquired by the ultrasound machine and stored into the central system.

Channel 5 (data-scraping techniques adoption) is mainly based on software techniques able to emulate a human agent interacting with the user interface of a non-interoperable software in order to insert/extract relevant data for specific purposes or for massive ingestion.

This channel is very helpful in the starting stage, when a first data ingestion and data integration process is needed. Physicians have information about several patients on the personal computer in their office. Such channel allows to retrieve all data directly from web pages or electronic forms with no need for human entry.

Channel 6 (smart digital devices adoption) is in line with the current evolution of Internet of Things in which smart devices can help to transform clinical practice and to improve the delivery of care as in the "connected health".

Medical offices can be transformed into "smart rooms" which simplifies and enriches the collection of patients' data.

The maternal weight gain monitoring during pregnancy is a critical matter the health of pregnancy and for the maternal and fetal long-term health. It depends on several factors such as the woman's weight before pregnancy, the woman's height, the type of pregnancy (one baby or twins), etc.

A precise and continuous monitoring can serve to evaluate whether patients are gaining less than the recommended amount of weight (this is associated with delivering a baby who is too small, with consequences like difficulty starting breastfeeding, increased risk for illness, etc.) or if they are gaining more than the recommended amount of weight (this is associated with having a baby who will born too large, which can lead to delivery complications, cesarean delivery, obesity during childhood, etc.).

Medical offices can be equipped with smart and low-cost instruments which can allow to obtain and automatically store precise measures during visits.

A WiFi scale, using the 802.11g wireless standard, is able to transmit and store data relating to the weight, fat mass, lean mass and body mass index (BMI) of patients who stand on the scale itself. Such measures are automatically taken before the visit starts in order to collect them and to analyze the variation over time. The same is true for measuring height: a digital stadiometer is able to quickly, easily, and accurately measure the height of patients.

In Fig. 2 the overall architecture of the proposed approach is presented. It can be divided into two main parts:

- the patient area, which includes all the possible devices (PC, notebook, tablet and smartphone) that a mother can adopt to perform the web-based questionnaire and to follow her own visits and monitoring reports;
- the medical office area, which includes all the possible devices (ultrasound machine, PC, scale and stadiometer) that physicians can exploit to capture data directly at the source and to store data on a centralized server.

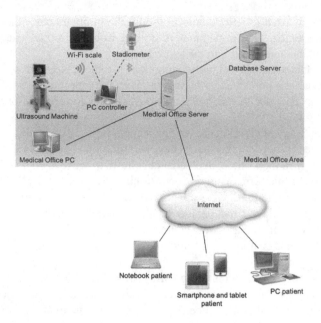

Fig. 2. Architecture of the proposed approach

4   Conclusions

The benefits coming from the combined adoption of the six above-mentioned channels in order to gather as much data as possible before, during and after each gynecological/ obstetrical visit are manifold: it saves physicians' time; it improves delivery of care to patients having special needs; it facilitates and expand the data collection, especially in case of potentially sensitive information (e.g. sexual history, alcohol consumption, etc.); it allows an easier availability and access to medical information for both patients and physicians and can also facilitate patients check their own data.

On the other hand, the extensive adoption of these methods in real medical settings is hindered by the lack of technical experience which frustrates both patients and physicians leading them to the preference for pen-and-paper methods; current regulations related on privacy and confidentiality and strong defensive medicine reasons.

The different channels have been tested separately in the context of two different projects: one carried out in collaboration with the the Operative Unit of Clinical Pathology of the main hospital of Lecce, in Italy, dealing with the possibility to exploits data-scraping techniques able to insert/extract massive amount of data from electronic documents in order to reduce the occurrence of inappropriate exams requests [18] and another one in collaboration with the Department of Gynecology and Obstetrics of the main hospital of Lecce, in Italy, dealing with the possibility to create dynamic and personalized fetal growth curves more appropriate for diagnostic purposes, by exploiting OCR techniques for massive data ingestion [19]. Channels have been subsequently adapted to the specific features of gynecological and obstetrical studies. As future work, we plan to perform the integration of the different technologies in a real case.

References

1. Engel, G.E., Morgan, W.L.: Interviewing and Patient Care. Saunders, Philadelphia (1973)
2. Roshan, M., Rao, A.P.: A study on relative contributions of the history, physical examination and investigations in making medical diagnosis. J. Assoc. Phys. India **48**(8), 771–775 (2000)
3. Peterson, M.C., Holbrook, J.H., Von Hales, D., Smith, N.L., Staker, L.V.: Contributions of the history, physical examination, and laboratory investigation in making medical diagnoses. West. J. Med. **156**(2), 163–165 (1992)
4. Keifenheim, K.E., Teufel, M., Ip, J., Speiser, N., Leehr, E.J., Zipfel, S., Herrmann-Werner, A.: Teaching history taking to medical students: a systematic review. BMC Med. Educ. **15**, 159 (2015)
5. Davenport, S., Goldberg, D., Millar, T.: How psychiatric disorders are missed during medical consultations. Lancet **2**, 439–441 (1987)
6. Palermo, T.M., Valenzuela, D., Stork, P.P.: A randomized trial of electronic versus paper pain diaries in children: impact on compliance, accuracy, and acceptability. Pain **107**, 213–219 (2004)
7. Pringle, M.: Preventing ischaemic heart disease in one general practice: from one patient, through clinical audit, needs assessment, and commissioning into quality improvement. Br. Med. J. **317**(7166), 1120–1123 (1998). discussion 1124
8. Mayne, J.G., Weksel, W., Sholtz, P.N.: Toward automating the medical history. Mayo Clinic Proc. **43**(1), 1–25 (1968)
9. Pappas, Y., Anandan, C., Liu, J., Car, J., Sheikh, A., Majeed, A.: Computer-assisted history-taking systems (CAHTS) in health care: benefits, risks and potential for further development. Inform. Prim. Care. **19**(3), 155–160 (2011)
10. Bowling, A.: Mode of questionnaire administration can have serious effects on data quality. J. Publ. Health **27**(3), 281–291 (2005)
11. Cash-Gibson, L., Pappas, Y., Car, J.: Computer-assisted versus oral-and-written history taking for the management of cardiovascular disease (Protocol). Cochrane Database Syst. Rev. 3, Art. no. CD009751 (2012)
12. Tiplady, B.A., Crompton, G.K., Dewar, M.H., Böllert, F.G.E., Matusiewicz, S.P., Campbell, L.M., Brackenridge, D.: The use of electronic diaries in respiratory studies. Ther. Innov. Regulatory Sci. **31**(3), 759–764 (1997)
13. Gaertner, J., Elsner, F., Pollmann-Dahmen, K., Radbruch, L., Sabatowski, R.: Electronic pain diary: a randomized crossover study. J. Pain Symptom Manage. **28**(3), 259–267 (2004)
14. Lauritsen, K., Degl', Innocenti A., Hendel, L., Praest, J., Lytje, M.F., Clemmensen-Rotne, K., Wiklund, I.: Symptom recording in a randomised clinical trial: paper diaries vs. electronic or telephone data capture. Control. Clin. Trials **25**(6), 585–597 (2004)
15. Bulpitt, C.J., Beilin, L.J., Coles, E.C., Dollery, C.T., Johnson, B.F., Munro-Faure, A.D., Turner, S.C.: Randomised controlled trial of computer-held medical records in hypertensive patients. Br. Med. J. **1**(6011), 677–679 (1976)
16. Vaira, L., Bochicchio, M.A., Navathe, S.B.: Perspectives in healthcare data management with application to maternal and fetal wellbeing. In: 24th Italian Symposium on Advanced Database Systems (SEBD 2016), Ugento, Lecce, 19–22 June 2016 (2016)
17. Bochicchio, M.A., Vaira, L.: Fetal growth: where are data? It's time for a new approach. Int. J. Biomed. Healthc. **4**(1), 18–22 (2016)

18. Vaira, L., Bochicchio, M.A.: Can ICT help to solve the clinical appropriateness problem? An experience in the Italian public health. J. Commun. Comput. **12**(6), 303–310 (2015)
19. Bochicchio, M.A., Vaira, L.: Are static fetal growth charts still suitable for diagnostic purposes? In: 2014 IEEE International Conference on Bioinformatics and Biomedicine (BIBM), Belfast, UK, 2–5 November 2014 (2014). doi:10.1109/BIBM.2014.6999260

Mobile Agent Service Model for Smart Ambulance

Sophia Alami-Kamouri[✉], Ghizlane Orhanou, and Said Elhajji

Laboratory of Mathematics, Computing and Applications, Faculty of Sciences,
Mohammed V University in Rabat, BP1014, Rabat, Morocco
sophia.alami.kamouri@gmail.com, {orhanou,elhajji}@fsr.ac.ma

Abstract. In a highly connected world, widespread networking has imposed new needs that require new paradigms and new technologies. The mobile agent is an emerging technology that is gaining ground in the field of distributed computing for the processing and transfer of information on the network. In our previous article we study the mobile agent model which thanks to its autonomy, mobility and adaptability, can send and retrieve data in real time using a local and or distant interaction with other agents on the network. In this paper, we will discuss the case of the use of mobile agent model in a connected ambulance. This paper aims to give a brief description of the mobile agents model and illustrates some existing systems that use this model in telemedecine. Then we present the new concept of the ambulance of the future and our proposal of mobile agent model service in smart ambulance able to diagnose the patients condition and the appropriate service and data transmission to get an accurate response in real time.

Keywords: Mobile agent · Smart environment · Smart ambulance · Lightweight agent · Heavy agent

1 Introduction

Mobile agent technology is an emerging concept that is gaining momentum in several fields of applications, like mobile computing, e-commerce, Internet applications, user modeling, etc. The power of these agents in solving complex problems is due to their autonomy and mobility, they can achieve their goals in a flexible way by using interaction with other agents on the network.

Indeed, there are several reasons for using mobile agents, like: reduce the network load, overcome network latency, encapsulate protocols, execute asynchronously and autonomously, adapt dynamically, naturally heterogeneous and robust, and fault-tolerant [1].

Mobile agents are used in different domains like:

- Smart environment to follow the users as they move through different smart spaces [2].

© ICST Institute for Computer Sciences, Social Informatics and Telecommunications Engineering 2018
A. Longo et al. (Eds.): IISSC 2017/CN4IoT 2017, LNICST 189, pp. 105–111, 2018.
https://doi.org/10.1007/978-3-319-67636-4_12

– In a wide variety of healthcare applications such as medical data management, medical information retrieval, health data integration, decision-making support, telemedicine, securing medical information and coordination of distinct medical activities [3].

In this paper, we aim first to give a flashback of the use of mobile agents in telemedecine and then the use of mobile agents in smart environment. We will focus on the use of mobile agent in the connected ambulance.

The paper is organized as follows: Sect. 2 describes the concept of smart ambulance, what this new ambulance is going to bring and using mobile agent in telemedicine. Section 3 presents our proposed model of smart ambulance using mobile agents. Finally, the paper is concluded in Sect. 4.

2   Telemedecine in Smart Environment

2.1   The Ambulance of the Future: A Conceptual Proposal

Ambulance concept is seeing a big shift, it passes an ambulance designed to transport patients to hospital, to an ambulance able to diagnose the patient's condition and the appropriate service. The ambulance of the future is a connected ambulance, intelligent, able to act quickly to save more lives. The most crucial aspect of the smart ambulance is its ability to send and receive data by contacting the hospital's doctors in real time. From here, we had the idea of using the mobile agent model to propose an efficient communication model based on Mobile Agents.

Related Works: Here we will talk about the different existing projects and ideas on the ambulance of the future:

Project SAEPP: brings together a group of European Emergency Medical Services and other healthcare organisations to form a consortium with the objective of designing and building a 21st century prototype of ambulance which will allow frontline clinicians to provide enhanced patient care on scene [4].

Smart Pods: the objectives of Smarts Pods are to understand current models of emergency care and provide the equipment and space they need to carry out more affective assesment and treatment on scene, thus minimising the number of patients admitted to hospital [5].

2.2   Use of Mobile Agents in Telemedicine

Recent studies have shown that mobile agents model facilitate medical and telemedecine applications. Its efficiency is due to its autonomy, capacity for adaptation and ability to communicate with other agents.

Mobile Agent: There are several types of mobile agent. In our case, we will use the following types of Mobile Agents:

- lightweight agents: small agents that have the ability of a very short displacement due to a very short transmission times because of their low cost bandwidth. These lightweight agents can migrate to any accessible item before it disappears.
- heavy agents: These agents are called heavy because of the size of the executable code and that of the transported data. They perform a task requiring lengthy periods of local treatments.

Related Works: In this part, we will provide examples of work that links mobile agents to telemedicine:

Secure Mobile Agent for Telemedicine Based on P2P Networks: to be able to communicate with patients remotely, telemedicine has opted to use mobile agents which operate in networks and have the ability to move from one server to another to find the right result. In this article, they talked about the construction of a secure telemedicine based on the P2P network architecture implementing 2 types of service model [6].

Mobile Agent based Ubiquitous Health Care (UHC) monitoring platform: is a mobile agent based ubiquitous healthcare platform so that patients could benefit from an automatic and real-time follow-up on their health without moving each time to the hospital(for patients who require medical follow-up) [7].

3   Proposed Model Based on Mobile Agents in Smart Ambulance

3.1   Using Mobile Agent in Smart Ambulance

Improvements made in the ambulance service focus on managing information and documentation aspects of medical incidents and patient care. The session is not interactive. Our objectives are divided into 2 parts: immediate objectives and objectives once arrived at the hospital.

Immediate objectives(along the way to hospital)

- Knowing the hospital to which the patient is associated thanks to the name of the patient.
- knowing the urgent care (current state) to be administered to the patient in the ambulance before arriving to hospital, according to his previous conditions and the information in his medical file.

Objectives once arrived at the hospital

– Prepare in advance the resuscitation room and the staff at the appropriate
  department of the hospital to which the patient is attached.
– Adequate device according to the declared state of the patient.

   We will present a service model (Figs. 1 and 2) concern the case where the
patient is attached to one hospital where he has his medical history.

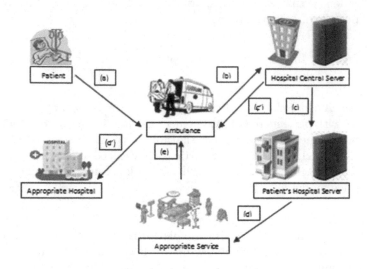

Fig. 1. Proposed Architecture for the first service model

(a) Once the patient is taken by the ambulance, the nurse identifies the patient
    and take his health parameters such as heartrate, body temperature, blood
    pressure, level of blood.
(b) This data are sent to the Hospital Central Server to see if the patient is
    attached to a hospital or not.
(c') Hospital Central Server sends to the ambulance the name of the hospital of
    the patient.
(c) Hospital Central Server sends to the appropriate hospital the name of the
    patient.
(d) The appropriate service looks for the patient's medical record to prepare
    the staff and sends to the ambulance the recommendations of patient.
(d') The ambulance takes the patient to the appropriate hospital.
(e) Appropriate service sends to the nurse of the ambulance the first care to
    make while awaiting the arrival of the patient.

3.2 Proposed Models Description

The diagram (Fig. 2) explains the role of the mobile agent model for data transmission to get an accurate response in real time.

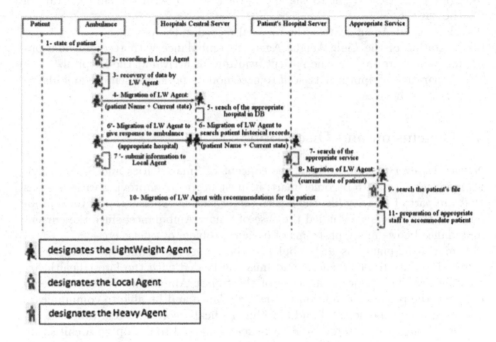

Fig. 2. Data transmission diagram for the first model sevice

1- When the patient is in the ambulance, the nurse takes the patient's name and current state (health parameters such as heart rate, body temperature, blood pressure, level of blood).
2- This data is recorded in the Local Agent in the ambulance.
3- The LightWeight Agent retrieves this data(patient Name + current data).
4- and thanks to its migration capacity, the LightWeight Agent migrates to the Hospitals Central Server, where is stocked which contain for each patient, the name and the hospital to which it is attached.
5- The LightWeight Agent looks in the database if the patient's name is already registered with its appropriate hospital.

Once found and thanks to the capacity of mobile agent to clone, the agent will clone to be able to do 2 tasks at the same time:

6'- Send to the ambulance the name of the hospital to which the patient is attached,
7'- and record the name of the appropriate hospital in the local agent to take the patient directly to it.

6- Migration of the LightWeight Agent to the patient's hospital to seek the appropriate service to have his medical record.

7- The LightWeight Agent will charge the Heavy Agents to search where each patient is registered with his identifier and the appropriate service.

8- Migration of the agent to the appropriate service with the current state of the patient.

9- Lightweight Agent searchs the medical record of the patient.

10- Migration of the LightWeight Agent to ambulance with recommendations for immediate care for the patient, waiting his arrival at the hospital.

11- Preparation of appropriate staff to accomodate patient when the ambulance arrives to hospital.

4   Conclusion and Discussion

Nowadays, everyone talks about the concept of Smart Cities and Smart Environment. For a city to become smart, it must begin by improving various areas that are part of the city like the health sector that is experiencing several problems. In this article we studied the case of Smart Ambulance, since the current ambulance knows many problems of design, problem of safety, etc.

Smart Ambulance is an ambulance that must be connected and able to respond quickly to emergencies and must be loaded with the latest healthcare technologies. The major challenges of the Smart Ambulance is to be able to diagnose the patient's condition in the ambulance and be able to communicate his condition to the hospital and have his medical record in a real time.

Our proposal is to send the data in real time and to set up an architecture that allows this using Mobile Agents which thanks to their autonomy and their ability to migrate and to clone allow to face these challenges.

We opted to work with the Mobile Agent model because of its ability to move, it allows to reduce as far as possible the remote communications to mobile agent transfers only and during the collection of Information in distributed databases and in the management of networks, it reduces the consumption of bandwidth.

There are several types of mobile agents and in this article we have choosen 3 types: local agent, light agent and heavy agent.

- The lightweight agents ensure the exploratory part, i.e. the agent migrates from one server to another to fetch the information and then retrieve it and each time it repeats the same behavior.
- The local agent ensures the reconstruction part, this part to which the light agent addresses when depositing his information.
- The heavy agent has the same principle of the light agent except that, as the name indicates, it carries several tasks.

In our future work, we will focus on the security aspects of our proposed service models.

References

1. Schoder, D., Eymann, T.: Technical opinion: the real challenges of mobile agents. Commun. ACM **43**(6), 111–112 (2000)
2. Marsa-Maestre, I., Lopez-Carmona, M.A., Velasco, J.R., Navarro, A.: Mobile agents for service personalization in smart environments. J. Netw. **3**(5), May 2008
3. Bagga, P., Hans, R.: Applications of mobile agents in healthcare domain. Int. J. Grid Distrib. Comput. **8**(5), 55–72 (2015)
4. Smart Ambulance European Procurers Platform. http://www.smartambulance project.eu
5. Hignett, S., Jones, A., Benger, J.: Portable and mobile clinical pods to support the delivery of community based urgent care. In: Include09 Conference London, UK, April 2009
6. Hsu, W.-S., Pan, J.-I.: Secure mobile agent for telemedicine based on P2P networks. J. Med. Syst. **37**(3), 9947 (2013)
7. Chuan-Jun, S., Chang-Yu, C.: Mobile Agent Based Ubiquitous Health Care (UHC) monitoring Platform. Advances in Humain Factors and Ergonomics Series, Chap. 64. CRC Press, Boca Raton (2010)

Extension to Middleware for IoT Devices, with Applications in Smart Cities

Christos Bouras[1,2(✉)], Vaggelis Kapoulas[1,2], Vasileios Kokkinos[1,2],
Dimitris Leonardos[3], Costas Pipilas[3], and Nikolaos Papachristos[3]

[1] Computer Technology Institute and Press "Diophantus", Patras, Greece
{bouras,kapoulas,kokkinos}@cti.gr
[2] Department of Computer Engineering and Informatics,
University of Patras, Patras, Greece
[3] ECONAIS, Patras, Greece
{dleonardos,cpipilas,nikolas}@wubby.io

Abstract. This work proposes extensions to Wubby (a device-level software platform for IoT devices, a technology developed by Econais A.E.) to support wireless modules for mobile networks (4 G / LTE-A, and also supporting the forthcoming 5 G). The proposed extension leverages the use of such modules, as it allows easy programming and existing code re-use. It thus adds a compatibility layer across the different modules as it a common set of classes for the wireless modules. The system can be used to support the networking aspects of a variety of IoT applications, including applications for Smart Cities, using a variety of IoT devices. This work suggests such a case focusing on air quality monitoring.

Keywords: Wireless modules · Middleware · Python · Internet of Things · IoT

1 Introduction

The ever increasing interest in the Internet of Things (IoT) and its immense growth over the last years [1–3], has led to the implementation of various computing devices of very small size (intended to be incorporated into various 'smart' objects), as well as numerous modules intended to enhance the functionality of these devices.

An important type of these kind of modules is the one for wireless network connectivity modules. With the technological progress in wireless communication already be in its 4th generation (4 G / LTE-A) of cellular networks and directed towards the 5th generation (5 G) of wireless networking, respective wireless networking modules are implemented for objects of the IoT (in addition to these for Wi-Fi, etc.) [4]. An important feature of the wireless modules is their diversity, both in terms of the wireless technology used, and the way they are implemented (design, chipsets, etc.).

Programming of these modules is usually done at a very low level, and this is generally "tied" to the chipset used. So the programs, in general, are not

© ICST Institute for Computer Sciences, Social Informatics and Telecommunications Engineering 2018
A. Longo et al. (Eds.): IISSC 2017/CN4IoT 2017, LNICST 189, pp. 112–118, 2018.
https://doi.org/10.1007/978-3-319-67636-4_13

transferable to other wireless modules. In addition, programming in low level requires considerable expertise, which the companies that manufacture devices for the IoT, do not have or do not want to acquire.

Companies using such modules to build devices for the IoT show a preference for higher-level programming languages; one of their most important preference being the Python programming language [5].

Currently, the IoT market is dominated by approaches where the devices are "built" around one or more modules. The role of these modules is to add intelligence and connectivity with previous-generation devices. As mentioned however, in these approaches software is "tied" to the hardware and they require the customer familiarity with each manufacturer's software and libraries, making the development of new products difficult. On the other hand, in cloud controlled approaches the cloud service providers offer an infrastructure for storing and managing information, together with software to link the data with a range of services. To allow different devices to connect and make use of these services, the cloud service providers give source code snippets or libraries to popular languages (such as PHP, Python, Java, etc.), which are incorporated in the software of the devices during the development process. Main drawback of the cloud controlled approaches is that there are serious risks of data security and privacy [6–8].

This work proposes an extension to Wubby, an existing Python-based middleware, to also support wireless modules for mobile networks, that are used in IoT devices. The middleware is upgraded to support wireless modules of various cellular network technologies (e.g. 3G, 4G, etc.) and is ready to integrate the forthcoming 5 G modules. The extension exposes a consistent well-defined set of common functions that capture the features and the use of the wireless modules, that are accessible through some common classes for networking. Thus the extension hides from the (higher-level) programmer both the wireless module's implementation details and the underlying networking technology used. The resulting system allows easy programming of these modules, leading to programs that are reusable with different wireless networking modules.

The remainder of the paper is organised as follows: Sect. 2 presents the proposed middleware, its architecture, and its interfaces/APIs; Sect. 3 presents the features and characteristics of the middleware; Sect. 4 discusses one use case / application; finally, Sect. 5 summarises the paper and outlines future work.

2   The Middleware and the Proposed Extension

When we talk about IoT devices, we usually mean embedded electronics, a microprocessor to provide intelligence used in conjunction with an RF chip or module providing connectivity. In that context, when it comes to IoT development, for the most part we are talking about Embedded Development. The products are designed in the Device Makers or Design Houses labs and their software development stays there, remains static and unable to change by someone else, other than the manufacturer himself. The contribution of the development community is minimum or zero, and this is because the products are closed, not following any standards, and the development of embedded applications remains challenging.

The proposed solution is literally changing this by drastically broadening the audience of developers that can contribute, extending an existing offering to address the emerging 5 G market, specifically targeting Smart Cities applications.

The idea behind Wubby is that future solutions should be based on a Virtual Machine that runs on a list of supported microcontrollers and provides a runtime environment for python code execution. Wubby will be used as the root infrastructure, but the software stack will be enhanced with APIs and libraries focused on the integration of 5 G solutions, targeting applications in Smart Cities.

2.1   Wubby

Wubby (pronounced Wha-bee) [9] is a software platform that simplifies the development of IoT devices by providing a programming environment that supports Python code execution directly in the devices microcontroller. This introduces several advantages: (a) It allows a broader set of developers to contribute, giving them the opportunity to design and develop new everyday objects based on a popular programming language like Python. (b) It speeds up the development process (c) It reduces development costs (d) It results in smarter, interoperable everyday objects Wubby separates hardware from software, abstracting the hardware complexity, while at the same time allowing developers to contribute by writing simple python scripts, rather than having to deploy the whole device image.

2.2   Architecture

The architecture makes use of the existing Wubby development environment, providing extensions in the Wubby VMs that focus on the use of mobile networking (i.e. 4 G / LTE-A, and the forthcoming 5 G) solutions. The high-level architecture is shown in Fig. 1.

The *Wubby VM* runs in the 'smart' object (actually in its microcontroller), and abstracts the hardware (i.e. provides a hardware agnostic environment).

In order to support application creation the environment includes:

Wubby Cloud: provides all the services for application deployment and backend device management

Wubby Client: allows a user to control and configure each device. This can be either a smart phone app or web service.

Wubby IDE: platform independent development environment that allows easy application development (debugging, code uploading, simulation, etc.) with Wubby.

Every Wubby enabled product is registered at the Wubby Cloud and is assigned to a default Wubby Application, a device-level application written in Python that can be uploaded on the Wubby Cloud and run in any Wubby enabled device. Wubby Cloud acts as a market place for Wubby Applications in

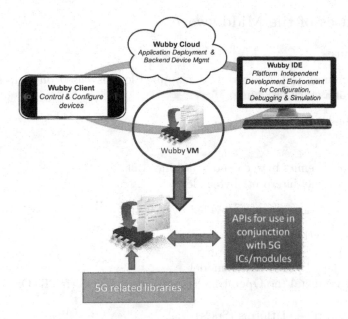

Fig. 1. High-level architecture of the system

the same way as iOS Apple Store and Google Play and the access to it is possible from the Wubby Clients (Web or Android/iOS Apps). For this purpose, owners of Wubby devices (end users) can register them in the Wubby Cloud in which they can select one of the compatible applications to install in their devices.

2.3 The Proposed Extension

The proposed extension involved changes in the Wubby VM to support the mobile (cellular) network wireless modules. These changes regard:

– supporting the relevant modules by installing and activating the necessary drivers,
– implementing the python classes to communicate with the module / chip set, and manage it. this is done by providing an implementation of the corresponding class for the specific module,
– implementing the additions/changes to the wlan class to support inquiring link status for the mobile (cellular) network modules,
– installing the network stack for these mobile networking technologies, and
– implementing the additions/changes socket class in order to support networking over the newly supported modules.

3 Features of the Middleware

3.1 Features

The programming of the Smart Cities applications is based on scripts, which run on top of a stack providing:

- Lexical analyzer
- Parser
- Compiler
- Code emitter: emits byte code or machine code
- Virtual machine: interprets bytecode

Some characteristics (already provided by Wubby) are:

- support for Python 3.4
- almost entire Py3 standard library
- subset of the CPython object model
- runs on bare metal (no Operating System) or on RTOS (freeRTOS is already supported)
- supports multiple platforms (SoCs)
- RF independence
- small footprint (75-250KB flash, can run with 8KB RAM)
- supports optimizations to create native code for cortex and others (native bitwise operations, dynamic type handling etc.)
- Python has special commands that interface directly with assembly (specifically, the ARM Thumb-2 instruction set)
- Python in Wubby targets any environment with ANSI C99 support (works on 8-bit or even 1-bit microcontrollers, given enough code storage and RAM)
- Inline assembler
- is written in C99 ANSI C
- runtime helper functions, etc.

3.2 Benefits

Wubby already offers several benefits, as it:

- reduces the overall development time, offering a much simpler programming environment, language syntax and restrictions,
- provides a separation between software and hardware, thus making applications (scripts running on top of the middleware) re-usable among different hardware platforms,
- reduces the after-sales support needs,
- dramatically broadens the developer audience that is able to contribute in the development of such applications,
- adds intelligence at the device level, contributes in the efficiency of device-cloud communications, reducing the amount of data that needs to be transferred, as a pre-processing phase is executed at the lowest level, and

– supports networking using various WiFi and BTLE modules. With the proposed extension, support will be added for networking using mobile (cellular network wireless modules), which is of great importance for Smart Cities applications.

4   Example Application: Air Quality Monitoring

This case study aims to give citizens a comprehensive view of the air quality, using smart sensors and base stations established in different places (see, e.g. [10,11]). Wubby enabled devices, equipped with various air-quality embedded sensors, which are small in size and exploit the features offered by mobile networks, are used to monitor the collected air quality data in real time, and upload the data to remote servers for further analysis.

The first step in this scenario is the installation of a sensor network that provides real-time measurements of carbon dioxide, temperature, pressure and humidity. Each sensor can collect the data and transmit them over a low power wide area network, exploiting the high speeds of modern cellular networks (e.g. LTE, LTE-A, etc.) and further 5 G features.

The above study could be designed to cover entire cities or hundreds of square kilometers giving many capabilities for air quality monitoring for indoor and outdoor conditions, independent of the location. The application provides the end user with intelligence and better understanding of the environment that one lives in.

5   Conclusions and Future Work

This works proposes an extension to the Wubby Python-based middleware for IoT devices, to support wireless modules for mobile (cellular) networks. The extension actually concerns the Wubby Virtual Machine, which is enhanced to support 4 G / LTE-A wireless modules. The extension integrates seamlessly with the existing networking classes of Python, and allows existing applications to work with the enhanced Wubby VM. Thus it promotes code reuse and extends the scope and of existing applications to more networking domains.

Future work will focus on the support of specific 4 G / LTE-A wireless modules by the Wubby VM, as well as preliminary support for 5 G wireless modules (based of course on the availability of the expected development boards for the respective modules).

References

1. Castillo, A., Thierer, A.D.: Projecting the growth and economic impact of the Internet of Things. Economic perspectives, pp. 1–10 (2015)
2. Verizon: State of the market: Internet of Things 2016, pp. 1–24 (2016)
3. Popescu, G.H.: The economic value of the industrial Internet of Things. J. Self-Governance Manag. Econ. **3**, 86–91 (2015)

4. Wang, S., Hou, Y., Gao, F., Ji, X.: A novel IoT access architecture for vehicle monitoring system. In: 3rd IEEE World Forum on Internet of Things, pp. 639–642. IEEE, Reston (2016)
5. Python. http://www.python.org
6. Gubbi, J., Buyya, R., Marusic, S., Palaniswami, M.: Internet of Things (IoT): a vision, architectural elements, and future directions. Elsevier Future Gener. Comput. Syst. **29**, 1645–1660 (2013)
7. Tao, F., Cheng, Y., Xu, L.D., Zhang, L., Li, B.H.: CCIoT-CMfg: cloud computing and Internet of Things-based cloud manufacturing service system. IEEE Trans. Industr. Inf. **10**, 1435–1442 (2014)
8. Rao, B.B.P., Saluia, P., Sharma, N., Mittal, A., Sharma, S.V.: Cloud computing for Internet of Things & sensing based applications. In: 6th International Conference on Sensing Technology, pp. 374–380. IEEE, Kolkata (2012)
9. Wubby documentation. http://www.wubby.io/docs
10. Cho, H., Kyung, C.-M., Baek, Y.: Energy-efficient and fast collection method for smart sensor monitoring systems. In: International Conference on Advances in Computing, Communications and Informatics, pp. 1440–1445. IEEE, Mysore (2013)
11. Postolache, O.A., Dias Pereira, J.M., Silva Girao, P.M.B.: Smart sensors network for air quality monitoring applications. IEEE Trans. Instrum. Meas. **58**, 3253–3262 (2009)

An Analysis of Social Data Credibility for Services Systems in Smart Cities – Credibility Assessment and Classification of Tweets

Iman Abu Hashish[✉], Gianmario Motta, Tianyi Ma, and Kaixu Liu

Department of Electronics, Computer Science and Electrical Engineering,
University of Pavia, Pavia, Italy
{imanhishamjami.abuhashish01,tianyi.ma01,
kaixu.liu01}@universitadipavia.it, motta05@unipv.it

Abstract. In the "Information Age", Smart Cities rely on a wide range of different data sources. Among them, social networks can play a big role, if information veracity is assessed. Veracity assessment has been, and is, a rather popular research field. Specifically, our work investigates the credibility of data from Twitter, an online social network and a news media, by considering not only credibility, and type, but also origin. Our analysis proceeds in four phases: Features Extraction, Features Analysis, Features Selection, and Classification. Finally, we classify whether a Tweet is credible or incredible, is rumor or spam, is generated by a human or a Bot. We use Social Media Mining and Machine Learning techniques. Our analysis reaches an overall accuracy higher than the benchmark, and it adds the origin dimension to the credibility analysis method.

Keywords: Smart cities · Smart citizens · Social data · Twitter · Twitter bot · Credibility · Veracity · Classification · Social media mining · Machine learning

1 Introduction

Smart cities rely on a wider and wider range of Internet information, which includes sensor data, public data, and human generated data, as social networks and crowdsourced data [1]. In human generated data, relevance and credibility need to be addressed since in social networks, feeds can be propagated without being controlled nor organized.

Our research addresses credibility evaluation techniques for smart mobility support systems. The targeted online social media is Twitter, a widely popular social media as well as a news medium. It enables its users to send and read short messages named Tweets. It is a platform for live conversations, live connections and live commentary. It is accessed daily by 313 million active users with 1 billion of unique visits monthly to websites with embedded Tweets [2]. Twitter users express their opinions, share their thoughts, celebrate religious events, discuss political issues, create news about ongoing events, and provide real time updates about ongoing natural disasters, etc. In addition, Twitter is a rich source for social data because of its inherent openness to public

© ICST Institute for Computer Sciences, Social Informatics and Telecommunications Engineering 2018
A. Longo et al. (Eds.): IISSC 2017/CN4IoT 2017, LNICST 189, pp. 119–130, 2018.
https://doi.org/10.1007/978-3-319-67636-4_14

consumption, clean and well-documented API, rich developer tooling and broad appeal to users [3].

We approach the issue of credibility when, in the larger project called IRMA (Integrated Real-Time Mobility Assistant), we started to consider feeds coming from social networks as information sources for mobility information systems. That issue implied credibility assessment, and on another side Big Data technologies given the huge number of feeds in social networks [4].

In section two, we compare the previous implementations. In section three, we illustrate the methodology, and we continue in section four with a comprehensive explanation of our implementation. In section five, we discuss our results, and section six sketches conclusion and future work.

2   State of the Art

To obtain a comprehensive assessment of State of the Art, we used the paradigm of systematic literature review [5]. (See Table 1).

Table 1. Related works

Author/Reference	Approach
Gupta et al. [6]	Used features related to Tweets, users and events to develop an automatic approach for credibility assessment, enhanced by an event graph-based optimization
Gupta et al. [7]	Developed "TweetCred" a real-time, web-based system to assess credibility of Tweets based on 45 features using Machine Learning, specifically, they proposed a semi-supervised ranking model
Skidar et al. [8]	Provided a comprehensive explanation of a better mechanism to extract credible from noisy data and argued the absence of a standard definition of credibility for making such studies more useful for the research community
Namihira et al. [9]	Proposed a method for assessing the credibility of a Tweet automatically based on topic and opinion classification using Latent Dirichlet Allocation and the analysis of semantic orientation dictionary named Takamura
Batool et al. [10]	Proposed a methodology for precise extraction of valuable information from Tweets to facilitate the extraction of keywords, entities, synonyms, and parts of speech from Tweets which are used after for classification

Most of the related works can be divided into two categories: Classification-based analysis as [11–14] adopting supervised classification, [15] or unsupervised classification or a hybrid of the both [16], and Pattern-based analysis as [17].

3   Methodology

Here below we illustrate the steps of our methodology, which includes (Sect. 3.1) Problem Definition and (Sect. 3.2) Proposed Algorithm.

3.1   Problem Definition

The definition of credibility in this work combines different perspectives, namely (Sect. 3.1.1) Users' Perception, (Sect. 3.1.2) Tweets' Content, and (Sect. 3.1.3) Tweets' Origin.

3.1.1   Credibility Based on Users' Perception

Users' perception in defining a credible Tweet varies. Some users trust what is shared on Twitter and start propagating, while other users question what they read, based on the apparent features of a user's profile. With respect to a comprehensive study, users assess credibility from content, creator, and other available features provided by user interface, while neglecting implicit features [18]. Thus, credibility in User's Perception stems from the features of the user interface of Twitter, namely from explicit features.

3.1.2   Credibility Based on Tweets' Perception

A Tweet consists of a user name, text, and possibly a URL, image, and video. Twitter includes four types of API objects, namely Tweets' objects, users' objects, entity objects, and place objects, which are used to extract a set of implicit features corresponding to a single Tweet. In this case, the degree by which a Tweet's content can convey the truthfulness of an event stems from implicit features.

3.1.3   Credibility Based on Tweets' Origin

If we assume that a credible user provides credible information, the origin is a key for credibility. Accordingly, through of a set of implicit features, the user account that originates the Tweets is classified as a Human or a Bot. A human account is a Twitter account whose Tweets are published by an actual user, while a Bot account Tweets are published by a robot. Thus, the truthfulness stems from both explicit and implicit features, which help in identifying the origin of the Tweet.

3.1.4   Spam and Rumor

Spam is unsolicited, unwanted, and malicious content; harmful URLs or simply text-based, mislead, deceive and negatively influence other users on an event. It is directly connected to automated accounts targeting naïve inexperienced users. While Rumor is a widely propagated misinformed content.

3.2 Proposed Algorithm

Our work, which is a part of a wider analysis framework we are working on, includes: Users' score, Tweets network score, and Sentiment score. Our current work focuses on Users' score, calculates features, identifies spam, and detects bots. Accordingly, the related algorithm includes four phases; Features Extraction, Features Analysis, Features Selection and Classification (Features Classification includes credibility and type/origin classification). (See Figs. 1 and 2).

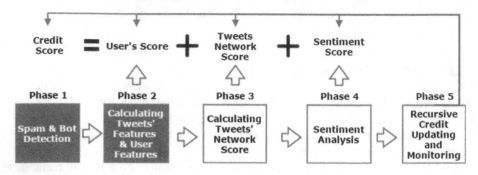

Fig. 1. Overall process

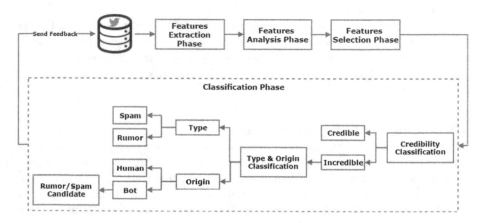

Fig. 2. Details of Phases 1 and 2

3.2.1 Features Extraction

The algorithm starts with a dataset of collected Tweets. When Twitter API is accessed, a target Tweet can be extracted with explicit and implicit features. This phase collects metadata of Tweets to provide contextual information (see Table 2). In Twitter API Documentation [19], the features to be extracted are divided into three sections: Users, Tweets, and Entities. Each is called an object, and each object is composed of a set of fields. Accordingly, those fields are interpreted as features or used for further deriving additional features.

Table 2. Features extraction phase output

Type	Name
From user	created_at, description, id_str, location, default_profile, default_profile_image, favourites_count, following, followers_count, friends_count, geo_enabled, listed_count, protected, screen_name, statuses_count and verified
From tweet	created_at, favorite_count, id_str, in_reply_to_screen_name, lang, possibly_sensitive, retweet_count, retweeted, retweeted_status and truncated
From entity	hashtags, URLs, media and user_mentions

3.2.2 Features Analysis

This phase analyzes the features extracted from the previous phase by considering the nature of Twitter environment as suggested in [20], namely information flow and content propagation, as well as possible interactions such as replying, retweeting, etc. Thus, another set of features can be derived and quantified to address the previously mentioned aspects (see Table 3).

Table 3. Features analysis phase output

Feature name	Description
Friends to followers ratio	Indicates the ratio of the number of people a user is following to the number of people following that user
Followers to friends ratio	Indicates the ratio of the number of people following a user to the number of people followed by the same user
Account reputation	Indicates an estimate of how popular a user account is
Users retweet ratio	Indicates the ratio of the number of retweets propagated by the user to the number of tweets originally published by the same user
External URL ratio	Indicates the ratio of the number of external URLs contained in a Tweet
Value of a retweet	Gives a value based on the deviation of a user's retweet ratio from the average retweet ratio in a target topic

3.2.3 Features Selection

This phase mines the set of features extracted and analyzed to select the features that affect the final judgment on Tweets credibility. Accordingly, a learner-based feature selection technique is applied. It is based on the use of learning algorithms, and the evaluation of the performance on the dataset with different subsets. Accordingly, the subset of features that will achieve the best results will be selected.

3.2.4 Classification

The classification process starts by classifying Tweets in terms of credibility, type as spam and rumor, and finally origin like human accounts and Twitter harmful bots. This phase is divided into two sub-phases, Credibility Classification classifies Tweets into credible or incredible depending on the features obtained. Type and Origin Classification analyzes the incredible Tweets furthermore by classifying them as rumor or spam, and as humans or bots account.

4 Implementation

The first two phases, Features Extraction and Features Analysis, were implemented using social media mining techniques while the final two phases, Features Selection and Classification, were implemented by using machine learning algorithms explained as follows. (See Fig. 3).

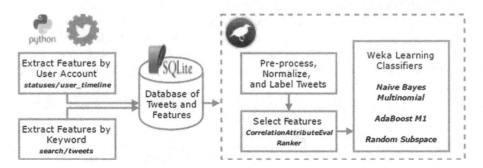

Fig. 3. Overall implementation of the proposed method

4.1 Social Media Mining Techniques

Social data, or human generated data, are big, unstructured and noisy with abundant social relations such as friendships, followers, following, etc. Consequently, using Social Media Mining enables combining social theories with statistical and data mining methods for extracting useful and meaningful data. In our implementation, we used Python and Twitter API.

4.1.1 Features Extraction by User Account
Using this approach, and by providing a list of target user handles, the Tweets of a specific account can be extracted. This approach analyzes the behavior of the target user in terms of posting behavior and Tweets propagated. Twitter proposes a public API, named GET status/user_timeline, which returns a collection of the most recent Tweets posted by the user, indicated either by user_id or screen_name and in our case, screen_name. This API can only return up to 3,200 of users' most recent Tweets, (retweets included).

4.1.2 Features Extraction by Keyword
The second approach is extracting Tweets by a keyword. The keyword is represented by the hashtag. Based on Twitter support [21] a hashtag is used to categorize Tweets by keywords. This approach is implemented by using GET search/tweets API.

4.2 Machine Learning Algorithms

For the last two phases, Features Selection and Classification, machine learning algorithms are exploited using Weka, a data mining software. Features Selection was implemented by applying correlation attribute evaluator, that evaluates the worth of an attribute by measuring Pearson's Correlation between the attribute and the class, using the Ranker in conjunction with the evaluator to rank the features by their individual evaluations, and in our case, their importance in credibility assessment. For Classification, we used several classifiers provided by Weka.

4.3 Twitter Bot Development

As a final step, we created a robot account to enrich the dataset with diverse contents and more robotic behaviors. The developed bot searches Twitter API by using a keyword, once the results are found, the bot retweets them, favorites them, follows their creator and adds the user accounts to a list, thus, reflecting a typical robotic behavior.

5 Evaluation

5.1 Dataset Creation

For the evaluation process, we chose USA 2016 Presidential Elections, then we chose several Twitter accounts covering the elections, along with few related hashtags to create a dataset with a diverse content. We also considered the bot that we have developed. Then, the extracted Tweets were manually labeled in terms of credibility, type and origin. A dataset, of around 2000 Tweets, was created, pre-processed, normalized, and labeled.

5.2 Experiment Setup and Task Preparation

To test performance and efficiency of the proposed algorithm, we performed three tasks: (1) classifying based on credibility, (2) classifying based on type and (3) classifying based on origin, including the following steps:

- Loading the dataset to Weka and assigning the target label as a class.
- Applying Features Selection phase by using correlation attribute evaluator as a subset evaluator and Ranker as a search method.
- Performing the Classification Phase by using the desired classifier.

5.3 Results and Discussion

5.3.1 Credibility Classification
The feature with the highest impact on credibility classification is *from_user_default_profile* which indicates that users have not altered the theme or background of their profiles. When a user first creates an account on Twitter, the default settings are set with an egg picture as an avatar, that is related to *from_user_default_profile_image*. Going on, *from_user_verified*

indicates whether the user account is verified or not. Obviously, a verified account is taken for granted as an official account to propagate credible feeds regarding a specific topic. Other selected features show that, when the user account has a profound network that interacts with what the user propagates, in terms of retweeting or following the user, the level of credibility and trust are higher, which explains the other features that were selected (see Table 4).

Table 4. Features selected for credibility classification

Rank	Feature
1	from_user_default_profile
2	from_user_verified
3	from_user_follower_count
4	from_user_listed_count
5	followers_to_friends
6	user_retweet_ratio
7	from_user_retweet_count
8	from_user_default_profile_image
9	friends_to_followers
10	value_retweet

5.3.2   Type Classification

We modified the original dataset by keeping the Tweets classified as incredible, labeling them as spam, and substituting the credible classified Tweets with a set that was labeled as rumors, while maintaining the total number of instances. However, before going on with the Features Selection, we applied N-Gram Features to consider the text of Tweets. Based on the average weights of the first 10 ranked features, *user_retweet_ratio* is the first attribute that contributes to the final classification, *from_user_retweet_count*, *retweeted_status* and *TXT_rt* behave in the same way. Other network related features were selected, namely *friends_to_followers* and *account_reputation* which also convey

Table 5. Features selected for type classification

Rank	Feature
1	user_retweet_ratio
2	from_user_retweet_count
3	from_user_default_profile_image
4	friends_to_followers
5	from_user_location
6	account_reputation
7	retweeted_status
8	TXT_rt
9	entities_mentions
10	TXT_#election2016

a robotic behavior by following many accounts, leading to a very small ratio between the friends and the followers count. The reason behind this ranking (see Table 5) is that, rumored and spammed Tweets are most likely to be originated by bot accounts. Finally, what distinguishes a rumored Tweet from a spammed one is how fast it gets propagated, thus, the *retweet_count* attribute.

5.3.3 Origin Classification
The features that contribute the most in classifying the origin are almost identical to the features selected in classifying credibility (see Table 6). This proves that the credibility of the Tweet is directly related to its origin.

Table 6. Features selected for origin classification

Rank	Feature
1	from_user_default_profile
2	from_user_verified
3	from_user_followers_count
4	from_user_listed
5	followers_to_friends
6	user_retweet_ratio
7	from_user_default_profile_image
8	from_user_retweet_count
9	friends_to_followers
10	value_retweet

Once the features are selected for each task, the Classification phase directly follows. The results obtained for each task are detailed in Table 7. As can be seen from the detailed accuracy results (see Figs. 4 and 5), Credibility and Type tasks provided higher accuracy measures than our baselines, [20] and [12] respectively. At the best of our knowledge, this is the first classification of Tweets with respect to their origins. Thus, considering only features that can be extracted and analyzed to investigate the robotic behavior, our algorithm looks accurate.

Table 7. Detailed classification results

Criteria	Precision	Recall	F-measure	MCC	ROC area
Credibility	0.902	0.885	0.883	0.783	0.921
Type	0.923	0.918	0.918	0.841	0.984
Origin	0.897	0.879	0.876	0.772	0.926

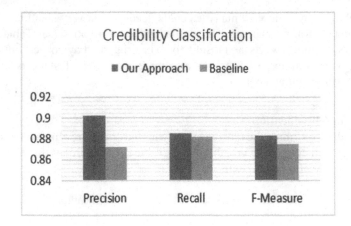

Fig. 4. Credibility task accuracy results vs. baseline

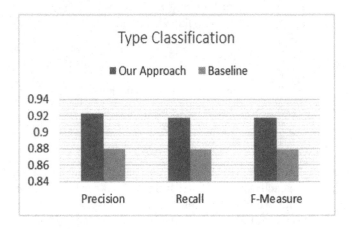

Fig. 5. Type task accuracy results vs. baseline

6   Conclusion and Future Work

Our work intends to provide a profound and comprehensive analysis on social data credibility, and, specifically, on Tweets credibility assessment. The feeds vary very much, they may represent a thought, a mood or an opinion, as well as on-going political news, sports, and natural disasters. Unlike other social networks, Twitter is an open nature that enables everyone to publish thoughts that reach a wide range of people. Because of these elements, credibility is relevant.

Therefore, we propose a comprehensive analysis from three points of view; Tweets' credibility, type and origin. Our analysis, which is implemented using Social Media Mining Techniques and Machine Learning Algorithms with Weka Software, includes four phases;

1. Features Extraction Phase: a set of features, attributes and characteristics of Tweets are extracted;
2. Features Analysis Phase: features are further analyzed and quantified;
3. Features Selection Phase: the list of features that contribute the most to the assessment of Tweets are selected;
4. Classification Phase: Tweets are classified with respect to our viewpoints.

We tested the correctness of our assumptions and the accuracy of our algorithm by conducting an experiment of three tasks that correspond to our three-fold classification phase. To accomplish this, we created a dataset of ~2000 Tweets, each Tweet is associated with 40 features. Our dataset concerned the 2016 USA Presidential Elections.

The accuracy of our algorithm is around ~89% for credibility classification, around ~92% for type classification and around ~88% for origin classification. These results are higher than our baseline for the first two classifications, while the final classification is new at the best of our knowledge.

Of course, our work may be extended by:

- Creating a larger dataset with more diverse content.
- Extending the number of the derived features to investigate the importance in the final assessment of Tweets credibility.
- Deepening the analysis of features from different perspectives such as: the representativeness of the hashtags to the content of Tweets, image processing techniques to explore the media published within Tweets, and Natural Language Processing to process the holistic semantics of Tweets.
- Designing an automatic system that assesses the credibility of Tweets as a browser add-on and a mobile application.

References

1. Motta, G.: Towards the Smart Citizen, New and smart Information Communication Science and Technology to support Sustainable Development (NICST) (2013)
2. Twitter Statistics. https://about.twitter.com/company
3. Russel, M.A.: Mining the Social Web, 2nd edn. O'Reilly, Beijing (2014)
4. Motta, G., Sacco, D., Ma, T., You, L., Liu, K.: Personal mobility service system in urban areas: the IRMA project. In: 2015 IEEE Symposium on Service-Oriented System Engineering (2015)
5. Okoli, C., Schabram, K.: A guide to conducting a systematic literature review of information systems research. SSRN Electron. J.
6. Gupta, M., Zhao, P., Han, J.: Evaluating event credibility on Twitter. In: Proceedings of the 2012 SIAM International Conference on Data Mining, pp. 153–164 (2012)
7. Gupta, A., Kumaraguru, P., Castillo, C., Meier, P.: TweetCred: real-time credibility assessment of content on Twitter. In: Aiello, L.M., McFarland, D. (eds.) SocInfo 2014. LNCS, vol. 8851, pp. 228–243. Springer, Cham (2014). doi:10.1007/978-3-319-13734-6_16
8. Sikdar, S., Kang, B., Odonovan, J., Hollerer, T., Adah, S.: Understanding information credibility on Twitter. In: 2013 International Conference on Social Computing (2013)

9. Namihira, Y., Segawa, N., Ikegami, Y., Kawai, K., Kawabe, T., Tsuruta, S.: High precision credibility analysis of information on Twitter. In: 2013 International Conference on Signal-Image Technology & Internet-Based Systems (2013)
10. Batool, R., Khattak, A.M., Maqbool, J., Lee, S.: Precise tweet classification and sentiment analysis. In: 2013 IEEE/ACIS 12th International Conference on Computer and Information Science (ICIS) (2013)
11. Castillo, C., Mendoza, M., Poblete, B.: Information credibility on Twitter. In: Proceedings of the 20th International Conference on World Wide Web (WWW 2011) (2011)
12. Sahana, V.P., Pias, A.R., Shastri, R., Mandloi, S.: Automatic detection of rumored tweets and finding its origin. In: 2015 International Conference on Computing and Network Communications (CoCoNet) (2015)
13. Zhang, Q., Zhang, S., Dong, J., Xiong, J., Cheng, X.: Automatic detection of rumor on social network. In: Li, J., Ji, H., Zhao, D., Feng, Y. (eds.) NLPCC 2015. LNCS, vol. 9362, pp. 113–122. Springer, Cham (2015). doi:10.1007/978-3-319-25207-0_10
14. Al-Dayil, R.A., Dahshan, M.H.: Detecting social media mobile botnets using user activity correlation and artificial immune system. In: 7th International Conference on Information and Communication Systems (ICICS) (2016)
15. Sivanesh, S., Kavin, K., Hassan, A.A.: Frustrate Twitter from automation: how far a user can be trusted? In: International Conference on Human Computer Interactions (ICHCI) (2013)
16. Gupta, A., Kaushal, R.: Improving spam detection in online social networks. In: International Conference on Cognitive Computing and Information Processing (CCIP) (2015)
17. Wang, S., Terano, T.: Detecting rumor patterns in streaming social media. In: IEEE International Conference on Big Data (Big Data) (2015)
18. Morris, M.R., Counts, S., Roseway, A., Hoff, A., Schwarz, J.: Tweeting is believing? In: Proceedings of the ACM 2012 Conference on Computer Supported Cooperative Work (CSCW 2012) (2012)
19. Twitter API Documentation. https://dev.twitter.com/overview/documentation
20. Kang, B., O'donovan, J., Höllerer, T.: Modeling topic specific credibility on Twitter. In: Proceedings of the 2012 ACM International Conference on Intelligent User Interfaces (IUI 2012) (2012)
21. Twitter Support: Using Hashtags in Twitter. https://support.twitter.com/articles/49309

Data Management Challenges for Smart Living

Devis Bianchini$^{(\boxtimes)}$, Valeria De Antonellis, Michele Melchiori,
Paolo Bellagente, and Stefano Rinaldi

Department of Information Engineering, University of Brescia,
Via Branze 38, 25123 Brescia, Italy
{devis.bianchini,valeria.deantonellis,michele.melchiori,
p.bellagente,stefano.rinaldi}@unibs.it

Abstract. An information infrastructure for modern Smart Cities must
be able to integrate data from multiple heterogeneous sources such as private and public energy consumption, garbage collection and environmental conditions (pollution, citizens' safety and security). In this context,
citizens themselves become providers of data, in the form of comments,
opinions and suggestions that should be integrated within the infrastructure. A vast amount of data must be collected, organized and analysed
to extract useful insights that can be transformed into actions aimed at
improving the quality of life in the city. In this paper, we discuss data
management issues to be addressed for bringing benefits to different categories of stakeholders in a Smart City, ranging from citizens to the Public
Administration and energy providers.

Keywords: Data management issues · Information infrastructure ·
Smart Cities · Brescia Smart Living

1   Introduction

Improving the quality of life of citizens and supporting Public Administrations
(PA) and energy providers to deliver innnovative services through the adoption
of modern technologies are primary goals of modern Smart Cities [1]. Citizens
become actively part of their city life, providing suggestions, opinions and comments about administration actions (e.g., through e-Participation tools). They
receive timely information about their city, the effects of PA actions, public as
well as private energy consumptions, and information about the environmental
conditions where they live (pollution and public security). On the other hand,
PA has new tools and techniques to deeply understand dynamics of phenom-
ena that characterise the administrated city, being able to take actions that
might improve citizens daily life. Furthermore, energy providers might have the
opportunity of implementing smart grids for improving their delivery services
and save costs. In this framework, the national research project Brescia Smart
Living (BSL) - MIUR "Smart Cities and Communities and Social Innovation"
is currently being performed. The main goal of the BSL project is to move from
a model based on a single monitored entity (a street, the electrical supply grid,

© ICST Institute for Computer Sciences, Social Informatics and Telecommunications Engineering 2018
A. Longo et al. (Eds.): IISSC 2017/CN4IoT 2017, LNICST 189, pp. 131–137, 2018.
https://doi.org/10.1007/978-3-319-67636-4_15

the hydric system) to an integrated view of the Smart City. Every aspect is seen as part of a more complex system, and different types of data have to be collected, properly integrated and organized in order to provide new services to both citizens and PA. The effectiveness and the quality of the services is enabled by applying advanced solutions for managing large amounts of data. Data about energy consumptions on the electrical and methane supply grids, hydric system, street lighting, heating are collected from proper sensors and technological equipment of modern city, according to the Internet of Things (IoT) paradigm. These data are stored within proprietary platforms managed by single energy providers. Further information coming from external sources (e.g., weather and pollution data) are integrated and organized in integrated platforms in order to: (a) aggregate information at city level, mainly devoted to energy providers and Public Administration to give a global view of data concerning the smart city; (b) enable personalized access to data of interest for private citizens at the level of single district, building or apartment. Data from social media are integrated as well, where citizens become themselves data producers through their comments, suggestions and preferences. To meet research goals, the project is being developed over the following phases: (i) collection and identification of requirements from citizens, energy providers and Public Administration, through the submission of proper questionnaires; (ii) design and specification of functionalities, in terms of use cases focused on services provided to the actors of integrated platforms; (iii) design of data models underlying the platforms; (iv) implementation and experiments. Experiments will be performed on two districts identified in Brescia, Italy. The aim is to provide an integrated observatory over the Smart City, for different kinds of information, at different levels of aggregation, for heterogeneous although interleaved categories of users (citizens, energy providers and Public Administration). In this paper we focus on challenges that raised in the project for managing data in the context of a Smart City and we provide some hints about possible solutions to address these issues.

This paper is organized as follows: in Sect. 2 we discuss the functional architecture of Brescia Smart Living project; Sect. 3 presents data management issues; Sect. 4 lists related projects; conclusions and future directions are sketched in Sect. 5.

2   General Architecture

Figure 1 shows an overview of the general architecture adopted in the BSL project. Data are collected from both energy consumption domain (electricity, heating, hydric and natural gas supply grids) and urban services domain (garbage collection and security). This information is stored within domain-specific platforms, owned by the energy and service providers that are participating to the project. Both historical data and (near) real-time data collected from sensors installed on-field (home automation hardware equipment, new generation meters for supply grids, wearable devices for security and safety monitoring) have been considered. The architecture also includes data coming from external sources, for weather forecasting and air pollution estimation.

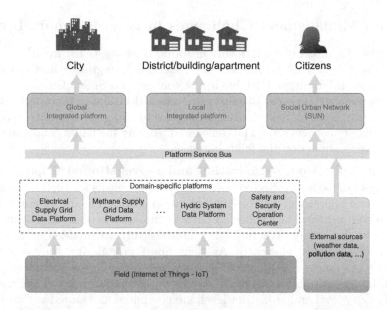

Fig. 1. Overview of the Brescia Smart Living general architecture.

Data coming from domain specific platforms and external datasources are organized within integrated platforms through a Platform Service Bus, that is in charge of managing message exchange between all the architectural components. Communication between domain-specific datasources and integrated platforms may be either synchronous (for instance, concerning historical data of supply grids) or asynchronous (e.g., events raised from home automation hardware or wearable devices, to be promptly showed on the platforms).

The visualisation of average energy consumptions (properly aggregated to preserve citizens' privacy), the visualisation of information about the pollution, the statistical data on crime rate, information about the status of garbage collection points are in charge of the *Global Integrated platform*. Its role is to provide a global view at city level about consumption and services for citizens and Public Administration. The platform also supports PA to take decisions given the current environmental conditions (e.g., weather and pollution conditions, to take effective and timely actions to preserve the health of fragile citizens).

Citizens can register themselves and access services of the *Local Integrated platform*. This platform enables the visualisation of the personal energy consumptions, as well as comparison of these data against benchmarks and average values locally at district/building/apartment level. It also enables citizens of smart homes to monitor, control and analyse data collected by smart plugs and the new generation meters on supply grids.

Finally, mobile applications and a dashboard of proper Key Performance Indicators will be designed and implemented on top of the integrated platforms.

3   Data Management Challenges in Brescia Smart Living

The aim of the integrated platforms introduced above is to provide citizens, energy providers and PA with a tool for collecting, integrating and visualizing heterogeneous information available in the context of a Smart City, at different levels of aggregation, in order to help them to take decisions in their daily life and stimulate their virtuous behaviour in using private and public resources. Several interdisciplinary aspects should be considered. Among the issues concerning data management, we mention the following ones.

(Big) data collection, organization and aggregation. The quantity and velocity of data to be collected pose not trivial problems for their efficient collection and organization, in order to speed up data access and exploration [2]. In the BSL project, data collected on-field through the domain-specific platforms present a poor structure (they are basically schemaless) and must be stored and indexed efficiently. At their finest granularity, they are stored within a document-oriented NoSQL database (using JSON documents). The Local Integrated platform is based on this database. Aggregated information, both at city level and at district level, are computed and stored within a relational database, that provides a more structured organization of information to enable exploration and visualisation facilities [3].

User-driven information service design. Supplied information should be accessed through proper services built on top of the underlying resources. Services design must be driven by the needs of the final users, ranging over PA, citizens and categories of users with specific requirements, such as fragile subjects. In the BSL project, service design started from a classification of users into stakeholders (Public Administration, energy providers) and citizens. The latter ones have been in turn distinguished according to the typology of collected data (traditional meters, new generation electric and methane meters, smart meters for home automation). Considering different categories of users, services designed for the BSL project range from data visualisation services to decision support services: (i) to help stakeholders to take actions in the context of the smart city; (ii) to enable citizens to compare their personal data with average values at building, district and city level.

Data privacy and ownership aspects. The above mentioned issues necessarily require to pay attention to the ownership of data, their retention and the protection of sensitive information. Proper data access mechanisms have to be defined for the different categories of users, according to recent national and European laws that address data privacy and preservation [4]. Within the BSL project, these aspects will be considered according to the European GDPR 2016/679 (General Data Protection Regulation). In particular, this regulation focuses on principles like privacy by design, that requires that data protection is included in the development of business processes for products and services, the right to be forgotten applied to personal data and the principle of data portability.

Data Security and Integrity. The integrity of the information should be always guaranteed or, at least, problems must be detected. For example, sensors deployed all around the city might get uncalibrated for some reasons. The system must be able to detect and manage this wrong data to avoid a decision-making process on wrong basis. A full digital description of the plants (including information about measurement accuracy of each device, certificate of calibration when available) and an history of measurements are needed to achieve this target. Using this set of data, it is possible to design algorithms able to analyze the system behavior and to provide suitable metrics that can highlight malfunctions as well as any data integrity issues, in a similar way as Intrusion Detection Systems (IDS) in cybersecurity identify network attacks.

System scalability and interoperability. The system must have the ability to integrate new data-collecting sub-systems or to create new sub-systems exploiting the existing hardware. A city grows in long periods and the data-collecting technologies advance faster, therefore managing the heterogeneity of the technologies over time is fundamental to build a robust system. Interoperability between different systems into the smart city must be achieved [6]. In the BSL project, to address this issue, a new generation of Discovery Services should be developed. As the Domain Name System (DNS) records matching information about IPs and domains, a Service Discovery System (SDS) for IoT will record the topology and the characteristics of the network nodes, including their communication, measurement and actuation capabilities. In this way, a new node is able to recover the resources it needs, ensuring flexibility, interoperability and reuse of existing hardware [5].

4   Related Work

Compared to recent and on-going Smart Cities projects, BSL provides a wider spectrum of services (as summarised in the previous sections), considering not only the energy consumption data, but also crime rate data, as well as data about environmental conditions. Moreover, BSL brings together the integration platforms at multiple levels, thus giving relevance both to the Smart Cities services meant for PA and the ones designed for citizens (also considering support for decisions devoted to fragile users).

Smart Cities projects. The Optimus project [7] aims to support Public Administration to optimise energy consumption. The focus here is on a semantic-based data acquisition module, to integrate heterogeneous data sources into a relational database, and Decision Support System to enforce an energy manager while taking his/her decisions. The project has been tested on three pilot cases in Italy (city of Savona), Spain (Sant Cugat del Vallès) and The Netherlands (Zaanstad). Similarly, the BESOS project [8] is focused on the implementation of distributed Energy Management Systems (EMS) for energy saving. BESOS is mainly devoted to PA and energy service companies, while the citizens' involvement is more marginal compared to the BSL project. The SFpark project [9] is focused on public transportation for the city of San Francisco. The project aims to provide advanced data mining and planning facilities for the PA to improve urban public mobility services. Primary goal of the Res Novae project [10] was to provide an integrated platform for visualising and monitoring the energy consumption at a city scale. The Res Novae project has been tested in the city of Bari, Italy. The ROMA project [11] aims to integrate data from heterogeneous sources (security, mobility and weather) to increase city resilience and support the PA in management of emergency situations.

Enabling technological infrastructure. The research topics addressed within Brescia Smart Living and related projects also rely on the availability of integration platforms and infrastructures that are able to address the data management issues we underlined in this paper. Available platforms must be based on standards, be scalable and modular, flexible enough to allow ease extension of functional and non functional requirements imposed by the dynamic environment of Smart Cities. Oracle and IBM proposed their own solutions for implementing Smart Cities projects. In particular, the Oracle Smart City Platform provides a set of front-office functions over multiple communication channels (e.g., telephone, web, chat), big data management solutions and analytical tools. It has been configured for several projects (such as the SFpark project mentioned above). IBM proposed a platform that integrates many tools for managing data in the context of smart cities, like the Intelligent Operations Center IOC [12], providing functions to visualise data on a tabular, graphical and map-based interface, SPSS [14] for stochastic and predictive analysis of data and CPLEX [13] for solving optimisation problems. IOC has been applied in the Res Novae project and has been chosen also for implementing the global integration platform within the BSL project. Compared to these Smart Cities platforms, middleware solutions provide communication drivers, data management facilities and APIs, but require additional development efforts to create new applications and services on top of them. Indra proposed a cross-platform and multi-device middleware called SOFIA2 [15]. This middleware is devoted to the development of smart applications that use real-time information according to a big data approach. It has been applied in two pilot projects for the cities of La Coruña and Turin. Tridium Niagara Framework [16] offers a development platform that connects and translates data from nearly any device or system, managing and optimizing performance when dealing with heterogeneous data formats and protocols. It also enables the development of software objects to manage data at cloud and edge computing.

5   Conclusions and Future Directions

Design and implementation of the Brescia Smart Living project poses complex data management issues. The overall target of the project is to develop and innovate services through the integration of heterogeneous data at various levels of aggregation and provided to citizens and PA to take decisions in their daily life and stimulate virtuous behaviour. Future efforts will be devoted to the extension of the infrastructure with new services (mobility, healthcare and education services), as well its application to new districts and smart cities.

Acknowledgments. The BSL consortium is leaded by A2A and includes as partners: Beretta Group, Cauto, Cavagna Group, the Municipality of Brescia, University of Brescia, Enea, STMicroelectronics and an association of private companies (see www. smartcityitalia.net/projects/brescia-smart-living/).

References

1. Khatoun, R., Zeadally, S.: Smart cities: concepts, architectures, research opportunities. Commun. ACM **59**(8), 46–57 (2016)
2. Chauhan, S., Agarwal, N., Kar, A.: Addressing big data challenges in smart cities: a systematic literature review. Info **18**(4), 73–90 (2016)
3. Bagozi, A., Bianchini, D., De Antonellis, V., Marini, A., Ragazzi, D.: Summarisation and relevance evaluation techniques for big data exploration: the smart factory case study. In: Dubois, E., Pohl, K. (eds.) CAiSE 2017. LNCS, vol. 10253, pp. 264–279. Springer, Cham (2017). doi:10.1007/978-3-319-59536-8_17
4. Li, Y., Dai, W., Ming, Z., Qui, M.: Privacy protection for preventing data over-collection in smart city. IEEE Trans. Comput. **65**(5), 1339–1350 (2016)
5. Bellagente, P., Ferrari, P., Flammini, A., Rinaldi, S.: Adopting IoT framework for Energy Management of Smart Building: a real test-case. In: 2015 IEEE 1st International Forum on Research and Technologies for Society and Industry (RTSI), Turin, Italy, pp. 138–143 (2015). doi:10.1109/RTSI.2015.7325084, ISBN 978-1-4673-8166-6
6. Ahlgren, B., Hidell, M., Ngai, E.: Internet of Things for smart cities: interoperability and open data. IEEE Internet Comput. **20**(6), 52–56 (2016)
7. OPTIMising the energy USe in cities with smart decision support systems. http://optimus-smartcity.eu
8. Building Energy decision Support systems fOr Smart cities. http://besos-project.eu
9. San Francisco Park project. http://sfpark.org
10. Res Novae Project. http://resnovae-unical.eu
11. Resilience enhancement Of a Metropolitan Area. http://www.progetto-roma.org
12. IOC - Intelligent Operations Center. http://www-03.ibm.com/software/products/it/intelligent-operations-center
13. C-PLEX Optimizer. http://www-01.ibm.com/software/commerce/optimization/cplex-optimizer/
14. SPSS. http://www-01.ibm.com/software/it/analytics/spss/
15. Indra, SOFIA2 Web site. http://sofia2.com/
16. Tridium Niagara Framework. http://www.tridium.com/en/products-services/niagaraax

Conference on Cloud Networking for IoT (CN4IoT)

Investigating Operational Costs
of IoT Cloud Applications

Edua Eszter Kalmar and Attila Kertesz$^{(\boxtimes)}$

University of Szeged, Dugonics ter 13, Szeged 6720, Hungary
keratt@inf.u-szeged.hu

Abstract. With the appearance of things of the Internet of Things (IoT) area, IoT Cloud systems have been formed that are supported by cloud technologies, but still needs a significant amount of research. Data users produce with IoT devices are continuously posted to online services, which require the use of cloud providers to efficiently handle, and meaningfully visualize these data. In this paper we analyze the pricing schemes of four corresponding providers, and perform usage cost calculations for a concrete IoT scenario to help users to better understand their operation. We also compare these IoT Cloud providers by estimating service costs for operating an application of a smart city use case. We also validate our cost estimation by simulating the smart city scenario in the IBM Bluemix Platform.

Keywords: Cloud computing · Internet of Things · Cost estimation

1 Introduction

The Cluster of European Research Projects on the Internet of Things [1] defined the Internet of Things (IoT) as a dynamic global network infrastructure with self-configuring capabilities based on standard and interoperable communication protocols. Things in this network interact and communicate among themselves and with the environment by exchanging data and information sensed, and react autonomously to events and influence them by triggering actions with or without direct human intervention. Recent trends and estimations call for an ecosystem that provides means to interconnect and control these devices. With the help of cloud solutions, user data can be stored in a remote location, and can be accessed from anywhere. There are more and more PaaS cloud providers offering IoT specific services (e.g. Amazon AWS IoT Platform, Azure IoT Suite). Some of these IoT features are unique, but every PaaS provider addressing IoT has the basic capability to connect to and store data from devices.

In this paper first we analyze the pricing schemes of four corresponding providers: the Microsoft Azure IoT Hub, the IBM Bluemix platform, the Amazon AWS IoT and the Oracle's IoT platform. We compare their pricing methods, and perform cost-efficient calculations for a concrete IoT application of a smart city use case to help users to better understand their operation. We also compare

© ICST Institute for Computer Sciences, Social Informatics and Telecommunications Engineering 2018
A. Longo et al. (Eds.): IISSC 2017/CN4IoT 2017, LNICST 189, pp. 141–150, 2018.
https://doi.org/10.1007/978-3-319-67636-4_16

these selected IoT Cloud providers by estimating service costs for operating an application of a smart city use case. We also validate our cost estimation by simulating the smart city scenario in the IBM Bluemix Platform.

The remainder of this paper is as follows: Sect. 2 introduces related approaches in the field of IoT Clouds. Section 3 presents the pricing schemes of four providers, and Section Sect. 4 details our method to estimate resource usage costs and its results. Section 5 presents real cost usage validations for a concrete provider, and the contributions are summarized in Sect. 6.

2   Related Works

The integration of IoT and clouds has been envisioned by Botta et al. [2] by summarizing their main properties, features, underlying technologies, and open issues. A solution for merging IoT and clouds is proposed by Nastic et al. [3]. They argue that system designers and operations managers face numerous challenges to realize IoT Cloud systems in practice, due to the complexity and diversity of their requirements in terms of IoT resources consumption, customization and runtime governance. They propose a novel approach to IoT Cloud that encapsulates fine-grained IoT resources and capabilities in well-defined APIs in order to provide a unified view on accessing, configuring and operating IoT Cloud systems, and demonstrate the framework for managing electric fleet vehicles.

Atzori et al. [4] examined IoT systems in a survey. They identified many application scenarios, and classified them to five application domains: transportation and logistics, healthcare, smart environments (home, office, plant), personal and social, finally futuristic domains. They described these domains in detail, and defined open issues and challenges to all of them. Concerning privacy, they stated that a lot of information about a person can be collected without the person being aware, and control on all such information is impossible with current techniques.

Based on these works we selected the smart city environment to investigate further, and to provide operational cost estimations at different providers. The following section define our model of cost calculations based on publicly available pricing information.

3   Calculating IoT Cloud Operation Costs of Four Providers

In this section, we introduce and compare pricing models of IoT Cloud providers. We considered the following, most popular providers: (i) Microsoft and its IoT platform called Azure IoT Hub [5], (ii) IBM's Bluemix IoT platform [7], the services of (iii) Amazon (AWS IoT) [9], and (iv) Oracle's IoT platform [8]. We took into account the prices publicly available on the websites of the providers and when we found it necessary we asked for further information or clarifications via email from the providers. The calculation of the prices depends on different methods. Some providers bill only according to the number of messages sent, while others also charge for the number of devices used. The situation is very similar if we consider the virtual machine renting or application service prices. One can be charged after GigaByte-hour (GB-hour) (uptime) or according to a fix monthly service price. This price also depends on the configuration of the virtual machine or the selected application service, especially the mount of RAM used or the number of CPU cores or their clock signal.

	MS Azure IoT	IBM Bluemix IoT	Amazon IoT	Oracle IoT
IoT fix prices and device side				
Pay as you go	+	+	+	+
Extras at start	+	+	+	-
In tiers	+	-	-	+
Device price / month	-	-	-	+
"Price / message" pricing	-	-	+	-
"X messages / month" pricing (tears)	+	-	-	+
Data exchanged (in MegaBytes)	-	+	-	-
Message size limit	+	-	+	-
Cloud side				
Instance price (VM, App/Compute service)	+	+	-	+
GB-hour price	-	+	+	(+)

Fig. 1. Pricing information of the considered providers

In our model we consider a real world smart city use case for cost estimations with following parameters: total number of sent messages in a certain period of time, the number of devices used, and the capacity of the virtual machine used to provide gateway services. We estimated how our application would be charged after a whole month of uptime running in the cloud of the providers mentioned before. In our model, the total cost of executing an application consists of two price categories: (1) IoT and device prices and (2) cloud side prices. In case (1), we may be charged after the tier (a package) used or only after the resources used. The latter is also called "pay as you go" billing method, it means that we only pay for what we really use. At some particular providers, we need to pay for both of these two methods. Moreover, there are message prices as well. If we pay for a tier (if it is possible at the particular provider) then the price of a message is not so important because the tier includes prices of a fix number of messages. However, the price of the tier depends on the number of messages we want to send; more messages are covered by bigger tiers. If we use a provider with a "pay as you go" category, then the price of a message becomes more important. In some cases, we are charged after data exchanged not the number of messages sent but the data used can also be covered by a tier. Finally, it may occur that we need to pay for the number of devices used. To run an IoT application we also need to pay for a virtual machine or application/compute service or runtime to operate a gateway service – covered by case (2). There can be a fix monthly price for a service but GB-hour price can be charged as well. In our investigation, we considered the most popular cloud providers, the pricing categories and their availability at different providers are depicted in Fig. 1. Our investigation estimates prices for executing the smart city application for traffic light control to compare the pricing methodology of the providers.

Azure IoT Hub [5] charges one after the chosen edition/tier. Figure 2 details the available Tiers and also shows the size restriction for messages. This means that there are intervals for the number of messages used in a month. Azure also comes with some extras when we start to use its services, as well as some of the providers do so, but we do not take extras into consideration because we investigate general situations. There is a restriction for message sizes which depends on the chosen tiers. One can choose from four tiers, Free, S1, S2, S3. Each of them vary in price and the total messages allowed per day. Message size of the Free tier also differs from the other tiers. In the Free edition, devices can only send a lot smaller messages than in the other editions. Regarding to the cloud side prices we need to count with an application service price and there is no GB-hour price because the service is in full uptime. We have the opportunity to choose from a wide variety of configurations, selecting the number of processor cores, RAM used and storage capacity, affecting the price of the application service.

Tier	Tier price / month (€)	Total messages / day	Message size / unit (KB)
Free	0	8 000	0.5
S1	42.17	400 000	4
S2	421.65	6 000 000	4
S3	4215.5	300 000 000	4

Fig. 2. Tier prices of MS Azure

As depicted in Fig. 3, the IBM Bluemix IoT platform's pricing method follows completely the "pay as you go" method, and it can be read in Bluemix's pricing sheet under the Internet of Things section and at Internet of Things platform [7]. Bluemix only charges after the MegaBytes (MB) exchanged. We differentiate three categories and each of them comes with a different price per MB. There are three categories for the data used in MegaBytes and each category has its own price per the MBs exchanged. The more MBs we use and thus select a bigger category, the less price per MB we get. Working with Bluemix we need to pay for the runtime as well to run our applications. It is configurable, depends on the number of instances and the RAM used, and has a fix monthly price. On the top of that, we will be charged for GB-hour price, too.

Amazon's IoT platform can also be classified as a "pay as you go" service. Its billing method [9] works out incredibly easily. Prices are based on publishing cost (the number of messages published to AWS IoT) and delivery cost (the number of messages delivered by AWS IoT to devices or applications). A message is a 512-byte block of data and the pricing in EU and US regions denotes $5 per million messages. In addition, there is no charge for deliveries to some other AWS Services. So, there is only price per message billing which can be affected by the size of messages because there is a limit for message size. Using Amazon's IoT solution we also need a virtual machine for the gateway service. We can choose from a wide range of virtual machine configuration affecting its price and GB-hour price will be charged as well. In our calculations 1 USD converts to 0.914039185 €.

From (MB)	-	To (MB)	Price / MB
1	-	499 999	0.00097
450 000	-	6 999 999	0.00068
7 000 000	-		0.00014

Fig. 3. Pricing for data exchange in IBM Bluemix

Finally, we investigated how prices can be calculated at Oracle's IoT solution. Its pricing can be seen in Fig. 4. The pricing method is slightly different from the three providers described before. We can say that its rather similar to Azure's tiers than a completely "pay as you go" billing like in Bluemix. The information was gathered from [8] and we calculated with the so-called Metered Services. There are four product type categories regarding the used devices (wearable, consumer, telematic, commercial/industrial). Each category type has a price per used device type. The four device/product type category determine the monthly device price and the number of messages that can be sent by that particular type of device. In addition, there is a restriction on how many messages can a particular type of device deliver per month. In case, the number of messages sent by a device is more than the device's category permits, an additional price will be charged according to a predefined price per thousand of messages. Concerning the cloud side, in Oracle we should also pay for a compute service and daily uptime of our application. The number of CPU cores also affect the price of this service.

Product type	Device price / month (€)	Messages / Month / Device
Wearable	0.46015	1 500
Consumer	0.93	15 000
Telematic	2.32	100 000
Commercial / Industrial	3.47	100 000
Additional messages	0.02344	1 000

Fig. 4. Device pricing in Oracle

Concerning cloud-based cost requirements of our smart city use case, we estimated that about 2–4 GBs of RAM and 2 CPU cores could run our application
smoothly. We also collected pricing information for these cloud gateway services
from the providers' official sites. The pricing of Azure's application service can
be found at [10], Bluemix's runtime is in its pricing sheet under the Runtimes
section [7], Amazon EC2 On-Demand prices are described at [11] and we can
find the pricing of Oracle's compute service at [12]. We used the prices of the
Metered Services. By clicking on the Buy Now button next to Metered Services
sign we can navigate to a detailed pricing calculator [13].

Scenario II	MS Azure IoT	IBM Bluemix IoT	Amazon IoT	Oracle IoT
VM / Service / Engine / Runtime	app service	runtime	VM (US East) linux	compute service
Instances	1	1	1	1
Category name	Basic B2	Liberty for Java	EC2 t2.medium	compute service
RAM (GB)	3.5	3.5	4	?
CPU Cores	2	?	2	2
GB-hour price	0	0.0526	0.0475300376	+
Fix price	94.11	112.83	0	139

Fig. 5. Virtual machine related configuration and prices for our use case

In Fig. 5 we can see the detailed cloud-side parameters. We decided to take
3.5 GBs of RAM for this scenario in the case of Azure and Bluemix, and 4 for
the virtual machine at Amazon. For Oracle we could not manage to find out the
exact amount of RAM used by the compute service, it is probably 7.5 GBs as
defined for the provided OCPU. The number of CPU cores of Bluemix's runtime
is not clear (denoted by "?"). GB-hour price is used by Bluemix and Amazon
but Azure does not charge for GB-hour. The price of the compute service used
for Oracle IoT is also affected by the uptime, we illustrate this with the "+" sign
in the column of Oracle. Amazon is the cheapest in the cloud-side, and Oracle
is the most expensive.

4   Estimating Operational Costs for a Traffic Light System Use Case of a Smart City

To perform our cost estimation we chose a use case of a traffic light control system in a smart city. This scenario represents a relatively large system, its detailed
information concerning a monthly operation period is depicted in Table 1. We
use 128 devices referring to a study and implementation of a smart city in
Messina [14]. We perform the estimation for running the application for a whole
month (744 h mean 31 days). We worked with message sizes up to a maximum
of 0.05 KiloBytes (KB). Devices send messages in every 20 s which means 180
messages in an hour. From the previously mentioned value we can assume that

Table 1. Basic configuration information

Devices	128
Device type	Telematic
Message size	0.05
Messages/month/device	133920
Total messages/day	552960
Total messages/month	17141760
MB exchanged/month	837
Messages transferred/device/hour	180
Test duration (days)	31
Full uptime (hours)	744

to get the total number of messages per device for the whole month we need to determine the messages sent by a device during a day (180 * 24) and then multiply it by the number of days (31) while we run this scenario resulting in 133920 messages per month per device. The total messages per day is counted by the number of the messages sent by a device during a day (180 * 24) multiplied by the number of devices (128), so the result is 552960. Furthermore, we can count out the total messages per month including all the devices by just easily multiply the number of devices by the number of messages per month per device which means 128 * 133920 = 17141760. We can estimate the exchanged Megabytes if we multiply the number of total messages per month by the message size given in KBs so we then divide with 1024 and then we get the result of 837 MBs.

Our estimated calculations are shown in Table 2. In our investigation Azure seemed to be really expensive compared to the other providers. Bluemix and Amazon cost less than a half of the price of Azure, and Oracle is just a little cheaper than Azure.

Table 2. Cost estimation for the smart city use case

Provider/Cost	Azure	Cost	Bluemix	Cost	Amazon	Cost	Oracle	Cost
IoT fix prices and device side								
Device price/month	−		−		−		+	296.96
"Price/message" pricing	−		−		+	78.19	+	
"X messages/month" pricing	+	421.65	−		−		+	0.79
Data exchange (in MegaBytes)	−		+	0.81	−		−	
Message size limit	4		−		0.512		−	
Total messages/day with size limit	552960				552960			
Cloud side								
Instance prices	+	94.11	+	112.83	−		+	139
GB-hour prices	−			0.0526	39.134	0.04	35.36	(+)
TOTAL PRICE/MONTH		515.76		152.77		113.55		436.75

5   Validating the Cost Estimations with IBM Bluemix

As the next step, we performed experimental measurement of the defined IoT scenarios to confirm our former investigation. To accomplish this goal, we used IBM's Bluemix IoT Platform [6]. After registration for Bluemix, we created a Cloud Foundary Application runtime for a Node.JS application with 1 GB RAM and 1 instance. We also needed an IoT Service to handle the messages between the application and the devices; it lets our application communicate with and consume data collected by our connected devices, sensors and gateways. Finally, we created a device-side program to connect to the IoT service. We developed special scripts to simulate the 128 devices and their messages sent in every 20 s, with the message size of 0.053 KBs. A sample message we used is the following:
{ "d":{ "id":"1uz6", "s":"1", "t":"2016-12-01 09:00:00"}}

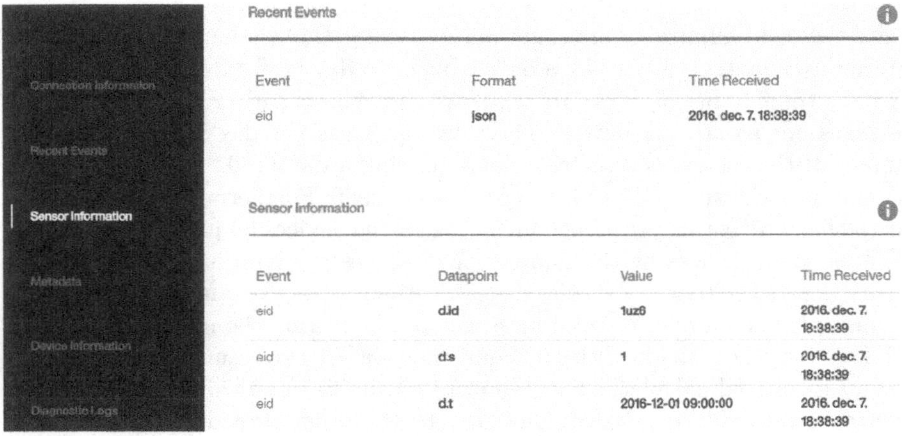

Fig. 6. Live event log of Bluemix devices

Bluemix provides a live event log for devices where we can trace the actual incoming messages from them. Figure 6 shows an example event log for a message received. In our simulated case, each device sends 180 messages in an hour to the IoT gateway service. The data usage of 180 messages was 61.44 KBs according to the Bluemix metering. This means that 0.3412 KB (i.e. 61.44/180) was logged by Bluemix for a message in contrast to the originally created text file with size of 0.053 KB. From this point, we can count that using 128 devices we have 17141760 messages for the whole month. We can calculate the total data exchanged by multiplying the number of the total messages with the size of one message which gives 5711.688 MBs. This is significantly larger than the estimated amount because of the additional information added to messages by Bluemix (that we found out later). Bluemix charges up 0.00097 € for each MB exchanged, so it means 5.54 € after that nearly 6 thousand MBs exchanged. This price is also larger than the estimated one (∼0.81 €) as well as the amount of data exchanged. The cloud side prices are the same as we estimated. The conclusion is that we need to pay some more Euros than estimated due to the larger message size the Bluemix system introduces, otherwise our prior calculations were right.

6   Conclusions

Data users produce with IoT devices are continuously posted to online services, which require the use of cloud providers to efficiently handle, and meaningfully visualize these data. Users also need to be aware of corresponding cost introduced by service providers, which can be very diverse.

In this work, we investigated pricing schemes of four popular IoT Cloud providers to help users to better understand their operation. We also performed usage cost calculations for a concrete IoT use case of a smart city, and compared them by estimating service costs for operating this application. Finally, we validated our cost estimation by simulating the smart city scenario in the IBM Bluemix Platform.

In general, we can conclude that Bluemix and Amazon is the cheapest due to the cheap message prices of Bluemix and the cheap virtual machine-related prices in case of Amazon. If we want to use a large number of devices, Oracle should be avoided, because of its expensive device prices. Nevertheless, for small systems Azure can be a good choice.

Acknowledgment. The research leading to these results was supported by the UNKP-UNKP-17-4 New National Excellence Program of the Ministry of Human Capacities of Hungary.

References

1. Sundmaeker, H., Guillemin, P., Friess, P., Woelffle, S.: Vision, challenges for realising the Internet of Things. CERP IoT - Cluster of European Research Projects on the Internet of Things, CN: KK-31-10-323-EN-C, March 2010
2. Botta, A., de Donato, W., Persico, V., Pescape, A.: On the integration of cloud computing and Internet of Things. In: The 2nd International Conference on Future Internet of Things and Cloud (FiCloud-2014), August 2014
3. Nastic, S., Sehic, S., Le, D., Truong, H., Dustdar, S.: Provisioning software-defined IoT cloud systems. In: The 2nd International Conference on Future Internet of Things and Cloud (FiCloud-2014), August 2014
4. Atzori, L., Iera, A., Morabito, G.: The Internet of Things: a survey. Comput. Netw. **54**(15), 2787–2805 (2010)
5. Pricing of Microsoft Azure IoT Hub, December 2016. https://azure.microsoft.com/en-gb/pricing/details/iot-hub/
6. IBM Bluemix IoT Platform, December 2016. https://www.ibm.com/cloud-computing/bluemix/internet-of-things
7. Pricing of IBM Bluemix IoT Platform, December 2016. https://console.ng.bluemix.net/?direct=classic/#/pricing/cloudOEPaneId=pricing&paneId=pricingSheet

8. Pricing of Oracle's IoT Platform, December 2016. https://cloud.oracle.com/en_US/opc/iot/pricing
9. Pricing of Amazon IoT, December 2016. https://aws.amazon.com/iot/pricing/
10. Pricing Calculator of Microsoft Azure, December 2016. https://azure.microsoft.com/en-gb/pricing/calculator/
11. Pricing of Amazon EC2 Instance, December 2016. https://aws.amazon.com/ec2/pricing/on-demand/
12. Pricing of Oracle's Compute Service, December 2016. https://cloud.oracle.com/en_US/opc/compute/compute/pricing
13. Pricing Calculator of Oracle's Compute Service, December 2016. https://shop.oracle.com/cloudstore/index.html?product=compute
14. Smart city of Messina, December 2016. http://smartme.unime.it/

Nomadic Applications Traveling in the Fog

Christoph Hochreiner[1(✉)], Michael Vögler[1], Johannes M. Schleicher[1],
Christian Inzinger[2], Stefan Schulte[1], and Schahram Dustdar[1]

[1] Distributed Systems Group, TU Wien, Vienna, Austria
{c.hochreiner,m.voegler,j.schleicher,s.schulte,
s.dustdar}@infosys.tuwien.ac.at
[2] S.E.A.L, University of Zürich, Zürich, Switzerland
inzinger@ifi.uzh.ch

Abstract. The emergence of the Internet of Things introduces new challenges like network congestion or data privacy. However, it also provides opportunities, such as computational resources close to data sources, which can be pooled to realize Fogs to run software applications on the edge of the network. To foster this new type of resources, we revisit the concept of mobile agents and evolve them to so-called nomadic applications, which allow addressing vital challenges for the Internet of Things.

In this paper, we propose a system design to realize nomadic applications and discuss several challenges that need to be addressed in order to apply them to real-world scenarios.

Keywords: Fog computing · Cloud computing · Internet of Things · Mobile agents

1 Introduction

With the growing maturity of Internet of Things (IoT) concepts and technologies over the last years, we see an increase in IoT deployments. This increase fosters the integration of IoT devices and Cloud-based applications to realize information aggregation and value-added services. While the first IoT devices were only capable of emitting sensor data, today more and more IoT devices as well as network infrastructure, e.g., routers, provide computational resources to process and store data. To cope with the large volumes of data originating from IoT sensors in geographically distributed locations, IoT devices can pool their resources to create Fogs based on the Fog computing paradigm [1]. Fogs are inspired by the principles of Clouds [8], such as virtualization and pooling of resources but due to their location on the edge of the network and the limited amount of computational resources, they can not support the concepts of rapid elasticity and broad network access. However, they excel at other aspects such as low latency, location awareness, or data privacy [1].

Today's software applications are typically running in public Clouds, like Amazon EC2, or within private Clouds. Clouds provide on-demand resource scalability as well as easy software maintenance and have become the de-facto

© ICST Institute for Computer Sciences, Social Informatics and Telecommunications Engineering 2018
A. Longo et al. (Eds.): IISSC 2017/CN4IoT 2017, LNICST 189, pp. 151–161, 2018.
https://doi.org/10.1007/978-3-319-67636-4_17

standard for today's software deployments. However, the Cloud computing paradigm is also confronted with several challenges, especially in the area of the IoT.

Due to the fact that applications are running in a remote data center, it is required to transfer all data to these data centers over the Internet. This approach is feasible for applications that process low volumes of data, but it becomes infeasible for IoT scenarios. In IoT scenarios, sensors produce large volumes of data, which cannot be processed by today's network infrastructure in real-time. Cloud-based applications are furthermore often in conflict with tight security restrictions since data owners want to ensure that no privacy-sensitive data leaks outside their companies' premises [9]. Therefore, it is often not feasible to transfer data to Cloud-based applications, because the data owner cannot control the data access after the data leaves the premises of the company.

To solve these challenges, it is required to refrain from deploying Cloud-based applications only in centralized remote data centers, but to consider a federated cloud architecture [2], and evolve Cloud-based applications into nomadic applications. In contrast to Cloud-based applications, which often require dedicated runtime environments, nomadic applications are self-contained software applications, which can transfer themselves autonomously among Fogs and Clouds and run directly on hypervisors due to unikernel architectures [7].

The idea is inspired by the principles of temporary workers or consultants, who move from one workplace to another to perform activities and led to the architectural design of mobile agents [5]. Mobile agents carry out operations in close proximity to the data source to reduce latency and network traffic [6]. These properties make them a perfect fit to tackle today's challenges for the IoT. Nevertheless, although mobile agents have been proposed around two decades ago, this concept never took off, mainly due to security considerations and the need for dedicated execution environments [4].

Since the initial proposal of mobile agents, the technological landscape has advanced and the Cloud computing paradigm has fostered the technical foundation for the execution of arbitrary applications on virtualized and pooled resources. Given the technical requirements for nomadic applications, Fogs provide a controlled and secure execution environment, which is managed by the owner of the data. Therefore, nomadic applications allow for a more efficient data transfer among IoT devices and processing applications due to the elimination of the transfer over the Internet. Furthermore, due to the fact that Fogs are often fueled by IoT devices who are already within the control of the data owner, it is also feasible to enforce strict privacy policies.

Although nomadic applications are the most promising approach to process privacy-sensitive data on already existing computational resources on the edge of the network, there are still a number of challenges, like data transfer or data recovery, which need to be resolved as discussed in Sect. 5.

The remainder of this paper is structured as follows: First, we provide a short discussion on the related work in Sect. 2. Then, we provide a motivational scenario in Sect. 3. Based on the motivational scenario we identify several requirements and present the foundation of our system design in Sect. 4. Furthermore, we discuss open research challenges in Sect. 5 before we conclude the paper in Sect. 6.

2 Related Work

The only recent manifestation of Fog computing, which is often also considered as edge computing, leads to a plethora of definitions (e.g., [1,3,11,12]). Literature as well as the OpenFog Consortium[1] consider Fog computing as an evolution of Cloud computing, which extends established data centers with computational resources that are located at the edge of the network. This enables Fog computing to bridge the currently existing geographic gap between IoT devices and the Cloud by providing different deployment locations to cater for the different requirements of data processing applications, e.g., low latency or cost efficiency [1].

Bonomi et al. [1] propose a layered model, which categorizes the different computing platforms ranging from embedded sensors from IoT devices over field area networks to data centers, where each layer provides a distinct level of quality of service. Furthermore, Dastjerdi et al. [3] provide a reference architecture for Fog computing that can be used to leverage the computational resources at the edge of the network and outline several research challenges, such as security and reliability. Another challenge for the realization of Fogs is the heterogeneity of devices that are used to build Fogs [12]. Nevertheless, there is already some preliminary work, such as the LEONORE framework proposed as part of our previous work, which accommodates the diversity for the deployment of applications on IoT devices [13].

3 Motivational Scenario from the Manufacturing Domain

Our motivational scenario originates from the manufacturing domain, which is one of the most advanced areas regarding the realization of the IoT. Today's manufacturing companies operate specialized manufacturing machines in different geographic locations [10], as depicted in Fig. 1. These machines are continuously monitored by sensors to assess their status as well as the quality of the manufactured products. The product quality often decreases over time, because expendable parts wear off and the machines need to be recalibrated from time to time. This recalibration requires the use of a dedicated application that analyzes sensor data and calculates the optimal configuration for each machine. Furthermore, the application maintains a knowledge base that is continuously updated to improve recalibration results based on reinforced learning. Now, there are two approaches on how to execute the recalibration application.

The first approach is to run the application within the factory's premises. This approach is optimal in terms of data privacy since the data never leaves the

---

[1] https://www.openfogconsortium.org.

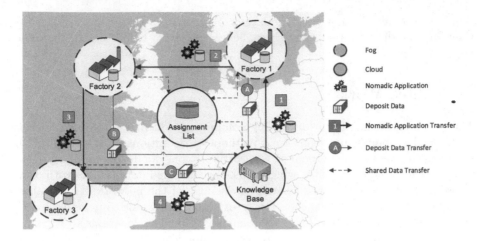

Fig. 1. Motivational scenario

company. However, this approach requires dedicated computational resources to perform the recalibration. To reduce the cost for the recalibration, it is also possible to operate the recalibration application in a Software-as-a-Service manner on Cloud resources in a remote data center.

Although this second approach reduces the cost, it also has its disadvantages. For this approach, the data needs to be transferred to a data center over the Internet. This data transfer potentially conflicts with legal or organizational policies, which may forbid any data transfer to remote locations or it simply may not be feasible to transfer a huge volume of sensor data over the Internet.

Fortunately, the concept of nomadic applications running in Fogs combines the benefits of the two previously described approaches. Whenever a machine is in maintenance mode to perform the recalibration, some of its computational resources are not used and can be contributed to a local Fog to host applications, such as the nomadic recalibration application. Another benefit of hosting the application on the Fog is that the recalibration is performed within the companies' premises and the data owner can control all activities performed by the application. The high trust level facilitated due to the tight control, entitles the recalibration application to also access internal interfaces of the machine, which is not possible for Cloud-based applications (due to security and data privacy reasons).

Figure 1 shows an exemplary order of events for a nomadic application, which travels among three factories to recalibrate machines. At the beginning of the journey, the application is residing at the knowledge base, since it is not required for any recalibration. Here, the application updates its configuration, i.e., becomes a stateful application, for future calibrations based on historic data.

Then, the application relocates immediately, as depicted by number 1, from the knowledge base to its first working assignment at Factory 1. At Factory 1, the application is running on the Fog of Factory 1, where it can access the sensor data as well as any other factory-specific configuration data. This data is then processed using the Fog, i.e., pooled and virtualized computational resources provided by different IoT devices. After completing its task, the application is ready to relocate to the next working assignment based on the information from a remote assignment list.

Due to the fact that the recalibration operation at Factory 1 generated new insights, which can be used to refine the recalibration operation, it is required to transfer these insights to the knowledge base. This transfer may contain a large amount of non-privacy-sensitive data, which does not exhibit any time-related transportation constraints and can be carried out independently from the travel route of the nomadic application as shown by migration A in Fig. 1.

These two operations are repeated twice, to also recalibrate the machines for Factory 2 respectively Factory 3 and collect the obtained insights in the knowledge base for future refinement. At the end of the journey, the nomadic application returns to the knowledge base to update its configuration and to be ready for future recalibration activities.

4   System Design

Our system design to realize a nomadic application infrastructure encompasses Clouds and Fogs, which are connected by a network, i.e., the Internet. To address the requirements, we propose the Nomadic Application Infrastructure, as depicted in Fig. 2. For our discussion, we distinguish between application management aspects, which are designed to run in the Cloud, and data management-oriented ones because these two management topics expose different requirements.

4.1   Application Management

Requirements. The requirements for the application management ensure that nomadic applications can travel from Fog to Fog over the Internet and cover all aspects of the nomadic application lifecycle. The first requirement is that applications need a location where they can reside, whenever they do not run on any Fog. Furthermore, the application management also needs to provide a mechanism to upgrade applications, e.g., to fix faulty applications or improve existing ones.

While some applications carry application data, i.e., are stateful, and can only exist once, the majority of nomadic applications is stateless and can be replicated to operate in multiple locations at the same time. Here, the application management needs to ensure that stateful applications are never replicated, i.e., the management needs to keep track of all running applications and the number of instances thereof. Furthermore, the application management needs to provide a recovery mechanism when one application crashes or the Fog is permanently disconnected from the Internet.

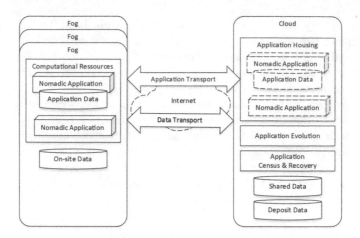

Fig. 2. Nomadic application infrastructure

Besides the infrastructural aspects, it is also required to support a fast and secure application transfer. Here, it is crucial to ensure the integrity of the application at any time so that the applications cannot be abused for malicious purposes, e.g., as attack vectors for sabotage operations or data leakage.

Architecture. Although nomadic applications are designed to operate in a decentralized manner, it is required to provide a centralized component to support the application management whenever they are not deployed on any Fog.

Application Housing and Transport. The housing component stores a shadow copy of each application to enable replication for stateless applications. Implementation-wise, we propose a similar infrastructure as the Docker Registry to cater for the required functionalities. Originating from the housing infrastructure, the applications can start their journey towards the Fogs over the Internet. These movement operations are supported by a dedicated application transport layer, which ensures a fast and reliable transport. Besides the basic transport aspects, this layer also ensures that applications are not modified or tampered with at any point in time, by validating the application's integrity based on cryptographic hash functions after each transport. The application housing also allows applications to update their application data, i.e., the state, before they continue their journey towards the privacy-sensitive Fogs.

Application Evolution. To comply with the need for continuous evolution for nomadic applications, the housing component furthermore needs to provide the possibility to update existing applications at any time and to inform applications that are running on Fogs about the update. These updates can be only applied when the applications have finished their tasks they must not be altered while processing data. To solve this challenge, we require the application hous-ing component to support versioning of applications to facilitate the update of applications in the housing component. The applications are required to regularly check whether a new version is available. If this is the case, stateful applications need to return to the application housing to transfer their application data to the evolved application and then they are able to continue their work.

For stateless applications, i.e., applications without application data attached, the housing component updates the shadow copy. The stateless appli-cation checks each time, before it moves to another location, whether the appli-cation has evolved. If this is the case, the application returns to the housing component to apply the updates or is discarded and new instances of the appli-cation are spawned from the updated shadow copy.

Application Census and Recovery. The application census and recovery compo-nent keeps track of all nomadic applications that are currently running on Fogs. This census is required to ensure that stateful applications are not replicated at any time. Besides the census functionality, this component is also required to provide a recovery mechanism for stateful applications. This recovery mecha-nism needs to decide whether a stateful operation will or will not return from the Fog, either due to an application crash or due to the fact that the Fog is perma-nently disconnected from the network. In this situation, the recovery mechanism restores the application alongside with its application data from a previous point in time and appoints the reconstructed application as the new sole instance of the nomadic application.

4.2   Data Management

Requirements. The data management is responsible for storing and transfer-ring data of different data types that are used by nomadic applications.

The first data type is the application data, which represents information that is stored within the application. This type is rather small, e.g., configuration settings or initialization values, does not contain any privacy-sensitive data, and remains the same for every Fog location. This application data only contains static information to avoid any data leakage, e.g., by embedding privacy sensitive information within the application data when the application is running in a Fog. Therefore, it must be ensured that this state can be only updated within a specific location that does not contain any privacy-sensitive information, e.g. the application housing.

The second type represents information that comprises both static data, which is stored in the Fog, and dynamic data, such as streaming data, e.g., sensor data, which cannot be stored due to its large volume. Although these two data types have entirely different requirements towards data management, both data types contain privacy-sensitive information, which must be processed according to the owner's policies. Due to the geographic colocation of this data and the application at runtime, this data is not moved outside the companies premises, which mitigates a potential data leakage.

Besides the application data and the owner's data, applications also require remote data repositories. Here, the data storage infrastructure needs to support two different scenarios. For the first scenario, the applications must be able to have a shared data storage, which can be used to either communicate with Fog providers, to retrieve new next job assignments or to share non-privacy-sensitive information with all replicas of an application.

This shared repository is required to be ACID-compliant and to support different access policies, e.g., a permissive one for the job assignments and a restricted one to restrict the access to a specific application. In addition to the shared repository, the application also requires a storage location, where it can deposit any arbitrary information that is generated while operating in one of the Fogs. This storage also needs to be partitioned into different segments, which can be only accessed by the assigned application. In contrast to the shared repository, this data storage only requires eventual consistency and any data transfer to this storage does not need to comply with any time-based restrictions. Nevertheless, the data needs to be persisted and provided at any point in time. The Fog operator needs to be able to check, whether the data transferred to the shared repository and the data deposit complies with the owner's policies and does not contain any privacy-sensitive information.

Architecture. To address the identified requirements for the different data types, we propose different data management techniques, as illustrated in Fig. 2.

Application Data. To realize tight coupling between the nomadic application and its application data, we propose to employ unikernels [7]. This tight coupling ensures that the data is always available for the application and the integrity check after the transfer over the network can be applied to the application and the application data at the same time.

On-site Data. Although the on-site data can be either static or dynamic, both data types must not leave the Fog, i.e., the premises of the data owner. Therefore, the data needs to be protected by methods originating from information rights management. These methods ensure that the data can be only read within the Fog and any data leakage outside the Fog renders the data useless due to the information rights management restrictions.

Shared Data. For the realization of the shared data, we propose a storage infrastructure similar to Amazon S3, where each application and potential replicas are able to read and write from a dedicated storage bucket. This storage infrastructure furthermore provides a high and instant availability regarding read and write operations, which distinguish the shared data from the deposit data.

Deposit Data. The deposit data follows the principles from Amazon Glacier. This makes it possible to store arbitrary information at any point in time, but it may take some time until the information is persisted within the storage respectively accessible for the application to be read. Furthermore, it is required to implement a data transport layer, which ensures both the integrity of the data as well as the compliance with the policy of the data owner at any time.

5   Discussion

Even though nomadic applications build on established principles and concepts, we have identified four research challenges, which are essential to realize them:

Scalable Privacy Protection for On-Site Data. One of the most important challenges is the development of a scalable privacy protection mechanism for dynamic data. While there are already solutions to enforce fine-grained access policies for static data, like office documents, there is still a lack of solutions for dynamic data. This is mainly due to the large volume of data that needs to be processed in real-time. Furthermore, it needs to be ensured that malicious applications cannot store any of this privacy-sensitive information within their own application data and transfer the data out of the owner's premises. Here, the data transport layer needs to ensure that only non-privacy-sensitive data, which is permitted to be sent to the deposit data, is transferred out of the Fog.

Target Scheduling for Stateful Applications. While stateless applications can be replicated on demand to be deployed in arbitrarily many Fogs, it is more complex for stateful applications to select their next assignment because they can exist only once and may be required at several locations at the same time. A first solution approach is the implementation of the first-come, first-served principle, but it is more desirable to implement a more flexible scheduling mechanism to avoid that one Fog operator occupies a specific application by spamming the waiting queue. To solve this issue it is desirable to implement an auctioning mechanism, which ensures a fair assignment of applications across all Fogs. This auctioning mechanism needs to be implemented on top of the transport layer in a decentralized manner to avoid any single point of failure.

Support Different Speeds in the Transport Layer. Due to the fact that the network transfer capabilities among the Fogs, application infrastructures, and storage facilities are limited, it is required to design a transport scheduling algorithm that ensures that each entity, i.e., a nomadic application or data, is transferred as efficiently as possible. Therefore it is required to design a transport protocol, which allows the different entities in the system to negotiate the transportation capabilities. This protocol should allow delaying those entities, which are not required to be transferred in a time critical manner, such as nomadic applications without any further job assignments returning to the housing component or deposit data. Nevertheless, it must be guaranteed that no entity suffers starvation in terms of transportation capabilities and all entities reach their destination eventually.

Recovery Mechanism. The final challenge is the development of a recovery mechanism which allows the reconstruction of application data. This reconstruction is required, when an application is unable to return to the housing component due to an application crash, a network disruption between the Fog and the network, or simply a failure of a single IoT device, which contributes to the Fog. Therefore, it is required to design a lightweight and efficient solution to track application states, e.g., data synchronization points, to be able to reconstruct applications. Furthermore, it is necessary to implement an algorithm to decide whether an application is lost forever and needs to be recovered or whether the application just needs longer than expected to finish its job. This functionality is crucial to avoid instances of a stateful application at any future point in time.

6   Conclusion

The growing use of IoT devices enables the emergence of the Fog computing paradigm which represents an evolution of the Cloud-based deployment model. In this paper, we identify opportunities of Fogs and introduce the concept of nomadic applications. These nomadic applications promise to solve both the challenges regarding the constantly growing volume of data and to enable a tight control of the data's privacy. In our future work, we will further develop the infrastructure for nomadic applications and apply them to real world scenarios.

Acknowledgements. This paper is supported by TU Wien research funds and by the Commission of the European Union within the CREMA H2020-RIA project (Grant agreement no. 637066).

References

1. Bonomi, F., Milito, R., Zhu, J., Addepalli, S.: Fog computing and its role in the Internet of Things. In: Proceeding of the MCC workshop on Mobile Cloud Computing, 1st edn., pp. 13–16. ACM (2012)
2. Celesti, A., Fazio, M., Giacobbe, M., Puliafito, A., Villari, M.: Characterizing cloud federation in IoT. In: 30th International Conference on Advanced Information Networking and Applications Workshops (WAINA), pp. 93–98. IEEE (2016)
3. Dastjerdi, A.V., Gupta, H., Calheiros, R.N., Ghosh, S.K., Buyya, R.: Fog Computing: principles, architectures, and applications. In: Buyya, R., Dastjerdi, A.V. (eds.) Internet of Things, pp. 61–75. Morgan Kaufmann (2016)
4. Kotz, D., Gray, R.S.: Mobile agents and the future of the internet. Oper. Syst. Rev. **33**(3), 7–13 (1999)
5. Lange, D.B., Mitsuru, O.: Programming and Deploying Java Mobile Agents Aglets. Addison-Wesley Longman Publishing Co., Inc., Boston (1998)
6. Lange, D.B., Mitsuru, O.: Seven good reasons for mobile agents. Commun. ACM **42**(3), 88–89 (1999)
7. Madhavapeddy, A., Mortier, R., Rotsos, C., Scott, D., Singh, B., Gazagnaire, T., Smith, S., Hand, S., Crowcroft, J.: Unikernels: library operating systems for the cloud. ACM SIGPLAN Not. **48**(4), 461–472 (2013)

8. Mell, P., Grance, T.: The NIST definition of cloud computing (2011)
9. Schleicher, J.M., Vögler, M., Inzinger, C., Hummer, W., Dustdar, S.: Nomads-enabling distributed analytical service environments for the smart city domain. In: International Conference on Web Services (ICWS), pp. 679–685. IEEE (2015)
10. Schulte, S., Hoenisch, P., Hochreiner, C., Dustdar, S., Klusch, M., Schuller, D.: Towards process support for cloud manufacturing. In: 18th International Enterprise Distributed Object Computing Conference (EDOC), pp. 142–149. IEEE (2014)
11. Shi, W., Dustdar, S.: The promise of edge computing. Computer **49**(5), 78–81 (2016)
12. Vaquero, L.M., Rodero-Merino, L.: Finding your way in the fog: towards a comprehensive definition of fog computing. ACM SIGCOMM Comput. Commun. Rev. **44**(5), 27–32 (2014)
13. Vögler, M., Schleicher, J.M., Inzinger, C., Dustdar, S.: A scalable framework for provisioning large-scale IOT deployments. Trans. Internet Technol. (TOIT) **16**(2), 11 (2016)

Fog Paradigm for Local Energy Management Systems

Amir Javed[1(✉)], Omer Rana[1], Charalampos Marmaras[2], and Liana Cipcigan[2]

[1] School of Computer Science and Informatics, Cardiff University, Cardiff, UK
javeda7@cardiff.ac.uk
[2] School of Engineering, Cardiff University, Cardiff, UK

Abstract. Cloud Computing infrastructures have been extensively deployed to support energy computation within built environments. This has ranged from predicting potential energy demand for a building (or a group of buildings), undertaking heat profile/energy distribution simulations, to understanding the impact of climate and weather on building operation. Cloud computing usage in these scenarios have benefited from resource elasticity, where the number and types of resources can change based on the complexity of the simulation being considered. While there are numerous advantages of using a cloud based energy management system, there are also significant limitations. For instance, many such systems assume that the data has been pre-staged at a cloud platform prior to simulation, and do not take account of data transfer times from the building to the simulation platform. The need for supporting computation at edge resources, which can be hosted within the building itself or shared within a building complex, has become important over recent year. Additionally, network connectivity between the sensing infrastructure within a built environment and a data centre where analysis is to be carried out can be intermittent or may fail. There is therefore also a need to better understand how computation/analysis can be carried out closer to the data capture site to complement analysis that would be undertaken at the data centre. We describe how the Fog computing paradigm can be used to support some of these requirements, extending the capability of a data centre to support energy simulation within built environments.

Keywords: Distributed clouds · Fog computing · Energy management · Built environments

1 Introduction

Buildings are considered to be one of the largest contributors towards total energy consumption and greenhouse gas production [15,28] in most IEA (International Energy Agency) countries [1]. Having said that, they are also considered to offer the greatest potential for achieving significant greenhouse gas emission reductions [27,40]. For these reasons, improving energy efficiency of buildings has

© ICST Institute for Computer Sciences, Social Informatics and Telecommunications Engineering 2018
A. Longo et al. (Eds.): IISSC 2017/CN4IoT 2017, LNICST 189, pp. 162–176, 2018.
https://doi.org/10.1007/978-3-319-67636-4_18

received a lot of attention globally [41]. On a smaller scale, improving energy use in buildings also leads to significant cost savings for the building manager, increasing the utility of the paid energy unit.

According to the US National Institute of Standards and Technology (NIST), buildings are an integral part of a Cyber-Physical system (defined as "a co-engineered interacting network of physical and computational components") [25]. Being part of this "smart" ecosystem, buildings need to integrate with future smart grids and transform their simplistic consumption-only profile to a complex one that includes local distributed energy resources (DER) and/or storage. Depending on the available assets, building managers must change from typical consumers to "prosumers", being able to both produce and consume energy on their premises. Nowadays building are equipped with building energy management systems (BEMSs), which control the heating, ventilation, air conditioning (HVAC) and lighting systems to reducing energy consumption while maintaining occupants' comfort [41]. However, due to these ever-changing and uncertain indoor and outdoor characteristics, the performance of typical BEMS often falls short of expectation, lacking the necessary data processing, evaluation, and control methodologies [2, 42].

In order to over come these challenges, there is a need to develop an efficient energy management system. An energy management system that allows a building to be part of a smart ecosystem. To be seen as an element of a miniature (local) energy system that interacts with the other elements of the system in a coordinated fashion. A typical BEMS that tries to optimise building energy efficiency will always fail (in the general context), if other elements of the system are not considered. On the other hand, considering the building in a local energy system with other buildings, distributed energy resources, energy storage and EVs, the energy management and coordination becomes more difficult. Over the years researchers have proposed many cloud based energy management system to overcome challenges such as single point of failure, prone to distributed denial of service attack, limited service capability due to single server, limited memory and computational resources [13, 16, 29, 44]. These cloud based energy management systems are capable for multidimensional data analysis for smart grids [19], data management and parallel processing in real time [18], or just data storage [30]. The rationale to use cloud in each scenario was to provide on-demand processing and storage capability to improve the services provided by energy management system.

However, as we move data processing and storage to cloud we are faced with issues like latency [5] and disruption of services due to host unreachability. One possible solution to overcome these challenges is by using fog computing [4] – an approach that extends cloud computing and service provision to the network edge. Fog computing enables developers to deploy services at the network edge using devices such as set-top-boxes or access points. The rationale of using fog computing is to process data at the network edge using a distributed architecture without effecting the quality of service. In the past we have seen evidence of Fog computing being used in the context of smart grids for load balancing [39] and real time processing of energy data [5].

However, it is necessary to better understand how to cope with the intermittent characteristics of the different elements of such a built environment, and handle the large amounts of data that is generated from various monitoring infrastructure associated with such an environment. Predictive models should also be incorporated in the coordination mechanism in order to deal with the associated uncertainties and increase the control efficiency. From a building manager's perspective, these algorithms must be able to facilitate different control strategies according to the overall coordination objective and enhance the (self-) awareness of the system. In this paper we propose a cloud based local energy management system that is used (i) to flatten the demand profile of the building facility and reduce its peak, based on analysis that can be carried out at the building or in its vicinity (rather than at a data center); (ii) to enable the participation of the building manager in the grid balancing services market through demand side management and response. Furthermore, the Local Energy Management System (LEMS) is extended using the Fog computing paradigm for the holistic management of buildings, energy storage and EVs.

2   Related Work

Over the year an efficient energy management system has been the focus of research for building or set of building using smart meters. Researchers have suggested improvement to energy management system by focusing and incorporating components such as building energy management system, home energy management system, shifting of energy load and looking at dynamic pricing [10]. To over come challenges in conventional energy management system, such as central point of failure or scalability due to limited memory and limited bandwidth to handle large request [3]. Researchers have proposed cloud based energy management system. Keeping these challenges in mind and to overcome them a cloud based demand response system was proposed that introduced data centric communication and topic based communication models [13]. Their model was based on a master and slave architecture in which the smart meters and energy management system at home acted as slave where as the utility acted as masters. The authors advocated that a reliable and scalable energy management system can be built using their model. In another approach the energy management system was built by considering the energy pricing to be dynamic [16]. While building this model the authors considered the peak demand of the building and incorporated the dynamic pricing while handling customer requests. [29] proposed an architecture for control, storage, power management and resource allocation of micro-grids and to integrate cloud based application for micro-grids with external one. The bigger and distributed the smart grid infrastructure become the more difficult it is to analyse real time data from smart meters. [44] suggested a cloud based system is most appropriate to handle analysis or real time energy data from smart meters. In another approach power monitoring and early warning system facilities were provided using cloud platform [12]. [34] proposed a mobile agent architecture for cloud based energy management system to handle customer request more efficiently. [32] proposed a dynamic cloud based demand response model to periodically forecast demand and by dynamically managing available resources to reduce the peak demand.

The concept of Fog computing has emerged to tackle issues relating to cloud latency, location awareness and improve quality of service for real time streamed data. Fog computing has been used in the context of smart grids in a number of ways. However, while using fog computing it is quite important to understand the energy sustainability for devices that are part of fog network. To address proper energy efficient management strategies, [9] proposed an energy-aware management strategy model that is able to improve the energy sustainability of entire federated IoT cloud ecosystem. Furthermore, fog computing has been applied in smart grids for enabling energy load balancing applications to run at the network edge, especially in close proximity to smart meters within micro-grids [39]. Fog-based infrastructure is used in this case to estimate energy demand, identify potential energy generation and the lowest energy tariff at that instant – this information is used to switch to alternate sources of energy in a dynamic manner. Furthermore, a fog infrastructure is also used as *collectors*, to gather energy related data, and subsequently process this in real time and generate command signals to consumer devices [5]. At the network edge the actual computational processing carried out is limited, while most of the data is pushed to a cloud data center to generate real time reports and for visualisation. Fog-based systems have also been used to *control* building energy consumption. In this scenario, sensors installed at various places read data related to humidity, temperature and various gases in the building atmosphere. Based on these readings, the sensors work together to reduce the temperature of the building by activating or deactivating various electrical devices [33].

Mobile Fog was proposed to tackle latency issues for geo-spatial distributed applications [11], comprising of a set of computational functions that an application executing on a device can invoke to carry out a task. However the functions supported by a *mobile Fog* infrastructure are not general purpose, but are application specific. Similarly, to tackle latency issues another proposal was presented in [26] by focusing on the placement and migration method of Fog and Cloud resources. This work describes how complex event processing systems can be used to reduce the network bandwidth of virtual machines that are migrating. In mobile Fog concept a local cloud is formed by combining capacity across neighboring nodes of a network [24] and one resource within these nodes acts as a local resource coordinator. In [24], the authors propose a framework to share resources based on the availability of particular service-oriented functions. [20] combine smart grid, Cloud, actuator and sensors together for a reliable fog computing platform. To address demand side response within a smart grids, [21] worked on maximizing the benefits to both consumer and power companies using a game theory approach. Their work was based on a Stackelberg game [14] between the consumers and the energy companies so that both the parties were able to satisfy their utility functions. In a similar approach, a cloud based framework was presented for a group of energy hubs, to manage two way communication between energy companies and consumers to reduce peak to average ratio of total electricity – while at the same time requiring consumers to pay less by using a game theory [31]. Similarly, [8] describe an approach for reducing the energy consumption by investigating the interaction of consumers and energy companies. Based on the interaction of the consumer and power companies they proposed an energy schedule based on game theory, the aim of which was to reduced the peak to average power ratio. In another approach a user aware demand management system was proposed [43] that manages residential load while taking into account user preferences. The proposed model used both energy optimization model and game theoretical model to maximize user saving without causing any discomfort.

The concept of cloud based energy system has been used to over come challenges that a conventional micro-grid based energy management system faces. However, while moving to cloud is advantages it has some challenges as well and one of them being loss of communication failure between the cloud based energy management system and endpoints (electric vehicles and energy storage units). We address this issue by suggesting how fog paradigm can be used along with cloud based energy management system to overcome situation of communication failure in a dynamic evironment.

3   Cloud Based Local Energy Management Systems

3.1   LEMS Components

The architecture of our cloud based local energy management system(LEMS) is shown in Fig. 1a and b we illustrate the core components of LEMS. The main objective of LEMS is to manage the demand from electric vehicles (EVs) and energy storage units (ESU's) at building premises by sending power set points through a Gateway to EV chargers. An electricity demand forecast (software)

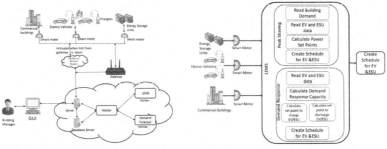

(a) Architectural layout of Cloud based Local Energy Management System and its components using Fog computing

(b) Architecture of Local Energy Management System

Fig. 1. Architecture of cloud based energy management system

tool was developed in order to work with the LEMS, which estimates the electricity demand of a building over a particular time period. This software tool uses historical data (collected from actual building use) and the weather measured in the proximity of the building.

Figure 1b gives an overview of the main components of LEMS. LEMS can be broadly divided into two modes of operation: peak shaving and demand response. The LEMS operates in timesteps during which the system is considered static, i.e. changes are only discovered at the end of the timestep. A timestep of 15 min is used in this work, providing a trade-off between a dynamic (semi-real time) and a reliable operation that allows the frequent capture of the building conditions and minimizes risk of communication lags. Data about EVs located at the building, such as their battery capacity, state of charge (SoC), expected disconnection times, charging/discharging power rate, charging/discharging schedule and available discharge capacity, is requested from charging stations upon the connection of every EV. Information regarding the available capacity, state of charge (SoC), charging/discharging power rate and charging/discharging schedule is requested from every ESU. This information is stored in a database, and is accessed from the LEMS after every timestep in order to define future power set points for charging stations.

A pre-forecast analysis stage was included in order to increase the performance of the demand forecast tool, by including weather information in the forecasting process [22]. The objective of this stage is to identify the optimal number of weather attributes to be considered by the model to improve accuracy. Using historical local weather data and building energy consumption data, an analysis was performed in order to calculate the correlation of the available weather data with the electricity demand of each building. The forecast model used an artificial neural network, implemented using the WEKA toolkit [27]. Electricity consumption on a random day was forecasted for each building for every timestep. The forecast accuracy was calculated using the mean absolute percentage error (MAPE) metric. For each building the set of attributes that resulted in the least MAPE was selected as the optimal one. The model performs a day-ahead power demand forecast using the optimal ANN configuration suggested by the pre-forecast analysis model [22].

LEMS has been deployed on the CometCloud [6] system. CometCloud enables federation between heterogeneous computing platforms that can support complete LEMS work, such as a local computational cluster with a public cloud (such as Amazon AWS). There are two main components in CometCloud: a *master* and (potentially multiple) *worker* node(s). In its software architecture, CometCloud comprises mainly three layers: the programming layer, a management layer and a federation or infrastructure layer. The programming layer identifies tasks that needs to be executed, the set of dependencies between tasks that enables a user to define the number of resources that are available along with any constraints on the usage of those resources. Each task in this instance is associated with the types of LEMS operation supported, or whether a demand forecast needs to be carried out. In the management layer policy and objectives are specified by the user that help in allocating the resources to carry out tasks. In addition to allocation of resources this layer also keeps a track of all tasks that are generated for workers, and how many of these have been successfully executed [7]. In the federation layer a lookup system is built so that content locality is maintained and a search can be carried out using wildcards [23]. Furthermore a "CometSpace" is defined that can be accessed by all resources in the federation [17]. CometCloud uses this physically distributed, but logically shared, tuple space to share tasks between different resources that are included in a resource federation.

The main task of the master node is to prepare a task that is to be executed and give information about the data required to process the task. The second component is the worker, which receives tasks from the master, executes the job and sends the results to the place specified by the master. In our framework there are two workers – one that will be running the LEMS algorithm that will generate the schedule to for the charging and discharging of the electric vehicles and the second that will forecast energy demand for the next day. There are two cloud-hosted servers that receive requests from a graphical user interface, and based on the requests call the appropriate function are executed via the master. The second server manages a database which contains information about building data, EVs and weather attributes around the building. The database is used to store historic data about power consumption, energy pricing etc. for each building and information regarding the weather is used to forecast (energy) demand for the next day. There is an intermediary gateway which intercepts all signals from the cloud server and forwards the schedule to EV's and ESU's or current energy reading of building, EV's and ESU's to database server.

The last component is the Fog server that contains sensors to read data at every time step from buildings, EVs and from energy storage units. There is a pre-generated model placed inside the Fog component to which the data read from the sensor are sent, and the output is the schedule for each EV for the time step. The rationale for using the Fog component is that in case there is network failure or latency, such that a signal is not able to reach the charging station, then with the help of sensors the current state of each asset can be read and a schedule can be prepared. The predictive model is updated every 24 h, replacing any previous estimation that was generated.

3.2   Energy Management System Operation

The LEMS maximizes its utility to the building manager by adjusting its operational target (objective) according to the system status and condition. Two scheduling algorithms for the management of the EVs and the ESUs were designed, namely Peak Shaving Schedule and Demand Response Schedule, refer Fig. 1b. Each algorithm serves one objective and the LEMS shifts from one scheduling strategy to another depending on the objective of the building manager:

- **Peak Shaving schedule:** This approach aims to flatten the aggregate demand profile of the building facility. This is achieved by *filling the valleys* (i.e. at periods of low demand) and *shaving the peaks* (i.e. at periods of high demand) of the demand profile using controllable loads (EVs, ESUs) of the building facility – this approach aims to shift energy load from periods where demand/tariff is likely to be high, to periods of low demand (e.g. night). Refer Fig. 1b the LEMS reads the building demand for next timestep, current charge in EV and ESU. Then calculates the charging/discharging schedules of the EVs and ESUs, and sends them, the corresponding power set points as charging or discharging schedule, at the beginning of every timestep. These power set points are messages with the exact power rate at which each EV/ESU must charge/discharge at each timestep.

– **Demand Response schedule:** This approach is intended to enable building managers to participate in the ancillary services market and provide demand response actions to the grid. It was assumed that the system operator sends requests to the building manager to either reduce or increase its aggregate demand in the next time step (of 15 min). Similar to peak shaving mode, refer Fig. 1b, in demand response mode LEMS read the current charge in EV's and ESU's to calculate available energy that can be used to increase or decrease demand. Then based on the request received the LEMS overrides the charging/discharging schedules of the available controllable assets by creating a charging/discharging schedule for all connected assets.

3.3   Fog Paradigm to Tackle Communication Failure Between LEMS and Charging Stations

In the *Peak Shaving* mode, the highest demand of a building is flattened by creating a schedule to manage the charging/discharging of EVs and ESUs, so that the discharging operation takes place when the building demand is highest, and charging operation takes place when the demand is low. A user can enter the peak shaving mode by making a selection from a graphical user interface (as illustrated in Fig. 1a, leading to the generation and submission of a computational task to the CometCloud system. On completion of these tasks, a peak shaving schedule is created and forwarded at the end points through the gateway. A day-ahead (24 h) schedule is created to ensure that charging stations can make local decisions even if there is a communication failure to the Cloud-hosted LEMS. The day-ahead schedule is based on the number of connected EVs and ESUs observed at the time of creation of the schedule (and estimating the number of EVs/ESUs to be observed for the next day).

However, as the number of EVs can change during the day, and the EV/building demand can be inaccurate, the LEMS is programmed to collect data from buildings and connected EVs/ESUs at regular intervals (defined by the timestep parameter previously described). For our experiment, this timestep is set to 15 min but can be changed by a building manager. At each time step, new data is read and the schedule updated for the next 24 h. This will ensure that any changes in the environment are taken into account (e.g. new EV arrival or departure) by LEMS and the charging station will always have a 24 h schedule updated every 15 min.

When LEMS operates in the demand response mode, a user can request an increase or decrease in total demand using a graphical interface. The computation of this request operates similarly to the previous scenario – i.e. a computational task is generated, executed on the cloud platform, and the result (a schedule) sent to the gateway. Based on the request a schedule is prepared to based on available EVs/ESUs, refer Fig. 1b. However, the demand response schedule (generated by LEMS) is only valid for one time step, with the schedule reverting back to peak shaving mode after this time step. For example, if a user has made a *demand down* request then LEMS will create a schedule that will discharge all available connected EVs/ESUs for one time step. However the schedule for other remaining intervals over the remaining 24 h will revert back to peak shaving operation. This indicates that during a communication failure (at a particular time step), the demand response request will not be executed and will have to be made again.

Currently LEMS handles communication failure by creating a 24 h moving window of charging/discharging schedule for connected EVs/ESUs. Furthermore, this schedule gets updated every time step, so that if the number of EVs has changed in the last 15 min then this change is taken into account. However, LEMS does not address a situation when there is a communication failure between LEMS and the charging point, and during this communication failure a new EV arrives. As there is no communication link available, no new schedule can be created for the new EV. To address this situation we create a forecasting model that can be hosted at the edge of the network (i.e. closer to the charging points for EVs) that will, by reading the environment data (information about EV, building energy and time) available locally, predict the charging schedule over one time step, or make adjustments (using pre-defined rules) to an existing schedule generated by LEMS if there is a communication failure.

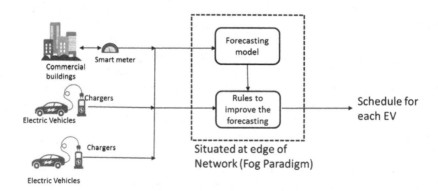

Fig. 2. Schedule forecasting model deployed at edge of network

Figure 2 summarises how an EV charging schedule is produced in case of a communication failure, and when the number of EVs have changed based on the originally generated schedule. There are two main components that interact to update the EV charging schedule:

- the forecasting model developed using the LEMS system – using attributes such as time of day, EV identity, state of charge of EV at that time, the current energy consumption of the building, in order to estimate the charging schedule for that EV at that time. A number of learning algorithms were used to determine the schedule, and the model with the lowest error rate was placed at the edge of the network. Once the model (used to derive a schedule) is created, a set of rules that govern the charging and discharging of the vehicle are used to update the model, providing an alternative means to alter the LEMS generated schedule using local information (in case of network failure).
- The rule based component is used to improve the accuracy of the forecasting model. The rule based component takes the LEMS-generated schedule that was saved at the charger, and produces a new charging schedule as output. Once all the attributes/parameters (as indicated above) are passed as input to the algorithm, it checks if there is already a previously generated schedule for the connected EV, and updates it according to the rules available. If there is no schedule for the connected EV (using an EV identifier), then this indicates that this EV arrived after the communication failure and the LEMS-generated schedule did not take this EV into account. The first things the algorithm checks is the state of charge of the vehicle (SOC_EV_{it}) at time instant 't', if this is less than the minimum state of charge (Min_SOC), then a charge event is generated (regardless of the LEMS-generated schedule) for that time step. Furthermore, the algorithm checks if the time to departure of the vehicle is less than 30 min, and the forecasting model is attempting to discharge the vehicle, then the schedule is updated to generate a charging event.

Furthermore, the algorithm checks if the State of charge for an EV has reached its maximum limit if it has and the forecasting model is signalling to still charge the vehicle a new schedule is set to idle for that vehicle. If none of the condition is met then the new schedule is set to the one forecasted by the machine learning model.

4   Results and Analysis

We simulated a scenario with ten EVs used to reduce the peak demand of one commercial building. In the simulation we had recorded the building energy consumption at a timestep of 15 min, along with details of each EV such as vehicle ID, state of charge of vehicle, minimum state of charge for that vehicle, maximum state of charge, transfer rate, time of arrival and time to leave. Based on these data our LEMS creates a charging/discharging schedule for each connected EV – along with a log file that contains values for each of the input parameters. We developed a forecasting model using the Weka toolkit. To identify the most appropriate

Algorithm 1. Algorithm

Input: Scheduling algorithm generated by forecasting model for each EV denoted by
Sch_EV_{it} (where i denotes the number of EVs and t denotes time instant t),
Schedule stored at Charger generated by LEMS $Old\_Sch\_EV_{it}$,
State of Charge of each EV SOC_EV_{it},
T: time of day,
Minimum State of Charge for each EV Min_SOC,
Maximum State of Charge for each EV Max_SOC,
Identifier for each connected EV EV_ID_i ,
time of (each) EV departure $Time\_EV_i$
Output: Output New Schedule for each EV as denoted by $New\_Sch\_EV_{it}$
1: **for** i in tolal EV **do**
2:    $charge = 3$
3:    $Discharge = -3$
4:    $idle = 0$
5:    **if** EV_ID_i in $Old\_Sch\_EV_{it}$ **then**
6:       set $New\_Sch\_EV_{it} = Old\_Sch\_EV_{it}$
7:    **else if** $Sch\_EV_{it} ==$ Discharge and $SOC\_EV_{it} < Min\_SOC$ **then**
8:       set $New\_Sch\_EV_{it} = charge$
9:    **else if** ($Sch\_EV_{it} ==$ Discharge or $Sch\_EV_{it} ==$ idle) and $(Time\_EV_i - t) < 30$ **then**
10:       set $New\_Sch\_EV_{it} = charge$
11:    **else if** $Sch\_EV_{it} ==$ charge and $SOC\_EV_{it} = Max\_SOC$ **then**
12:       set $New\_Sch\_EV_{it} = idle$
13:    **else**
14:       set $New\_Sch\_EV_{it} = Sch\_EV_{it}$
15:    **end if**
16: **end for**

classification algorithm to use for developing the model, we considered both generative and discriminative techniques to identify the most appropriate classifier. For generative models we looked at models that consider conditional dependencies (Bayesnet) [35] and those that looked at conditional independence (Naivebayes) [38] in the dataset. For discriminative model we considered decision trees (J48) [36] and a neural network (multilayer perceptron) [37].

While each model trained on the dataset to identify the best classifier we used the standard/default configuration for our classifier. Once the model was trained we created a log file to simulate the a scenario in which communication link was broken between the LEMS and the charging station and an EV had arrived after the communication failure. This log file was used as the testing dataset for the model. The log file considered arrival of the EV at different times with different states of charge. Based on their state of charge, time of day, energy consumption of building a charging schedule was forecasted. The accuracy of each model is shown in the table below. We can see from the table that the Bayesnet performed the best (85%) among the four models we created, which showed that data had conditional dependency and NaiveBayes performed worst (75%). Once the schedule was created, the rule based component compares the scheduling decisions made for the connected EV and updates the schedule. As we can see the accuracy of the forecasting model increased once the rules

Table 1. Accuracy of schedule forecasting algorithm at edge

Machine learning model (MLM)	Accuracy of MLM	Accuracy after applying rule based component
NaiveBayes	76%	82%
BayesNet	85%	87%
J48	82%	83%
Multilayer perceptron	80%	83%

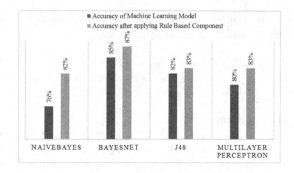

Fig. 3. Accuracy of machine learning model vs overall accuracy of model deployed at network edge

were applied. From Table 1 and Fig. 3, we can observe that the combination of Bayesian model and rule based component gave the highest accuracy of 87%.

5 Conclusion

We investigated the integration of a Local Energy Management System (LEMS), which is cloud hosted and needs to acquire data over a network to develop a charging/discharging schedule for EVs/ESUs, with capability that is located at the network edge. The LEMS system also made use of EV batteries/ESUs as an energy store, to flatten the peak energy demand of a building or to participate in an ancillary market. We looked at two scenarios in which there is a communication failure between the LEMS and that of charging stations. One scenario when no new EVs arrive at the building site is handled by developing a day-ahead schedule using the cloud-based LEMS and stored at the charging point. This schedule is then updated after each time step (set to 15 min in our simulation), and able to take account of any changes that might have occured in the system over this time period. In the second scenario we looked at a situation when a new EV arrives at a building site after a communications failure has occured between the LEMS and the charging point/gateway. In this situation we introduce a schedule generation capability that comprises of two components: (i) the LEMS-generated schedule and (ii) a rule-based component that is able to adapt the schedule based on locally recorded data. We tested our forecasting model by simulating a scenario in which an EV arrives at a site during a communication failure and found that our forecasting model can forecast the schedule for the new EV with 87% accuracy. Our approach demonstrates how a forecasting model that has been generated at a data center can be combined with an adaptation mechanism that is located at the network edge, and able to adapt the forecasting model in case of network failure (between the data center and the edge) and taking account of latency considerations (i.e. having to transfer data about recently arrived EVs to the cloud-based LEMS to update the schedule). The general approach described here can also be generalised to other similar types of applications.

Acknowledgment. This work was carried out in the InnovateUK/EPSRC-funded "Ebbs and Flows of Energy Systems" (EFES) project.

References

1. I.E. Agency: Energy efficiency (2017). http://www.iea.org/about/faqs/energyefficiency/. Accessed 11 Jan 2017
2. Amarasinghe, K., Wijayasekara, D., Manic, M.: Neural network based downscaling of building energy management system data. In: IEEE 23rd International Symposium on Industrial Electronics (ISIE), pp. 2670–2675. IEEE (2014)
3. Bera, S., Misra, S., Rodrigues, J.J.: Cloud computing applications for smart grid: A survey. IEEE Trans. Parallel Distrib. Syst. **26**(5), 1477–1494 (2015)
4. Bonomi, F.: Connected vehicles, the internet of things, and fog computing. In: The Eighth ACM International Workshop on Vehicular Inter-Networking (VANET), Las Vegas, pp. 13–15 (2011)
5. Bonomi, F., Milito, R., Zhu, J., Addepalli, S.: Fog computing and its role in the internet of things. In: Proceedings of the First Edition of the MCC Workshop on Mobile Cloud Computing, pp. 13–16. ACM (2012)
6. Diaz-Montes, J., AbdelBaky, M., Zou, M., Parashar, M.: CometCloud: enabling software-defined federations for end-to-end application workflows. IEEE Internet Comput. **19**(1), 69–73 (2015)
7. Diaz-Montes, J., Xie, Y., Rodero, I., Zola, J., Ganapathysubramanian, B., Parashar, M.: Exploring the use of elastic resource federations for enabling large-scale scientific workflows. In: Proceedings of Workshop on Many-Task Computing on Clouds, Grids, and Supercomputers (MTAGS), pp. 1–10 (2013)
8. Fadlullah, Z.M., Quan, D.M., Kato, N., Stojmenovic, I.: GTES: an optimized game-theoretic demand-side management scheme for smart grid. IEEE Syst. J. **8**(2), 588–597 (2014)
9. Giacobbe, M., Celesti, A., Fazio, M., Villari, M., Puliafito, A.: A sustainable energy-aware resource management strategy for IoT cloud federation. In: IEEE International Symposium on Systems Engineering (ISSE), pp. 170–175. IEEE (2015)
10. Green, R.C., Wang, L., Alam, M.: Applications and trends of high performance computing for electric power systems: focusing on smart grid. IEEE Trans. Smart Grid **4**(2), 922–931 (2013)
11. Hong, K., Lillethun, D., Ramachandran, U., Ottenwälder, B., Koldehofe, B.: Mobile fog: a programming model for large-scale applications on the internet of things. In: Proceedings of the Second ACM SIGCOMM Workshop on Mobile Cloud Computing, pp. 15–20. ACM (2013)
12. Ji, L., Lifang, W., Li, Y.: Cloud service based intelligent power monitoring and early-warning system. In: Innovative Smart Grid Technologies-Asia (ISGT Asia), pp. 1–4. IEEE (2012)
13. Kim, H., Kim, Y.-J., Yang, K., Thottan, M.: Cloud-based demand response for smart grid: architecture and distributed algorithms. In: IEEE International Conference on Smart Grid Communications (SmartGridComm), pp. 398–403. IEEE (2011)

14. Korzhyk, D., Conitzer, V., Parr, R.: Solving stackelberg games with uncertain observability. In: The 10th International Conference on Autonomous Agents and Multiagent Systems, vol. 3, pp. 1013–1020. International Foundation for Autonomous Agents and Multiagent Systems (2011)

15. Laustsen, J.: Energy efficiency requirements in building codes, energy efficiency policies for new buildings. Int. Energy Agency (IEA) **2**, 477–488 (2008)

16. Li, X., Lo, J.-C.: Pricing and peak aware scheduling algorithm for cloud computing. In: Innovative Smart Grid Technologies (ISGT), 2012 IEEE PES, pp. 1–7. IEEE (2012)

17. Li, Z., Parashar, M.: A computational infrastructure for grid-based asynchronous parallel applications. In: Proceedings of the 16th International Symposium on High Performance Distributed Computing, pp. 229–230. ACM (2007)

18. Lohrmann, B., Kao, O.: Processing smart meter data streams in the cloud. In: 2nd IEEE PES International Conference and Exhibition on Innovative Smart Grid Technologies (ISGT Europe), pp. 1–8. IEEE (2011)

19. Lv, H., Wang, F., Yan, A., Cheng, Y.: Design of cloud data warehouse and its application in smart grid. In: International Conference on Automatic Control and Artificial Intelligence (ACAI 2012), pp. 849–852. IET (2012)

20. Madsen, H., Burtschy, B., Albeanu, G., Popentiu-Vladicescu, F.: Reliability in the utility computing era: towards reliable fog computing. In: 20th International Conference on Systems, Signals and Image Processing (IWSSIP), pp. 43–46. IEEE (2013)

21. Maharjan, S., Zhu, Q., Zhang, Y., Gjessing, S., Basar, T.: Dependable demand response management in the smart grid: a stackelberg game approach. IEEE Trans. Smart Grid **4**(1), 120–132 (2013)

22. Marmaras, C., Javed, A., Cipcigan, L., Rana, O.: Predicting the energy demand of buildings during triad peaks in GB. Energy Build. **141**, 262–273 (2017)

23. Montes, J.D., Zou, M., Singh, R., Tao, S., Parashar, M.: Data-driven workflows in multi-cloud marketplaces. In: IEEE 7th International Conference on Cloud Computing, pp. 168–175. IEEE (2014)

24. Nishio, T., Shinkuma, R., Takahashi, T., Mandayam, N.B.: Service-oriented heterogeneous resource sharing for optimizing service latency in mobile cloud. In: Proceedings of the First International Workshop on Mobile Cloud Computing & Networking, pp. 19–26. ACM (2013)

25. National Institute of Standards and Technology. Cyber-physical systems — NIST (2016). https://www.nist.gov/el/cyber-physical-systems. Accessed 11 Jan 2017

26. Ottenwälder, B., Koldehofe, B., Rothermel, K., Ramachandran, U.: MigCEP: operator migration for mobility driven distributed complex event processing. In: Proceedings of the 7th ACM International Conference on Distributed Event-Based Systems, pp. 183–194. ACM (2013)

27. Pérez-Lombard, L., Ortiz, J., Pout, C.: A review on buildings energy consumption information. Energy Build. **40**(3), 394–398 (2008)

28. United Nations Environment Programme: Why buildings (2016). http://www.unep.org/sbci/AboutSBCI/Background.asp. Accessed 11 Jan 2017

29. Rajeev, T., Ashok, S.: A cloud computing approach for power management of microgrids. In: Innovative Smart Grid Technologies-India (ISGT India), 2011 IEEE PES, pp. 49–52. IEEE (2011)

30. Rusitschka, S., Eger, K., Gerdes, C.: Smart grid data cloud: a model for utilizing cloud computing in the smart grid domain. In: First IEEE International Conference on Smart Grid Communications (SmartGridComm), pp. 483–488. IEEE (2010)

31. Sheikhi, A., Rayati, M., Bahrami, S., Ranjbar, A.M., Sattari, S.: A cloud computing framework on demand side management game in smart energy hubs. Int. J. Electr. Power Energy Syst. **64**, 1007–1016 (2015)

32. Simmhan, Y., Aman, S., Kumbhare, A., Liu, R., Stevens, S., Zhou, Q., Prasanna, V.: Cloud-based software platform for big data analytics in smart grids. Comput. Sci. Eng. **15**(4), 38–47 (2013)

33. Stojmenovic, I., Wen, S.: The fog computing paradigm: scenarios and security issues. In: 2014 Federated Conference on Computer Science and Information Systems (FedCSIS), pp. 1–8. IEEE (2014)

34. Tang, L., Li, J., Wu, R.: Synergistic model of power system cloud computing based on mobile-agent. In: 3rd IEEE International Conference on Network Infrastructure and Digital Content (IC-NIDC), pp. 222–226. IEEE (2012)

35. University of Waikato: Bayesnet (2017). http://weka.sourceforge.net/doc.dev/weka/classifiers/bayes/BayesNet.html

36. University of Waikato: J48 (2017). http://weka.sourceforge.net/doc.dev/weka/classifiers/trees/J48.html

37. University of Waikato: Mlpclassifier (2017). http://weka.sourceforge.net/doc.packages/multiLayerPerceptrons/weka/classifiers/functions/MLPClassifier.html

38. University of Waikato: Naivebayes (2017). http://weka.sourceforge.net/doc.dev/weka/classifiers/bayes/NaiveBayes.html

39. Wei, C., Fadlullah, Z.M., Kato, N., Stojmenovic, I.: On optimally reducing power loss in micro-grids with power storage devices. IEEE J. Sel. Areas Commun. **32**(7), 1361–1370 (2014)

40. Weng, T., Agarwal, Y.: From buildings to smart buildings—sensing and actuation to improve energy efficiency. IEEE Des. Test **29**(4), 36–44 (2012)

41. Wijayasekara, D., Linda, O., Manic, M., Rieger, C.: Mining building energy management system data using fuzzy anomaly detection and linguistic descriptions. IEEE Trans. Ind. Inform. **10**(3), 1829–1840 (2014)

42. Wijayasekara, D., Manic, M.: Data-fusion for increasing temporal resolution of building energy management system data. In: 41st Annual Conference of the IEEE Industrial Electronics Society, IECON 2015, pp. 004550–004555. IEEE (2015)

43. Yaagoubi, N., Mouftah, H.T.: User-aware game theoretic approach for demand management. IEEE Trans. Smart Grid **6**(2), 716–725 (2015)

44. Yang, C.-T., Chen, W.-S., Huang, K.-L., Liu, J.-C., Hsu, W.-H., Hsu, C.-H.: Implementation of smart power management and service system on cloud computing. In: 9th International Conference on Ubiquitous Intelligence & Computing and 9th International Conference on Autonomic & Trusted Computing (UIC/ATC), pp. 924–929. IEEE (2012)

Orchestration for the Deployment of Distributed Applications with Geographical Constraints in Cloud Federation

Massimo Villari$^{(\boxtimes)}$, Giuseppe Tricomi, Antonio Celesti, and Maria Fazio

Department of Engineering, University of Messina, Messina, Italy
{mvillari,gtricomi,acelesti,mfazio}@unime.it

Abstract. This paper presents a system developed in the Horizon 2020 BEACON project enabling the deployment of distributed applications in an OpenStack-based federated Cloud networking environment. In such a scenario, we assume that a distributed application consists of several microservices that can be instantiated in different federated Cloud providers and that users can formalize advanced geolocation deployment constrains. In particular, we focus on an Orchestration Broker that is able to create ad-hoc manifest documents including application deployment instructions for the involved federated Cloud providers and users' requirements.

1 Introduction

Nowadays, federated Cloud networking [1] represents an interesting scenario for the deployment of distributed applications. In this paper, we describe the results obtained by the Horizon 2020 BEACON Project in terms of Cloud brokering for the deployment of distributed applications in federated OpenStack-based Cloud networking environments [2]. In such a scenario, we assume that a distributed application consists of several microservices that can be instantiated in different federated Cloud providers and that users can specify advanced geolocation deployment constrains. In particular, we present an Orchestration Broker that is able to create ad-hoc service manifest documents including application deployment instructions destined to selected federated Cloud providers and users' requirements. The Orchestration Broker interacts through RESTFUL communications with federated OpenStack Clouds through their own HEAT orchestration systems.

The purposes of this paper is not to define a new standard for addressing application deployment but to extend the Heat Orchestrator Template (HOT) [3] resource set in order to manage the federated deployment of distributed applications. The Orchestration Broker analyses the HOT service manifest of an application and automatically extracts the elements able to describe how microservices have to be deployed in federated OpenStack Clouds via their HEAT systems. An important feature of this approach is that the Orchestrator Broker is able to select target federated Clouds according to their geographic location. In fact,

© ICST Institute for Computer Sciences, Social Informatics and Telecommunications Engineering 2018
A. Longo et al. (Eds.): IISSC 2017/CN4IoT 2017, LNICST 189, pp. 177–187, 2018.
https://doi.org/10.1007/978-3-319-67636-4_19

a "borrower", i.e., a Cloud federation client, can exactly specify the application requirements along with the geographical locations where the microservices of a distributed application have to be deployed.

The rest of the paper is organized as follows: Sect. 2 describes related works. Section 3 presents the Orchestrator Broker design. Section 4 describes implementation highlights. Section 5 concludes the paper also providing lights to the future.

2   Related Work and Background

Cloud federation raises many challenges in different research fields as described in [4–7]. Most of scientific works focus on architectural models able to efficiently support the collaboration between different Cloud providers according to different points of view. The recent trend has been to use Cloud federation for new challenging scenarios including Internet of Things (IoT) [6], Fog, Edge, and Osmotic Computing [8]. In [9] it is proposed a mathematical algorithm to improve the automatic scaling capabilities of a Cloud provider, based on a brokering approach. The adopted approach focuses on the selection of Cloud providers in order to create a federation able to maximize profits. In [10], it is proposed a selection algorithm that allows federated Cloud providers to determine and choose the best destination where to migrate their VMs according to green computing policies. A parametric decisioning algorithms for the distribution of the computational workload in a federated Cloud environment was presented in [11]. An architecture for the setup of a Platform as a Service (PaaS) for the deployment of distributed application was described in [12]. The aforementioned initiatives focus on algorithms and architectures for the distribution of the computational workload of application s among different Cloud providers, but they lack of a concrete deployment orchestration mechanism able to consider geographical constrains.

3   Architectural Design

The federation management system requires to manage several OpenStack Clouds that cooperate each other according to specific federation agreements. In order to achieve such a goal, we designed a federation management component named OpenStack Federation Flow Manager (OSFFM) that acts as Orchestrator Broker. It is responsible to interact with OpenStack Clouds under specific assumptions and to lead the deployment and management of distributed applications. The OSFFM was designed according to the following assumptions:

- The system is composed by twin Clouds; this means that Virtual Machine (VM) images, networks, users, key pair, security groups and other configurations are the same in each Clouds.
- Each OpenStack Cloud interacts with a component called Federation Agent able to set up OVN tunnel between with other Clouds.

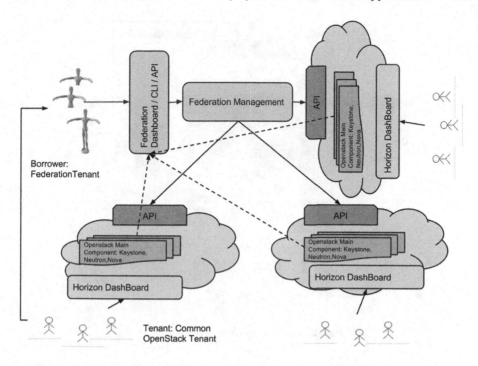

Fig. 1. Overall high-level federation architecture.

Figure 1 shows the logical high-level Cloud federation architecture.

We can identify two types of actors: *tenant* of a Cloud involved in federation, *borrower* of a federation. The tenant is a subject (a person or a society) who/which uses the resource and services provided by a Cloud in order to provide, in turn, services to his/her/its clients. Instead, the borrower is considered as a tenant of the Cloud federation having an agreement with a particular Cloud for accessing federated services.

The federation management is implemented by means of the OSFFM component that represents the core of the Orchestrator Broker. It includes several Application Program Interfaces (APIs) for the interaction among borrowers, tenants and users of the Clouds involved in the federation. It carries out a federation coordinator task managing virtual machines and virtual networks. All produced big data for management and federation status are stored in a NoSQL database. Each OpenStack Cloud involved in the federation is supported by a VM running a software component named Federation Agent, that is responsible to create virtual networks and virtual paths among them. In order to achieve such a goal, each OpenStack Cloud was equipped with a OSFFM component whose architecture is shown in Fig. 2.

The OSFFM is connected with the other actors by means of the following interfaces:

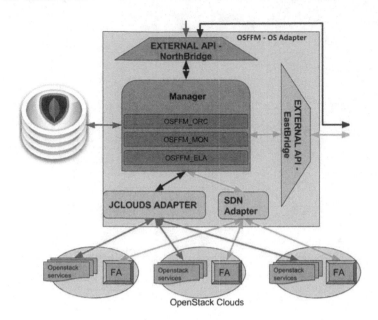

Fig. 2. OSFFM system architecture.

- **Southbridge.** It is used to send instructions to federated OpenStack Clouds. It includes two different adapters: jClouds and Software Defined Networking (SDN). The first one interacts with the OpenStack common module of each involved Cloud in order to retrieve information useful for the federation establishment process. Instead, the second one is used to provide information to the Federation Agent responsible to setup the federated network in which applications will be deployed.
- **Eastbridge.** It is used to send and receive instructions for the network management of the federated element involved in the application deployed. This interface acts both as REST server and client.
- **Northbridge.** It is used to receive application deployment instructions included in the service manifest.
- **Westbridge.** It is used to store status and management data, inside a NoSql database. In our example, it is represented by a MongoDB connector class.

The manager component includes three sub-modules that are OSFF Orchestrator (OSFFM_ORC), Monitoring (OSFFM_MON) and Elasticity Location Aware (OSFFM_ELA). All actions are performed by such sub-modules through the jClouds adapter that interacts with OpenStack Clouds.

OSFFM_ORC. This module is responsible to orchestrate all the tasks required for deploying a distributed application. In particular it receives as an input the HOT service manifest including guidelines for the deployment of a distributed application and builds several HOT microservice manifests that are sent to the heat modules of specific OpenStack Clouds for the instantiation of virtual resources in which microservices are deployed in. In order to do this it:

- pre-processes the pieces of information coming from others components and stores them in MongoDB,
- post-processes the pieces of information retrieved from MongoDB,
- creates connections between NorthBridge and SouthBridge interfaces in order to expose federated Clouds' data through a single point of inquiry;
- coordinates of the activity of the other OSFFM modules.

The OSFFM_ORC sub-module uses hash tables in order to store the result of its "manifest parsing" sub-elaboration activities; these activities are focused on retrieving pieces of federated deployment information and pieces information required to apply elasticity policies on the VM instantiated for the distributed application deployment. After such parsing activities of the HOT service manifest, OSFFM_ORC builds several HOT microservice manifests that are provided to specific federated Clouds. Figure 3 shows an example of HOT microservice manifest. The HOT standard has been extended in order to add new parameters that specify deployment requirements defined as resources. In this way, it is possible to compose a complex HOT service manifest by defining resources of

```
heat_template_version: '2014-10-16'          resources:
                                               B:
description: Microservice able to instantiate    type: OS::Nova::Server
a cirros VM with a fixed IP address              properties:
                                                   key_name: {get_param: key_name}
parameters:                                        flavor: m1.tiny
  key_name: {                                      image: {get_param: cirros}
      default: serviceKeypair,                     name: test
      description: Name of keypair to              networks:
                  assign to servers,              - fixed_ip: 10.0.0.61
      type: string                                  network: {get_param: private_network}
}
private_network: {                             outputs:
      default: private,                         out_B_private_ip:
      description: Network to attach             description: IP address of B server in
                  instance to.,               private network
      label: Private network name or ID,        value:
      type: string}                               get_attr: [B, first_address]
cirros: {
      default: cirros,
      description: description,
      type: string}
```

Fig. 3. Example of HOT microservice manifest.

other resources that can be queried by means of a simple "get_resource" function call. In particular, the following deployment requirements have been added: *(i)* service placement policies according to location constraints; *(ii)* location-aware elasticity rules; *(iii)* network reachability rules. The main methods involved for the HOT service manifest instantiation process are:

- *ManifestInstantiation.* This method is used to create an instance of a ManifestManager thread starting from an existing HOT service manifest. All ManifestManager threads are stored inside a hash map indexed through a service Manifest Unique IDentifier (UID).
- *ManagementGeoPolygon & ManagementRetrieveCredential.* These methods are used to retrieve from MongoDB, the credentials that borrowers hold in the Cloud datacenters placed particular geographical locations. These actions are complex because the credentials stored in the data model are stratified and are associate to a three-dimensional matrix whose dimension represents: Geographical Areas, Datacenters in Geographical Areas and Credentials valid in Datacenters. More specifically the first two levels of this structure are retrieved from the managementGeoPolygon method.
- *DeployManifest & SendShutSignalStack4DeployAction.* These methods are used to deploy a stack, i.e., a group of resources, in several federated Clouds belonging to a particular service group. The instantiated resources are all twins among them for fault-tolerance purposes. In fact, after the instantiation of VMs only a few of them are maintained in an active status, whereas the others ones are shut down.

OSFFM_ELA. This module is designed to control and maintain the performance of applications deployed in the federation. This goal is achieved by providing functions that allow to horizontally scale of resources in the federation. This module interacts with the target Cloud when a particular condition occurs in order to trigger a specific action. By interfacing this component with the monitoring one, it is possible to have the parameters needed to verify both the Cloud infrastructure and VMs internal states. When the previous information is correlated with other Clouds information, the module becomes able to make the required scalability decisions. The OSFFM_ELA interacts directly with OSFFM_ORC to accomplish the decision made and interacts with OSFFM_MON to receive status notifications about monitored condition.

OSFFM_MON. This module is designed as a collector of various monitoring flows coming from several monitoring components inside the federated clouds. The OSFFM_MON is interconnected with clouds via the SouthBridge interfaces and makes request in order to discover information needed to monitor resources state instantiated via the stacks. For OSFFM architecture, the monitoring solution is achieved by adapting the monitoring module used in OpenStack, that is the Ceilometer component, at a federation level and interconnected with the federated Ceilometer creating a hierarchical level structure.

4   OSFFM Orchestration Implementation

```
1 public void manifestinstatiation(String manName,String tenant){
2    JSONObject manifest=null;
3    this.addManifestToWorkf(manName, manifest);
4    ManifestManager mm=(ManifestManager)OrchestrationManager.mapManifestThr.get(manName);
5    this.manageYAMLcreation(mm, manName,tenant);
```

Listing 1. Function manifestinstatiation

The OSFFM was developed in JAVA, and exposes REST-API interfaces in order to avoid platform constraint during its usage. According to HEAT-API, also service manifest used in our solution are based on YAML, this makes OSFFM able to manipulate the manifest disrupting, and manifest composing, without problems.

```
1 public HashMap<String,ArrayList<ArrayList<String>>> managementgeoPolygon(
2    String manName,MDBInt.DBMongo db,String tenant)
3    {
4       HashMap<String,ArrayList<ArrayList<String>>> tmp=new
5       HashMap<String,ArrayList<ArrayList<String>>>();
6       ManifestManager mm=(ManifestManager)OrchestrationManager.mapManifestThr.get(manName);
7       Set s=mm.table_resourceset.get("OS::Beacon::ServiceGroupManagement").keySet();
8       Iterator it=s.iterator();
9       boolean foundone =false;
10      while(it.hasNext()){
11         String serName=(String)it.next();
12         SerGrManager sgm=(SerGrManager)mm.serGr_table.get(serName);
13         ArrayList<MultiPolygon> ar=null;
14         try{
15            ar=(ArrayList<MultiPolygon>)mm.geo_man.retrievegeoref(
16               sgm.getGeoreference());
17         }catch(NotFoundGeoRefException ngrf){...}
18         ArrayList dcInfoes=new ArrayList();
19         for(int index=0;index<ar.size();index++){
20            try{
21               ArrayList<String> dcInfo=
22                  db.getDatacenters(tenant,ar.get(index).toJSONString());
23               if(dcInfo.size()!=0){
24                  dcInfoes.add(dcInfo);
25                  foundone=true;
26               }
27            }
28            catch(org.json.JSONException je){...}
29         }
30         tmp.put(serName, dcInfoes);
31         if(!foundone) return null;
32      }
33      return tmp;
34 }
```

Listing 2. Implementation of the *managementGeoPolygon* method.

```
1  public ArrayList<ArrayList<HashMap<String, ArrayList<Port>>>> deployManifest(
2    String template,
3    String stack,
4    HashMap<String, ArrayList<ArrayList<OpenstackInfoContainer>>> tmpMapcred,
5    HashMap<String,ArrayList<ArrayList<String>>> tmpMap,
6    DBMongo m){
7      String stackName = stack.substring(stack.lastIndexOf("_") + 1 > 0 ?
8      stack.lastIndexOf("_") + 1 : 0, stack.lastIndexOf(".yaml") >= 0 ?
9      stack.lastIndexOf(".yaml") : stack.length());
10     ArrayList arDC=(ArrayList<ArrayList<String>>)tmpMap.get(stackName);
11     ArrayList arCr=(ArrayList<ArrayList<OpenstackInfoContainer>>)
12       tmpMapcred.get(stackName);
13     ArrayList<ArrayList<HashMap<String, ArrayList<Port>>>> arMapRes =
14       new ArrayList<>();
15     boolean skip = false, first = true;
16     int arindex = 0;
17     while (!skip){
18       ArrayList tmpArDC = (ArrayList<String>) arDC.get(arindex);
19       ArrayList tmpArCr = (ArrayList<OpenstackInfoContainer>) arCr.get(arindex);
20       ArrayList<HashMap<String, ArrayList<Port>>> arRes = new
21         ArrayList<HashMap<String, ArrayList<Port>>>();
22       for (Object tmpArCrob : tmpArCr) {
23         boolean result = this.stackInstantiate(template, (OpenstackInfoContainer)
24           tmpArCrob, m, stackName);
25         String region = "RegionOne";
26         ((OpenstackInfoContainer) tmpArCrob).setRegion(region);
27         HashMap<String, ArrayList<Port>> map_res_port =
28           this.sendShutSignalStack4DeployAction(stackName,
29           (OpenstackInfoContainer) tmpArCrob, first, m);
30         if(result){
31           first = false;
32           arRes.add(map_res_port);
33         }
34         arindex++;
35         arMapRes.add(arRes);
36         if(arindex > tmpArCr.size()) skip = true;
37       }
38     return arMapRes;
39   }
40 }
```

Listing 3. Implementation of the *deployManifest* method.

In our implementation we considered the OpenStack Mitaka release along with the OVN integration for Neutron. In the following, we provide a few implementation highlights regarding the main previously described OSFFM_ORC methods. The *manifestInstantiation* method is defined in the OrchestrationManager class and it is the manifest analysis workflow entry point. It allows to create a new object of ManifestManager moved inside a support HashMap used to bind Manifest with its ManifestManager thread. The manifest instantiation code is shown in Listing 1. After this Manifest splitting process, the ManifestManager starts the reconstruction in order to create the temporary template following the service groups directives written inside the service manifest. The *management-GeoPolygon* method is used to create a Hash Map storing three-dimensional parameters for each service group that has been found in the service manifest. Its implementation is shown in Listing 2. The *managementRetrieveCredential* method retrieves from MongoDB the access credentials related to the borrower that are valid in the Cloud selected by the previous function. Listings 3 and 4 respectively show the java code of the *deployManifest* and *sendShutSignal-*

Stack4DeployAction methods that are strictly linked. The first one prepares all information needed by the second one, the real executor of the deployment task. These methods are used to deploy a stack in the federation according to the service replication purposes. The performed actions are used for the resources instantiation on all Clouds selected in the service manifest for a particular service group.

```
1  public HashMap<String, ArrayList<Port>> sendShutSignalStack4DeployAction(
2       String stackName, OpenstackInfoContainer credential,boolean first, DBMongo m) {
3    try {
4       Registry myRegistry = LocateRegistry.getRegistry(ip,port);
5       RMIServerInterface impl = (RMIServerInterface) myRegistry.lookup("myMessage");
6       ArrayList resources =impl.getListResource(credential.getEndpoint(),
7            credential.getUser(),credential.getTenant(),credential.getPassword(),stackName);
8       boolean continua=true;
9       NovaTest nova = new NovaTest(credential.getEndpoint(), credential.getTenant(),
10               credential.getUser(), credential.getPassword(), credential.getRegion());
11      NeutronTest neutron = new NeutronTest(credential.getEndpoint(),
12          credential.getTenant(), credential.getUser(), credential.getPassword(),
13          credential.getRegion());
14      HashMap<String, ArrayList<Port>> mapResNet = new HashMap<String, ArrayList<Port>>();
15      Iterator it_res = resources.iterator();
16      while (it_res.hasNext()) {
17          String id_res = (String) it_res.next();
18          if(!first){
19              nova.stopVm(id_res);
20              m.updateStateRunTimeInfo(credential.getTenant(), id_res, first);
21          }
22          ArrayList<Port> arPort = neutron.getPortFromDeviceId(id_res);
23          mapResNet.put(id_res, arPort);
24          Iterator it_po = arPort.iterator();
25          while (it_po.hasNext()) {
26              m.insertPortInfo(credential.getTenant(),
27              neutron.portToString((Port)it_po.next()));
28          }
29      }
30      return mapResNet;
31  }catch (Exception e){
32      ...
33      return null;
34  }
35 }
```

Listing 4. Implementation of the *sendshutsignalstack4deployaction* method.

4.1   The New HOT Manifest

```
1 federation:
2    type: OS::Beacon::ServiceGroupManagement
3    properties:
4      name: GroupName
5      geo_deploy: { get_resource: geoshape_1}
6      resource:
7        groups:  {get_resource:  A}
```

Listing 5. New Model of resource OS::Beacon::ServiceGroupManagement

The HOT service manifest is typically provided by the borrower and it is an advanced version of HOT, because it is enriched with a set of new resource types that are extracted by the Orchestrator Broker and processed separately. These resources extend the HOT capabilities and are used by the OSFFM to compose a series of HOT microservice manifests. In addition, it is possible to use the HOT syntax in order to formalize the requirements for the deployment of a borrowers' distributed application. As previously discussed, such requirements include: *(i)* Service placement policies according to location constraints; *(ii)* Location-aware elasticity rules; *(iii)* Network reachability rules. In order to address the aforementioned requirements, in the context of the BEACON H2020 project we added to the HOT-based service manifest the following new definition of resources: OS::Beacon::ServiceGroupManagement and OS::Beacon::Georeferenced_deploy. *OS::Beacon::ServiceGroupManagement* is related requirements *(i)* and *(ii)*. This resource type allows to specify the geographical information for the deployment of a specific group by means of the geo_deploy field. Listing 5 shows an example of such a resource. Instead, *"OS::Beacon::Georeferenced_deploy"* allows to define an array of polygon (defined in GeoJSON format as MultiPolygon) that identifies the areas where a resource could be allocated. Listing 6 shows an example of such a resource.

```
1  geoshape_1:
2      type: OS::Beacon::Georeferenced_deploy
3      properties:
4        label: Shape label
5        description: description
6        shapes: [{"type":"Feature","id":"BEL","properties":{"name":"Belgium"},
7        "geometry":{"type":"Polygon","coordinates":[[[3.314971,51.345781],
8        [4.047071,51.267259],[4.973991,51.475024],[5.606976,51.037298],[6.156658,50.803721],
9        [6.043073,50.128052],[5.782417,50.090328],[5.674052,49.529484],[4.799222,49.985373],
10       [4.286023,49.907497],[3.588184,50.378992],[3.123252,50.780363],[2.658422,50.796848],
11       [2.513573,51.148506],[3.314971,51.345781]]]}}}]
```

Listing 6. New Model of resource OS::Beacon::Georeferenced_deploy

5   Conclusion and Future Work

In this paper, we proposed an approach for the orchestration deployment of distributed applications in federation Cloud environments. In particular, an Orchestration Broker is presented. It is able to process a HOT service manifest and to produce different corresponding microservice manifests destined to different federated OpenStack-based Clouds providers. An important feature of this approach is the ability to select target federated Clouds as function of their geographical position. In fact, a borrower can select exactly the geographical area where a distributed application has to be deployed. In future works, we will focus on the enhancement of the maintenance tasks performed by the OSFFM_ELA and OSFFM_MON modules on the virtual resources in which a distributed application is deployed.

Acknowledgment. This work was supported by the European Union Horizon 2020 BEACON project under grant agreement number 644048.

References

1. Moreno-Vozmediano, R., et al.: BEACON: a cloud network federation framework. In: Celesti, A., Leitner, P. (eds.) ESOCC Workshops 2015. CCIS, vol. 567, pp. 325–337. Springer, Cham (2016). doi:10.1007/978-3-319-33313-7_25
2. Celesti, A., Levin, A., Massonet, P., Schour, L., Villari, M.: Federated networking services in multiple OpenStack clouds. In: Celesti, A., Leitner, P. (eds.) ESOCC Workshops 2015. CCIS, vol. 567, pp. 338–352. Springer, Cham (2016). doi:10.1007/978-3-319-33313-7_26
3. Heat Orchestration Template (HOT) specification. http://docs.openstack.org/developer/heat/template_guide/hot_spec.html
4. Vernik, G., Shulman-Peleg, A., Dippl, S., Formisano, C., Jaeger, M., Kolodner, E., Villari, M.: Data on-boarding in federated storage clouds. In: 2013 IEEE Sixth International Conference on Cloud Computing (CLOUD), pp. 244–251 (2013)
5. Azodolmolky, S., Wieder, P., Yahyapour, R.: Cloud computing networking: challenges and opportunities for innovations. IEEE Commun. Mag. 51, 54–62 (2013)
6. Celesti, A., Fazio, M., Villari, M.: Enabling secure XMPP communications in federated IoT clouds through XEP 0027 and SAML/SASL SSO. Sensors 17, 1–21 (2017)
7. Celesti, A., Celesti, F., Fazio, M., Bramanti, P., Villari, M.: Are next-generation sequencing tools ready for the cloud? Trends Biotechnol. 35, 486–489 (2017)
8. Villari, M., Fazio, M., Dustdar, S., Rana, O., Ranjan, R.: Osmotic computing: a new paradigm for edge/cloud integration. IEEE Cloud Comput. 3, 76–83 (2016)
9. Mashayekhy, L., Nejad, M.M., Grosu, D.: Cloud federations in the sky: formation game and mechanism. IEEE Trans. Cloud Comput. 3, 14–27 (2015)
10. Giacobbe, M., Celesti, A., Fazio, M., Villari, M., Puliafito, A.: An approach to reduce carbon dioxide emissions through virtual machine migrations in a sustainable cloud federation. In: 2015 Sustainable Internet and ICT for Sustainability (SustainIT), Institute of Electrical & Electronics Engineers (IEEE) (2015)
11. Panarello, A., Breitenbcher, U., Leymann, F., Puliafito, A., Zimmermann, M.: Automating the deployment of multi-cloud application in federated cloud environments. In: Proceedings of the 10th EAI International Conference on Performance Evaluation Methodologies and Tools (2017)
12. Celesti, A., Peditto, N., Verboso, F., Villari, M., Puliafito, A.: DRACO PaaS: a distributed resilient adaptable cloud oriented platform. In: IEEE 27th International Parallel and Distributed Processing Symposium (2013)

Web Services for Radio Resource Control

Evelina Pencheva$^{(\boxtimes)}$ and Ivaylo Atanasov

Technical University of Sofia, Sofia, Bulgaria
{enp,iia}@tu-sofia.bg

Abstract. Mobile Edge Computing (MEC) supports network function virtualization and it brings network service intelligence close to the network edge. MEC services provide low level radio and network information to authorized applications. Communication between MEC services and applications is according to the principles of Service–oriented Architecture (SOA). In this paper, we propose an approach to design application programming interfaces for MEC Web Services that may be used by RAN analytics applications to adapt content delivery in real–time improving quality of experience to the end users. Web Service interfaces are mapped onto network protocols.

Keywords: Mobile Edge Computing · 5G · Radio Resource Control · Radio Network Information Services · Service oriented Architecture · Behavioral models

1   Introduction

Mobile Edge Computing (MEC) is a hot topic in 5 G. MEC supports network function virtualization and it brings network service intelligence close to the network edge [1]. MEC enables low latency communications, big data analysis close to the point of capture and flexible network management in response to user requirements [2,3]. MEC is required for critical communications which demand processing traffic and delivering applications close to the user [4,5]. MEC provides real-time network data such as radio conditions, network statistics, etc., for authorized applications to offer context-related services that can differentiate end user experience. Some of the promising real-time MEC application scenarios are discussed in [6].

MEC use cases and deployment options are presented in [7]. The European Telecommunications Standards Institute (ETSI) defined MEC reference architecture, where MEC deployment can be inside the base station or at aggregation point within Radio Access Network (RAN) [8]. Minimal latency for many applications can be achieved by integrating MEC server in base station [9,10].

The communications between applications and services in the MEC server are designed according to the principles of Service-oriented Architecture (SOA). The Radio Network Information Services (RNIS) provide information about the mobility and activity of User Equipment (UE) in the RAN. The information includes parameters on the UE context and established E-UTRAN Radio Access

© ICST Institute for Computer Sciences, Social Informatics and Telecommunications Engineering 2018
A. Longo et al. (Eds.): IISSC 2017/CN4IoT 2017, LNICST 189, pp. 188–198, 2018.
https://doi.org/10.1007/978-3-319-67636-4_20

Bearer (E-RAB), such as Quality of Service (QoS), Cell ID, UE identities, etc. This information is available based on the network protocols like Radio Resource Control (RRC), S1 Application Protocol (S1-AP), and X2 Application Protocol (X2-AP) [11].

ETSI standards just identified the required MEC service functionality, but do not define Web Service application programming interfaces (APIs). As far as our knowledge there is a lack of research on MEC service APIs, and the related works consider MEC applications that may use MEC services. In this paper we propose an approach to design APIs of SOA based Web Services for access to radio network information.

The paper is structured as follows. Section 2 provides a detailed Web Service description including definitions of data structure, interfaces, interface operation and use cases. Section 3 describes functionality required for mapping of Web Service interfaces onto network protocols. Device state models are described and formally verified. The conclusion summarizes the authors' contributions and highlights the benefits of the proposed approach.

2   Detailed Service Description

2.1   Device Context Web Service

Device Context service provides access to the UE context including EPS Mobility Management (EMM) state, EPS Connectivity Management (ECM) state, RRC state, UE identities, and Cell-ID. This information is provided through:

- Request for the UE context of a device;
- Request for the UE context of a group of devices;
- Notification change in the context of a device;
- Notification of device context on a periodic basis.

The response to a request for a group of devices may contain a full or partial set of results. The results are provided based on a number of criteria including number of devices for which the request is made and amount of time required to retrieve the information. Additional requests may be initiated for those devices for which information was not provided.

The EMM states describe mobility management states that result from the Attach and Tracking Area Update (TAU) procedures. The *EMMstatus* is of enumeration type with values of EMM-Deregistered (device is deregistered and it is not accessible) and EMM-Registered (device is registered to the network). The ECM states describe the signaling connectivity between the device and the core networks. The *ECMstatus* is of enumeration type with values of ECM-Idle (there is no non-access stratum signaling connection between the device and the network) and ECM-Connected (there is a non-access stratum signaling connection). The RRC states describe the connection between the device and the RAN. The *RRCstatus* is also of enumeration type with values of RRC-Idle (there is no RRC connection between the device and the network), and RRC-Connected (an RRC connection between the device and the RAN is established). The UE identity information is represented by C-RNTI (Cell Radio Network Temporary Identity) which identified the RRC connection. The Cell-ID uniquely identifies the E-Node B which currently serves the device.

StatusData structure contains the device context information. As this can be related to a query of a group of devices, the *ResultStatus* element is used. It is of enumerated type with values indicating whether the information for the device was retrieved or not, or if an error occurred. Table 1 illustrates the *StatusData* elements.

Table 1. Structure of device status data

Names	Types	Description
DeviceAddress	xsd:anyURI	Address of the device to which the UE context information applies
ReportingStatus	ResultStatus	Status of retrieval for this address
CurrentEMMstatus	EMMstatus	EMM status of the device if the ReportingStatus is equal to Retrieved
CurrentECMstatus	ECMstatus	ECM status of the device if the ReportingStatus is equal to Retrieved
CurrentRRCstatus	RRCstatus	RRC status of the device if the ReportingStatus is equal to Retrieved
CellID	integer	Cell-ID of the ENodeB which serves the device
CRNTI	integer	C-RNTI of the device

The Device Context Web Service supports the following interfaces:

The *UEContext* Interface requests the context information for a device. It supports two operations. The *GetUEContext* operation is intended to retrieve the context for a single device. The *GetUEContextForGroup* operation initiates a retrieval of context data for a group of devices.

The *UEContextNotificationManager* interface may be used to set up notifications about the events related to given device context. The operation *StartPeriodicNotifications* makes periodic notifications available to applications (the operation defines maximum frequency of notifications and the length of time notifications occur for). The *StartTriggeredNotification* operation makes triggered notifications available to applications (the operation defines maximum frequency of notifications, maximum number of notifications, period of time notifications are provided for, and the criteria). The *EndNotifications* operation ends either type notifications.

The interface to which notifications are delivered is *UEContextNotification*. It supports the following operations. The *UEContextNotification* operation is used to notify the application when the context of the monitored device changes. The *UEContextError* operation is used to inform the application that the notifications for a device or a group of devices are cancelled by the Web Service.

The *UEContextEnd* operation informs the application that the notifications have been completed when the duration or count for notifications have been completed. Figure 1 shows the sequence diagram for on demand access to device context information and triggered device context notification.

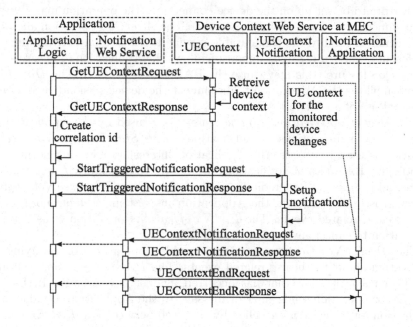

Fig. 1. Sequence diagram for on demand access to device context and triggered notifications

The Application queries for the device context and receives its context. The Application generates a correlator and starts triggered notifications. The Web Service sets up a notification to monitor changes in the device context. A notification is delivered to the Application when the device context changes. When the notifications are completed, the Application is notified.

2.2   Device Bearer Web Service

Device Bearer service provides access to information about active Radio Access Bearers (RABs) of the device and allows applications to dynamically manipulate device RABs. The information about devices RABs is provided on demand, periodically or upon event occurrence. An authorized Application may request RAB establishment, modification or release.

The Device Bearers Web Service supports the following interfaces:

The *ApplicationBearerControl* interface provides functionality for querying active RABs of the device, applying or modifying the QoS available on device connections. The *GetActiveRAB* operation retrieves the active RABs of the device. The *PutQoS* operation allows the Application to request a temporary QoS feature to be set up on the device connection (the operation may cause an establishment of a new RAB for the device). The *AlterQoS* operation allows the Application to modify the configurable service attributes on active temporary QoS feature. The *PutOffQoS* operation allows the Application to release a temporary QoS feature (this may cause the RAB bearer release). The *Disconnect* operation allows the Application to disconnect the device session (the operation causes release of all active RABs).

The *BearerNotificationManager* interface is used by the Applications to manage their subscriptions to notifications. The *StartPeriodicNotification* operation is used to register the Application interest in receiving notifications periodically. Examples of notifications are bearer establishment/ modification/ release, all bearers are lost, radio link failure. The *StartTriggeredNotification* operation is used to register the Application interest in receiving notifications about bearer related events. The *EndNotifications* operation is used by the Application to cancel any type of notifications.

The *BearerNotification* interface provides operation for notifying the Application about the bearer related events. The *RABNotification* operation reports a network event that has occurred against device active RABs. The *RABError* operation sends an error message to the Application to indicate the notification for a device is cancelled by the Web Service. The *RABEnd* operation informs the Application that the notifications have been completed when the duration expires or the count limit for notifications has been reached.

The *Bearer* interface supports one operation *GetRABAttributes* which allows the Application to query about device's bearer attributes.

3   Implementation Issues

As a mediation point between MEC applications and RAN the MEC server, which provides Web Services, needs to maintain the network and the application views on the device status. These views need to be synchronized. Furthermore, the MEC server needs to translate the Web Service interface operations into respective events in the network and vice versa.

3.1   Device State Models

Figure 2 shows the device state model as seen by the MEC server.

Table 2 provides a mapping between Web Services operations and network events.

Figure 3 shows the device state model as seen by the application.

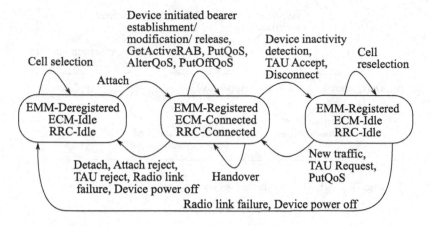

Fig. 2. Device's state model as seen by the MEC server

Table 2. Structure of device status data

Web service operation	Network events
UEContextNotification	Detach, Attach Reject, TAU Reject, Radio Link Failure, UE Power Off, New Traffic, TAU Request, Cell reselection
RABNotification	Device initiated bearer establishment/release/modification
PutQoS	Application initiated bearer establishment
AlterQoS	Application initiated bearer modification
PutOffQoS	Application initiated bearer release
Disconnect	Application initiated data session release

The proposed state model representing the Application view on the device state includes the following states.

In *AppDeregistered* state, the device is not registered to the network. The respective states in the network are RRC-idle, EMM-deregistered and ECM-idle. During attachment to the network (*Attach*), the network notifies the Application about the change in the device context ($N_{UEcontext}$), the device moves to *AppActive* state and the respective network states are RRC-connected, EMM-registered and ECM-connected. After successful mobility management event without data transfer activity e.g. TAU_{Accept}, the network notifies the Application about the change in device context ($N_{UEcontext}$), and the Application considers the device being in *AppIdle* state, where the respective network states are RRC-idle, EMM-registered and ECM-idle. In case of unsuccessful mobility management event (e.g. $Attach_{Reject}$, TAU_{Reject}), the Application is notified (N_{MMrej}) and the device moves to *AppDeregistered* state.

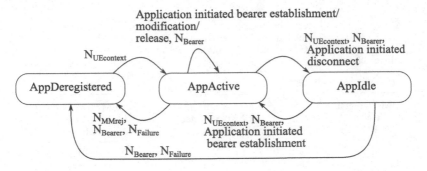

Fig. 3. Device's state model as seen by the MEC application

Application may decide to apply specific QoS ($App_{BearerEst}$) and it invokes the *PutQoS* operation. In *AppActive* state, the Application may decide to modify the established bearer ($App_{BearerMod}$) or to release it ($App_{BearerRel}$) and in these cases it invokes *AlterQoS* or *PutOffQoS* operations respectively. In *AppActive* state, the Application may decide to release all bearers i.e. to disconnect the device (App_{Discon}) and in this case it invokes *Disconnect* operation. The Application may also receive notifications about bearer related events (N_{Bearer}), e.g. notifications about device-initiated bearer establishment ($Device_{BearerEst}$), device-initiated bearer modification ($Device_{BearerMod}$), and device-initiated bearer release ($Device_{BearerRel}$).

During active data transfer, the device is in *AppActive* state. In this state, the Application may decide to apply specific QoS ($App_{BearerEst}$) and it invokes the *PutQoS* operation. In *AppActive* state, the Application may decide to modify the established bearer ($App_{BearerMod}$) or to release it ($App_{BearerRel}$) and in these cases it invokes *AlterQoS* or *PutOffQoS* operations respectively. In *AppActive* state, the Application may decide to release all bearers i.e. to disconnect the device (App_{Discon}) and in this case it invokes *Disconnect* operation. The Application may also receive notifications about bearer related events (N_{Bearer}), e.g. notifications about device-initiated bearer establishment ($Device_{BearerEst}$), device-initiated bearer modification ($Device_{BearerMod}$), and device-initiated bearer release ($Device_{BearerRel}$).

If the Application is notified that all bearers are lost ($N_{Bearers}$), it may initiate data session release on behalf of the device (*Disconnect*) and the device state becomes *AppIdle*. In *AppActive* state, when the network detects device inactivity, the Application is notified ($N_{UEcontext}$) and it considers the device being in *AppIdle* state.

In case the device detach (*Detach*) or device power is off ($Device_{PowerOff}$), the Application is notified ($N_{UEcontext}$) and it considers the device being in *AppDeregistered* state. In case of radio link failure, the network notifies the Application ($N_{Failure}$) and the device moves to *AppDeregistered* state.

3.2   Formal Verification of Device State Models

We use the mathematical formalism of Labeled Transition Systems (LTSs) to describe the device state models. An LTS is defined as a quadruple of set of states, set of inputs, set of transitions, and an initial state.

By $D_{App} = \left(S_{App}, Inp_{App}, \rightarrow_{App}, s_0^{App} \right)$ it is denoted an LTS representing the Application's view on device state where:

$$S_{App} = \{AppDeregistered, AppActive, AppIdle\};$$
$$Inp_{App} = \{N_{MMrej}, N_{Bearer}, N_{Bearers}, N_{Failure}, N_{UEcontext}, App_{BearerEst},$$
$$App_{BearerMod}, App_{BearerRel}, App_{Discon}\};$$
$$\rightarrow_{App} = \{(AppDeregistered\ N_{UEcontext}\ AppActive)\ [\tau_1^A], (AppActive$$
$$App_{BearerEst}\ AppActive)\ [\tau_2^A], (AppActive\ App_{BearerMod}$$
$$AppActive)\ [\tau_3^A], (AppActive\ App_{BearerRel}\ AppActive)\ [\tau_4^A],$$
$$(AppActive\ N_{Bearer}\ AppActive)\ [\tau_5^A], (AppActive\ N_{MMrej},$$
$$AppDeregistered)\ [\tau_6^A], (AppActive\ N_{Bearers}\ AppDeregistered)$$
$$[\tau_7^A], (AppActive\ N_{Failure}\ AppDeregistered)\ [\tau_8^A], (AppActive$$
$$N_{UEcontext}\ AppIdle)\ [\tau_9^A], (AppActive\ N_{Bearer}\ AppIdle)\ [\tau_{10}^A],$$
$$(AppActive\ App_{Discon}\ AppIdle)\ [\tau_{11}^A], (AppIdle\ N_{UEcontext}$$
$$AppActive)\ [\tau_{12}^A], (AppIdle\ N_{Bearer}\ AppActive)\ [\tau_{13}^A], (AppIdle$$
$$N_{BearerEst}\ AppActive)\ [\tau_{14}^A], (AppIdle\ N_{UEcontext}\ AppDeregistered)$$
$$[\tau_{15}^A], (AppIdle\ N_{Failure}\ AppDeregistered)\ [\tau_{16}^A]\};$$
$$s_0^{App} = \{AppDeregistered\}.$$

Short notations of the transitions are given in brackets.

Let us denote by *Deregistered* the device states in the network EMM-Deregistered, ECM-Idle, RRC-Idle, by *Connected* the device states in the network EMM-Connected, ECM-Connected, RRC-Connected, and by *Idle* the device states in the network EMM-Registered, ECM-Idle, RRC-Idle.

By $D_{MEC} = (S_{MEC}, Inp_{MEC}, \rightarrow_{MEC}, s_0^{MEC})$ it is denoted an LTS representing the MEC server's view on device state where:

$S_{MEC} = \{Deregistered, Connected, Idle\}$;

$Inp_{MEC} = \{Cell_{Selection}, Attach, Detach, Attach_{Reject}, TAU_{Reject}, TAU_{Accept},$
$\qquad Radio_{LinkFailure}, Device_{PowerOff}, Device_{BearerEst}, Cell_{Reselection},$
$\qquad Device_{BearerMod}, Device_{BearerRel}, PutOffQoS, GetActiveRAB,$
$\qquad AlterQoS, Disconnect, Handover, Device_{NewTraffic}, TAU_{Request},$
$\qquad PutQoS, Device_{Inactivity}\}$;

$\rightarrow_{MEC} = \{(Deregistered\,Cell_{Selection}\,Deregistered)\,[\tau_1^{MEC}], (Dere-$
$\qquad gistered\,Attach\,Connected)\,[\tau_2^{MEC}], (Connected\,Device_{BearerEst}$
$\qquad Connected)\,[\tau_3^{MEC}], (Connected\,Device_{BearerMod}\,Connected)$
$\qquad [\tau_4^{MEC}], (Connected\,Device_{BearerRel}\,Connected)\,[\tau_5^{MEC}],$
$\qquad (Connected\,GetActiveRAB\,Connected)\,[\tau_6^{MEC}], (Connected$
$\qquad PutQoS\,Connected)\,[\tau_7^{MEC}], (Connected\,AlterQoS\,Connected)$
$\qquad [\tau_8^{MEC}], (Connected\,PutOffQoS\,Connected)\,[\tau_9^{MEC}],$
$\qquad (Connected\,Handover\,Connected)\,[\tau_{10}^{MEC}], (Connected\,Detach$
$\qquad Deregistered)\,[\tau_{11}^{MEC}], (Connected\,Attach_{Reject}\,Deregistered)$
$\qquad [\tau_{12}^{MEC}], (Connected\,TAU_{Reject}\,Deregistered)\,[\tau_{13}^{MEC}],$
$\qquad (Connected\,Radio_{LinkFailure}\,Deregistered)\,[\tau_{14}^{MEC}],$
$\qquad (Connected\,Device_{PowerOff}\,Deregistered)\,[\tau_{15}^{MEC}], (Connected$
$\qquad Device_{Inactivity}\,Idle)\,[\tau_{16}^{MEC}], (Connected\,TAU_{Accept}\,Idle)\,[\tau_{17}^{MEC}]$
$\qquad (Idle\,Device_{NewTraffic}\,Connected)\,[\tau_{18}^{MEC}], (Idle\,TAU_{Request}$
$\qquad Connected)\,[\tau_{19}^{MEC}], (Idle\,PutQoS\,Connected)\,[\tau_{20}^{MEC}], (Idle$
$\qquad Cell_{Reselection}\,Idle)\,[\tau_{21}^{MEC}], (Idle\,Radio_{LinkFailure}\,Deregistered)$
$\qquad [\tau_{22}^{MEC}], (Idle\,Device_{PowerOff}\,Deregistered)\,[\tau_{23}^{MEC}]\}$;

$s_0^{MEC} = \{Deregistered\}$.

We use weak bisimulation to formally verify the suggested models.

Proposition 1. *The systems D_{App} and D_N are weakly bisimilar.*

Proof. As to definition of weak bisimulation, provided in [12], it is necessary to identify a bisimilar relation between the states of both LTSs and to identify respective matching between transitions.

Let the relation U_{MECApp} be defined as $U_{MECApp} = \{(Deregistered, AppDeregistered), (Connected, AppActive), (Idle, AppIdle)\}$, then:

1. In case of attachment, for $Deregistered \exists \{\tau_1^{MEC}, \tau_2^{MEC}\}$ that leads to $Connected$, and for $AppDeregistered \exists \{\tau_1^A\}$ that leads to $AppActive$.

2. In case of detach, or attach reject, or TAU reject, or radio link failure, or device power off, for $Connected \exists \{\tau_{11}^{MEC} \vee \tau_{12}^{MEC} \vee \tau_{13}^{MEC} \vee \tau_{14}^{MEC} \vee \tau_{15}^{MEC}\}$ that leads to $Deregistered$, and for $AppActive \exists \{\tau_6^A \vee \tau_7^A \vee \tau_8^A\}$ that leads to $AppDeregistered$.

3. In case of device initiated bearer establishment/modification/release, for $Connected \exists \{\tau_3^{MEC}, \tau_4^{MEC}, \tau_5^{MEC}\}$ that leads to $Connected$, and for the state $AppActive \exists \{\tau_5^A\}$ that leads to $AppActive$.

4. In case of $Application$ initiated establishment/modification/release, for state $Connected \exists \{\tau_6^{MEC}, \tau_7^{MEC}, \tau_8^{MEC}, \tau_9^{MEC}\}$ that leads to $Connected$, and for $AppActive \exists \{\tau_2^A, \tau_3^A, \tau_4^A\}$ that leads to $AppActive$.

5. In case of handover, for $Connected \exists \{\tau_{10}^{MEC}\}$ that leads to $Connected$, and for $AppActive \exists \{\tau_5^A\}$ that leads to $AppActive$.

6. In case of device inactivity detection or TAU accept or Application initiated disconnect, for $Connected \exists \{\tau_{15}^{MEC} \vee \tau_{16}^{MEC} \vee \tau_{17}^{MEC}\}$ that leads to $Idle$, and for $AppConnected \exists \{\tau_9^A \vee \tau_{10}^A \vee \tau_{11}^A\}$ that leads to $AppIdle$.

7. In case of device initiated new traffic, or TAU request, or Application initiated bearer establishment, for $Idle \exists \{\tau_{21}^{MEC}, \tau_{18}^{MEC} \vee \tau_{19}^{MEC} \vee \tau_{20}^{MEC}\}$ that leads to $Connected$, and for $AppIdle \exists \{\tau_{12}^A \vee \tau_{13}^A \vee \tau_{14}^A\}$ to $AppIdle$.

8. In case of device power off or radio link failure, for $Idle \exists \{\tau_{22}^{MEC} \vee \tau_{23}^{MEC}\}$ leads to $Deregistered$, and for $AppIdle \exists \{\tau_{15}^A \vee \tau_{16}^A\}$ to $AppDeregistered$. Therefore D_{App} and D_N are weakly bisimilar. □

4 Conclusion

In this paper we propose an approach to design APIs of Web Services for MEC. The approach is based on the RNIS provided by the MEC server. Two Web Services are proposed: Device Context Web Service and Device Bearers Web Service. The Device Context Web Service provides applications with information about device connectivity, mobility and data transfer activity. The Device Bearers Web Service provides applications with information about device's active bearer and allows dynamic control on QoS available on device's data sessions. Web Service data structures, interfaces and interface operations are defined. Some issues related to MEC service APIs deployment are presented. The MEC server functionality includes transition between Web Service operations and network events (signaled by respective protocol messages) and maintenance of device state models which has to be synchronized with the Application view on the device state. A method for formal model verification is proposed.

Following the same approach, other Web Services that use radio network information may be designed. Examples include access to appropriate up-to-date radio network information regarding radio network conditions that may be used by applications which minimize round trip time and maximize throughput for optimum quality of experience, access to measurement and statistics information related to the user plane regarding video management applications, etc.

Acknowledgments. The research is in the frame of project DH07/10-2016, funded by National Science Fund, Ministry of Education and Science, Bulgaria.

References

1. Nunna, S., Ganesan, K.: Mobile Edge Computing. In: Thuemmler, C., Bai, C. (eds.) Health 4.0: How Virtualization and Big Data are Revolutionizing Healthcare, pp. 187–203. Springer, Cham (2017). doi:10.1007/978-3-319-47617-9_9
2. Gupta, L., Jain, R., Chan, H.A.: Mobile edge computing - an important ingredient of 5G networks. In: IEEE Softwarization Newsletter (2016)
3. Chen, Y., Ruckenbusch, L.: Mobile edge computing: brings the value back to networks. In: IEEE Software Defined Networks Newsletter (2016)
4. Roman, R., Lopez, J., Mambo, M.: Mobile edge computing, fog et al.: a survey and analysis of security threats and challenges. J. CoRR, abs/1602.00484 (2016)
5. Beck, M.T., Feld, S., Linnhhoff-Popien, C., Pützschler, U.: Mobile edge computing. Informatik-Spektrum **39**(2), 108–114 (2016)
6. Ahmed, A., Ahmed, E.: A survey on mobile edge computing. In: 10th IEEE International Conference on Intelligent Systems and Control (ISCO 2016), pp. 1–8 (2016)
7. Brown, G.: Mobile edge computing use cases and deployment options. In: Juniper White Paper, pp. 1–10 (2016)
8. ETSI GS MEC 003, Mobile Edge Computing (MEC); Framework and Reference Architecture, v1.1.1 (2016)
9. Sarria, D., Park, D., Jo, M.: Recovery for overloaded mobile edge computing. Future Generation Computer Systems, vol. 70, pp. 138–147. Elsevier (2017)
10. Beck, M., Werner, M., Feld, S., Schimper, T.: Mobile edge computing: a taxonomy. In: Sixth International Conference on Advances in Future Internet, pp. 48–54 (2014)
11. 3GPP. TS 36.300 Evolved Universal Terrestrial Radio Access (EUTRA) and Evolved Universal Terrestrial Radio Access Network (E-UTRAN); Overall description; Stage 2, Release 14, v14.0.0 (2016)
12. Fuchun, L., Qiansheng, Z., Xuesong, C.: Bisimilarity control of decentralized nondeterministic discrete-event systems. In: International Control Conference, pp. 3898–3903 (2014)

Big Data HIS of the IRCCS-ME Future: The Osmotic Computing Infrastructure

Lorenzo Carnevale[1,2]([✉]), Antonino Galletta[1,2], Antonio Celesti[1], Maria Fazio[1], Maurizio Paone[2], Placido Bramanti[2], and Massimo Villari[1,2]

[1] Department of Engineering, University of Messina, Messina, Italy
{lcarnevale,angalletta,acelesti,mfazio,mvillari}@unime.it
[2] IRCCS Centro Neurolesi "Bonino Pulejo", Messina, Italy
{lcarnevale,angalletta,mpaone,pbramanti,mvillari}@irccsme.it

Abstract. Nowadays, we are observing a massive digitalization of clinical tasks in Hospital Information Systems (HIS). Even more medical devices belongs to Internet of Things (IoT) applications that generate a huge amount of clinical data. Therefore, the healthcare industry is looking at modern big data storage, processing and analytics technologies. In this context, traditional HIS presents several issues, such as a mismanagement of data generated from medical devices. Starting from the experience of IRCCS Centro Neurolesi "Bonino Pulejo" placed in Messina (Italy), i.e., a clinical and research center, in this paper, we motivate the need to move traditional HIS into an innovative infrastructure based on the Osmotic computing paradigm. In particular, studying the healthcare domain, we specifically focus on production and research tasks.

Keywords: Hospital Information System · Big Data · cHealth · IoT · Osmotic computing

1 Introduction

Nowadays, the healthcare industry is facing many challenges such as waste reduction, integration of a new generation of electronical medical systems, collection and communication of a huge amount of clinical data in a quick and safe fashion. Up to now, for the healthcare industry has not been easy to introduce new technological improvements in the daily work of the clinical personnel but, currently, medical and governmental authorities of many countries encourage the adoption of cutting-edge information technology solutions in healthcare. Typical examples of famous initiatives include Electronic Health Record (EHR), Remote Patient Monitoring (RPM) and tools for medical decision making.

The healthcare industry is looking at modern Big Data storage, processing, and analytics technologies. An analysis of the McKinsey Global Institute [1] studied the Big Data penetration for healthcare, highlighting a good potential to achieve insights. In the period between 2010 and 2015, it measured that the

© ICST Institute for Computer Sciences, Social Informatics and Telecommunications Engineering 2018
A. Longo et al. (Eds.): IISSC 2017/CN4IoT 2017, LNICST 189, pp. 199–207, 2018.
https://doi.org/10.1007/978-3-319-67636-4_21

number of connected nodes increased up to 50 million. In the same period, the Organisation for Economic Co-operation and Development (OECD) [2] measured about $100 billion, as a share of Gross Domestic Product (GDP) and total health spending, for the final consumption of healthcare goods and services (investments not included). The estimate takes into account both private and public financing. Moreover, in [3], Forbes highlights how Big Data is changing healthcare. Indeed, in addition to economical healthcare perspective, such as improving profits and cutting down on wasted overhead, healthcare operators are looking at Big Data analytics in the context of epidemics prediction and disease care in order to improve the quality of life of patients and avoid preventable deaths. New models of treatment delivery are rapidly changing because population and longevity grow and the decisions making about these changes are driven by data. Nowadays, the trend is to understand as much as possible the patients' status, collecting signals about serious illness in a preliminary stage in order to ensure simpler and cheaper treatment.

In this context, many healthcare organizations have evaluated the possible adoption of Cloud Computing solutions due to the intrinsic ability to access services through standard mechanisms that promote heterogeneous clients utilization and elastically provide services able to spatially and temporally scale up/down without limits [4]. Medical devices have been seen as part of Internet of Things (IoT) [5] applications either directly connected to the network or indirectly connected to the Hospital Information System (HIS) through clinical workflows. Nevertheless, this is still not enough. The emerging availability and complexity of various types of medical devices, along with large data volumes that such devices generate, can limit the current Cloud-centric IoT programming models. Thus, the current systems need to be revised into something that is more adaptable and decentralized in order to meet the emerging healthcare applications needs. The Osmotic Computing [6] paradigms aims to decompose applications into microservices [7,8] and to perform dynamic tailoring of microservices in smart environments exploiting resources in Edge and Cloud infrastructures. Application delivery follows an Osmotic behavior where microservices in containers are deployed opportunistically in Cloud and Edge systems.

This scientific work highlights the experience reported at IRCCS Centro Neurolesi "Bonino Pulejo" (Messina, Italy), a healthcare clinical and research centre. In particular, we talk about motivations that led the IRCCS' managers to invest in the modernization of their IT infrastructure. This experience has shown the importance of a lean planning in order to meet demanding requirements both for productive and research areas of dynamic healthcare environments. Moreover, we highlight the Osmotic Computing advantages for the creation of Big healthcare Data infrastructure.

The rest of the paper is organized as follows. Related works are summarized in Sect. 2. Section 3 discusses the reasons because a HIS should adopt Cloud technologies. The architecture is presented in the Sect. 4, whereas the aspects related to Osmotic Computing applied to Big healthcare Data analytics are presented in Sect. 5. Conclusion and lights to the future are presented in Sect. 6.

2   Related Work

Nowadays, Cloud computing into the healthcare domain is a really challenging topic. To demonstrate this, in the following we report several scientific works that aim to improve HIS solutions. In [9] authors focused on Digital Imaging and Communications in Medicine (DICOM), a standard for storing and managing medical images. They proposed a hybrid model for Cloud-based HIS focusing about public and private Cloud. The last one was able to manage and store computer-based patients records and other important information, while a public Cloud was able to handle management and business data. In order to share information among different hospitals, authors adopted VPN (Virtual Private Network). In [10] authors proposed a Cloud-based Tele-Medicine system that, thanks to wearable sensors, allows patients to send eHealth data, such as Blood Pressure (BP) and Electrocardiogram (ECG), into specific gateways in order to forward them to the Cloud. Here, data were processed and compared with existing results. If system founds suitable results, it sends back an automatic feedback, otherwise the appropriate physician is intimated via phone call or SMS (Short Message System). Using their PDA/smartphone, physicians can get patients' data in order to diagnose the disease and send back reports. Four services for a Healthcare as a Service (HaaS) model have been proposed in [11]:

1. Storage Archival and Indexing Services: using features of commercial Cloud providers (like Amazon, Microsoft Azure, etc.), authors proposed a Cloud-based Picture Archiving and Communication System (PACS) to stored both Medical Images and patient's personal data;
2. Image Processing Services: authors proposed an image processing service on a Virtual Machine that is able to retrieve images from Cloud storage, compute and encapsulate them into JavaScript Object Notation (JSON) format and, moreover, to send results to client applications.
3. Reporting Services: a mechanism to share medical reports among different hospitals.
4. Charting and Trend Analysis of Healthcare Data: a system that aggregates medical data and performs different kinds of analysis.

In [12] the authors presented a hybrid storage solution for the management of eHealth data, which proved the synergetic utilization of SQL-like strategies ad NoSQL document based approaches. Specifically, this scientific work adopted the proposed solution for neurologic Tele-Rehabilitation (TR) of patients at home. A Open Archivial Storage System (OAIS) for Cloud-based HIS able to manage Big Clinical Data through a NoSQL column oriented approach was presented in [13]. Finally, a Cloud-based next-generation sequencing (NGS) tool has been proposed in [14]. The authors investigated the existing NGS solutions, highlighting the necessary missing features in order to move toward the achievement of an ecosystem of biotechnology Clouds.

3   Motivation

Nowadays, traditional HIS are composed of several independent subsystems that perform specific tasks and store personal and medical patients' data into local repositories. Nevertheless, this kind of configuration presents several issues for patient, physician, technician and administrative staff. From the patient point of view, the management of exams outcomes is difficult. They can not retrieve results of their analysis. Indeed, at present, they have to request these to administrative staff of each ward. The mismanagement of HIS causes losing of a huge amount of clinical data generated both by human and machine sources. In this way, only a small quantity of gathered data can be analysed. Moreover, this quantity is managed through spreadsheets, causing difficulties to correlate clinical data and find out insights. As mentioned above, HIS is composed of several black-box subsystems that require specific servers and hardware/software configurations. This kind of infrastructure is really expensive for hardware, cooling and powering costs. Furthermore, it is difficult to be managed due to the fact that update operations are hard to be accomplished because system administrators have to replicate the same tasks several times.

4   IRCCS'. Infrastructure at a Glance

The objective of this scientific work is to describe a Cloud-based HIS, which integrates daily clinical activities along with digitalization and analysis processes in order to support healthcare professionals. Our case study is the IT infrastructure of IRCCS Centro Neurolesi "Bonino Pulejo" placed in Messina (Italy). It is a scientific institute for recovery and care with the mission in the field of neuroscience for the prevention, recovery and treatment of individuals with severe acquired brain injuries, besides spinal cord and neurodegenerative diseases, by integrating highly specialized healthcare, technological innovation and higher education. To this end, the clinical activities need to be divided into two categories: Production and Research. With reference to Fig. 1, the production side includes all services that facilitate the administrative and healthcare personnel; on the other hand, the research side includes all innovative services that support the IRCCS' healthcare research activities. Moreover, for each category, we thought several thematic areas such as Frontend & Communication, Security & Privacy, Microservices, Big Data and Storage.

All these services are supported from a powerful physical infrastructure. With reference to Fig. 2, the infrastructure is largely built using traditional systems because it is required to build a solid foundation for the production line. At the same time, research line is supported by the same infrastructure. It is composed by three layers (Storage, Network and Computation) linked together. Storage disks are network available thanks to the iSCSI internet protocol. Instead, computation is provided with different technologies. Xen Server is the hypervisor used to provide traditional virtual environment and it allows to run several Virtual Machine for different purposes. Docker and Kubernates provide a lighter

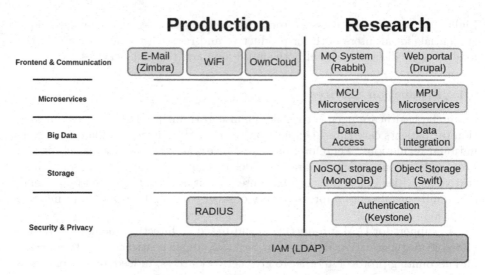

Fig. 1. Services list of IRCCS Institute.

virtual environment for each specific purpose. Finally, microcontroller devices mount firmware and provide another way to compute a specific purpose. All of these support RESTful/MQTT clients or servers for input/output network communications.

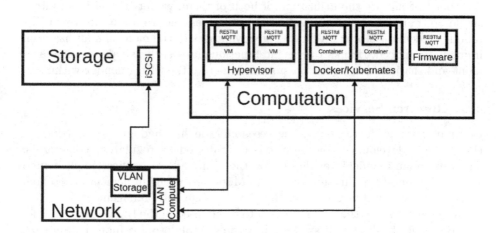

Fig. 2. Layers infrastructure of IRCCS institute

Following this section, we deepen the implemented services both for production and research sides. The only one service shared for both sides was the Identity and Access Management (IAM). It allows to manage users' authentication and authorization for the whole healthcare system. Indeed, thanks to

Lightweight Directory Access Protocol (LDAP), our IAM system provides unique credentials for all users both for productive and research Cloud services. In the following, we discuss in detail both production and research services.

4.1 Production Services

From the healthcare perspective, the main constraint for new services' production for patients care clinical support is given by the current national and international regulations. Therefore, our assistance was verifiable exclusively in the Frontend & Communication area in order to facilitate healthcare and administrative activities in low patient risk context or, if necessary, be used by patients and family members to improve quality of service during the time spent into the hospital.

As support for IAM, productive Cloud-based architecture includes RADIUS (Remote Authentication Dial-In User Service), an authentication, authorization and accounting protocol in order to give network access. Indeed, on top of this, a wireless communication was developed. The introduction of a stable and extensive wireless network, where there was only a wired network, has allowed the growth of heterogeneous devices connected to the Internet, besides to facilitate services access from any local Institute.

Other powerful tools for daily activities have been business email and web storage services. The first one is a Zimbra-based web mail software for messaging and collaboration; while the web storage services has been deployed using ownCloud, "an open source, self-hosted file sync and share app platform" [15]. In order to facilitate the utilization of both of them, we integrated them into a single Software as a Service (SaaS) web tool accessible from any browser using unique credentials stored on IAM. The advantages to the medical staff has been immediate. Indeed, thanks to specific functionalities such as calendar management and sharing files, it was possible to integrate the turn calendar within.

4.2 Research Services

Compared to productive side, the research side has had greater freedom of thought and development because it is not affected by regulatory constraints. The advantage is quickly evidenced by the multitude of services implemented and visible on the right side of Fig. 1. Moreover, each implemented research service follows a well-defined line: Big Data storage and management.

According to [16], the best approach to be adopted in the Big Data infrastructure design for healthcare is suggested by the lean philosophy. Indeed, after each software release, we provided research tools to healthcare personnel and gathered feedback useful to re-address our work. Therefore, we started with a well defined sandbox.

The first challenge was to acquire all data coming from medical devices considering that the low IT expertise of the clinical personnel can (potentially) be a limit. In this regard, our goal was to minimize the number of IT operations they have to perform. The first step of this clinical workflow was to move outcomes of medical devices inside shared directories. It is the only requirement requested by healthcare professionals. Data Access service continuously listen on shared directories to monitor the addition of new outcomes. Data collected from shared directories are parsed and integrated with unstructured storage systems such as MongoDB, i.e., a scalable NoSQL database. In order to accomplish this task we provided the Data Integration service. Moreover, as support of this clinical workflow we thought a message queue system such as RabbitMQ, which task is to maintain data acquisition requests in an ordered list of messages.

Along with text/numbers data, the pool of main generated data coming from healthcare industry includes also images [1], such as Magnetic Resonance Imaging (MRI), radiograph films, etc. In this domain file systems or block storage architecture have management limits because they manage, respectively, data as a file hierarchy and data as blocks with sectors and tracks. Instead, object storage manages data as object, including data itself, metadata and globally unique identifiers. For this purpose, our research Cloud-based architecture includes Swift's OpenStack as object storage, "a highly available, distributed, eventually consistent object store" [17]. This wide uses another OpenStack service for authentication and high-level authorization, namely Keystone. It supports integration with LDAP directories, extending the Identity and Access Management discussed in starting part of the Sect. 4.

Other clinical data and services are provided by MCU and MPU controllers. Their task is to extend the functionalities of medical devices in order to complete the set of data associated to patients during analysis. Thus, they are typical IoT applications for specific operations.

Finally, all services are available through a Drupal-based web portal. It allows to manage each service in terms of configuration and visualization.

5   Osmotic Evolution of the Infrastructure

The discussion in the previous Section, specially regarding to the set of services offered by the research branch of Cloud-based architecture, provides the foundations for a well-defined Big Data storage and management. As a result, we approve the creation of a new model service in addition to the three models (Infrastructure as a Service, Platform as a Service and Software as a Service) theorized by National Institute of Standards and Technology (NIST). This model is called Big Data as a Service and includes all operations useful to discover insights, from raw data access produced by medical devices and personnel up to displaying analysed data. More specifically, it includes several phases such as asynchronous and real-time data access, data integration and normalization, data cleaning in order to remove errors, inaccuracies or inconsistent data, data analysis and visualization of final outcomes. Moreover, we must not neglect data access security mechanisms. Among these phases, some are automated and repeatable while others have a different cycle of utilization and require more human interactions. Furthermore, in order to complete all Big Data operations, we need to add other technologies such as Hadoop and Spark.

The characteristic shared by these phases is that each of them can be handled as a stand alone system but, at the same time, as part of a well-defined healthcare workflow. Thus, it is easy to think about phases as microservices that are dynamically tailored on hosting smart environments. The Osmotic Computing was born from the dynamic movement of microservices that individually perform their tasks, but together complete an ensemble action. Indeed, like the movement of solvent molecules through a semipermeable membrane into a region of higher solute concentration to equalize the solute concentrations on the two sides of the membrane - that is, osmosis (in the context of chemistry) - in Osmotic Computing, the dynamic management of resources in Cloud and Edge datacenters evolves toward the balanced deployment of microservices satisfying well-defined low-level constrains and high-level needs. However, unlike the chemical osmotic process, Osmotic Computing allows a tunable configuration of involved resources, following resource availability and application requirements.

The advent of Osmotic Computing as management paradigm of microservices has been enabled by the proliferation of light virtualization technologies (such as Docker and Kubernates), alternatively to traditional approaches based on hypervisor (such as Xen and VMWare). Adapting microservices to the physical characteristics of underlying infrastructure by using decision making strategies that map them, the Osmotic Computing reduces waste in terms of systems administration and energy costs.

6   Conclusion and Future Work

In this paper, we discussed a novel technological approach to deploy a HIS able to store Big eHealth Data collected through several medical devices. In particular, the paper presents a collection of motivations in order to migrate from traditional legacy HIS to Osmotic-based HIS solutions, improving data sharing, energy management and system administration.

In order to accomplish these goals, our idea was to create a robust infrastructure based on new Osmotic Computing paradigm, implementing all hospital operations as specific microservices. Moreover, studying the healthcare domain, we decided to divide our infrastructure into two different branches: one for production and another one for research tasks. The first one offers facilities to healthcare and administrative personnel, while the latter exposes innovative tools to support mostly Big Data research activities. As union point between both sides, we deployed an IAM service in order to provide a unique authentication and authorization system.

Given the infrastructural platform built and described in this paper, in our future work we aim to design an agile Osmotic-based piece of middleware able to perform microservices for Big healthcare Data management.

Acknowledgment. The authors would like to thank IRCCS Centro Neurolesi "Bonino Pulejo" and all healthcare personnel that helped us during design and deploy of the infrastructure.

References

1. Big Data: The next frontier for innovation, competition, and productivity. McKinsey Global Institute, June 2011
2. OECD, Health spending (indicator) (2016). http://dx.doi.org/10.1787/8643de7e-en
3. How big data is changing healthcare. https://goo.gl/R0RIOb
4. Celesti, A., Peditto, N., Verboso, F., Villari, M., Puliafito, A.: Draco paas: a distributed resilient adaptable cloud oriented platform. In: 2013 IEEE International Symposium on Parallel Distributed Processing, Workshops and Phd Forum, pp. 1490–1497, May 2013
5. Celesti, A., Fazio, M., Giacobbe, M., Puliafito, A., Villari, M.: Characterizing cloud federation in IoT. In: 2016 30th International Conference on Advanced Information Networking and Applications Workshops (WAINA), pp. 93–98, March 2016
6. Villari, M., Fazio, M., Dustdar, S., Rana, O., Ranjan, R.: Osmotic computing: a new paradigm for edge/cloud integration. IEEE Cloud Comput. **3**(6), 76–83 (2016)
7. Enabling microservices: containers & orchestration explained, July 2016. https://www.mongodb.com/collateral/microservices-containers-and-orchestration-explained
8. Microservices: The evolution of building modern applications, July 2016. https://www.mongodb.com/collateral/microservices-the-evolution-of-building-modern-applications
9. He, C., Jin, X., Zhao, Z., Xiang, T.: A cloud computing solution for hospital information system. In: 2010 IEEE International Conference on Intelligent Computing and Intelligent Systems, vol. 2, pp. 517–520, October 2010
10. Parane, K.A., Patil, N.C., Poojara, S.R., Kamble, T.S.: Cloud based intelligent healthcare monitoring system. In: 2014 International Conference on Issues and Challenges in Intelligent Computing Techniques (ICICT), pp. 697–701, February 2014
11. John, N., Shenoy, S.: Health cloud - healthcare as a service (HaaS). In: 2014 International Conference on Advances in Computing, Communications and Informatics (ICACCI), pp. 1963–1966, September 2014
12. Fazio, M., Bramanti, A., Celesti, A., Bramanti, P., Villari, M.: A hybrid storage service for the management of big e-health data: a tele-rehabilitation case of study. In: Proceedings of the 12th ACM Symposium on QoS and Security for Wireless and Mobile Networks, pp. 1–8 (2016)
13. Celesti, A., Maria, F., Romano, A., Bramanti, A., Bramanti, P., Villari, M.: An oais-based hospital information system on the cloud: analysis of a NoSQL column-oriented approach. IEEE J. Biomed. Health Inform. **99**, 1 (2017)
14. Celesti, A., Celesti, F., Fazio, M., Bramanti, P., Villari, M.: Are next-generation sequencing tools ready for the cloud? In: Trends in Biotechnology (2017)
15. ownCloud. http://www.owncloud.org
16. The Big Big Data Workbook, Informatica (2016)
17. Swifts documentation. http://www.docs.openstack.org/developer/swift

Dynamic Identification of Participatory Mobile Health Communities

Isam Mashhour Aljawarneh[1], Paolo Bellavista[1], Carlos Roberto De Rolt[2], and Luca Foschini[1(✉)]

[1] University of Bologna, Bologna, Italy
{isam.aljawarneh3,paolo.bellavista,luca.foschini}@unibo.it
[2] Universidade do Estado de Santa Catarina, Florianópolis, Brazil
rolt@udesc.br

Abstract. Today's spread of chronic diseases and the need to control infectious diseases outbreaks have raised the demand for integrated information systems that can support patients while moving anywhere and anytime. This has been promoted by recent evolution in telecommunication technologies, together with an exponential increase in using sensor-enabled mobile devices on a daily basis. The construction of Mobile Health Communities (MHC) supported by Mobile CrowdSensing (MCS) is essential for mobile healthcare emergency scenarios. In a previous work, we have introduced the COLLEGA middleware, which integrates modules for supporting mobile health scenarios and the formation of MHCs through MCS. In this paper, we extend the COLLEGA middleware to address the need in real time scenarios to handle data arriving continuously in streams from MHC's members. In particular, this paper describes the novel COLLEGA support for managing the real-time formation of MHCs. Experimental results are also provided that show the effectiveness of our identification solution.

Keywords: Mobile healthcare · Middleware · Crowdsourcing · Mobile Health Communities · Community detection

1 Introduction

Today's proliferation of mobile technologies including networks, devices and software systems has caused the widespread creation of mobile healthcare services and systems. Mobile telemedicine, mobile patient's health status monitoring, location-based medical services and emergency response are just few examples, thus constituting an opportunity to provide anytime and anywhere healthcare services in a timely and location-based manner.

In the domain of health care, a challenging problem is to inject novel methods for health care assistance based merely on extemporaneous interactions and collaborations. Due to the unsuitability of traditional virtual health networks in handling today's anytime and anywhere healthcare scenarios, it is essential to activate novel forms of healthcare communities, the so-called Mobile Health Communities (MHC). As an example scenario, MHC can be created by forming a community that consists of passing-by

© ICST Institute for Computer Sciences, Social Informatics and Telecommunications Engineering 2018
A. Longo et al. (Eds.): IISSC 2017/CN4IoT 2017, LNICST 189, pp. 208–217, 2018.
https://doi.org/10.1007/978-3-319-67636-4_22

volunteers and professionals, who are willing to provide instantaneous assistance in case of emergency, and also patients who are geographically co-located. Participants may include health staff, friends, neighbors, and passing-by people who can provide instant aid or contribute to patient's rescue. As a simplified scenario, patients with illnesses like cardiopathy and asthma, who have the potential to alert anytime and anywhere, would wear sensor-enabled devices equipped with some kind of network connectivity support (wireless, Bluetooth, LTE, ..) in order to be able to send notifications in case of emergency. On the other side, passing-by volunteers, who are in a relatively nearby distance with that patient, and for whom specific constraints apply, would be notified to provide suitable assistance to that patient. Participants can either be trained enough to give instantaneous medical care, or act as information collectors of relevant data to provide to official medical staff upon arrival.

In the last decade, the use of Mobile CrowdSensing (MCS) has increased vastly, promoting a participatory approach for the management of MHCs. MCS is a community sensing method that collects information using people's sensor-equipped devices [1]. The purpose of those sensing technologies is not only sending emergency alerts, but also feeding specialized database servers with information necessary for disease's diagnosis and management. For instance, MCS's users can feed the system with information related to air pollution's measurements or allergens in some locations of a city, which, in turns, can alert patients with asthma to avoid those areas. Also, MCS support can be useful in proposing sensing activities to users belonging to MHCs based on their location, like taking photos or examining the availability of defibrillators, pharmacies and medical facilities within a city.

However, despite its increased adoption, many technological challenges hinder a proper implementation of participatory MHCs. Wireless-enabled monitoring, control health indicators, location discovery systems for identifying patient's location at the time where help is emergent, and appropriate crowdsensing platforms for supporting participatory mobile healthcare, to name but a few.

Specifically, today it is essential to find solutions that can dynamically form appropriate MHCs nearly on-the-fly, and upon arrival of an emergency event, which will offer a basement for a dynamic interaction among participants, which in turns, facilitates quick decisions suitable for those emergency situations. We define the main requirements that should be met to be able to speed up the decision making process. However, current methods fall short in achieving these requirements and that calls for a novel contribution to accomplish dynamic health's scenario-specific requirements.

Recently, a novel approach for analyzing large streams of data has emerged, the Apache Spark platform, which will be referred to as Spark for short hereafter. Spark has many features, including fast processing of streaming data, and parallel dynamic analysis [2]. These unique features and many others make Spark an excellent candidate for addressing the requirements of our specific mobile healthcare scenarios.

However, our main focus in this paper is not Spark as a core. Alternatively, we are interested in a genuine platform that has been built on the top of Spark, specifically for graph processing, the so-called GraphX. Its introducers claim that it acts faster than traditional programming paradigms in terms of performance and an ability to easily integrate with other platforms, which may need to act on constructed graphs for more specific analysis [3]. Spark through an implementation for GraphX facilitates a construction of MHC's dynamically. Compared to traditional programming paradigms, it is the best current choice available for forming MHCs for many reasons. First, it enables near real-time formation of MHCs by applying functionalities of its GraphX. Second, it easily enables the system to apply intelligent algorithms on the constructed MHCs, then to find best rescue plan depending on a specific situation of a patient in the presence of emergency. For example, this includes, but not limited to, discovery of a most suitable passing-by participant, discovery of a best hospital that is nearby a location of a patient, and which hosts medical staff and contains equipment appropriate for a specific case of a patient.

As far as we know, currently there are no specific integrated platforms capable of achieving all of the requirements for dynamic mobile healthcare. In this paper, we extend our middleware architecture, called COLLEGA (COLLaborative Emergency Group Assistant) [4] with an innovative MHC formation support. Based on the analysis of requirements for dynamic MHC creation, we have developed and integrated a Spark's-based community detection support for MHCs.

The rest of the paper is divided into the following sections. First, we provide some background of participatory MCS and its application in the construction of MHCs. This is followed by detailed explanations of the COLLEGA middleware and our community detection support based on Spark. In last sections, we present experimental results and conclude the paper reporting future development directions.

2 Background

The high-quality performance of participatory healthcare together with the minimized associated costs have motivated an extended research in the field. Different related aspects have been researched, including wireless area networks, monitoring systems, virtual health community management and construction. In the following subsections, we focus on crowdsensing and community detection in mobile healthcare scenarios.

2.1 Crowdsensing for Mobile Healthcare

The widespread of wireless networks technologies and sensor-enabled devices encourages the emergence of healthcare scenarios, where patients are sending continuous timely and location-based health indicators while moving. As a consequence, novel forms of communities referred to as MHCs should be activated. In addition, the unprecedented smartphone sensing and communication capabilities facilitate healthcare delivery, diagnosis and control of diseases that potentially may disseminate quickly. The emergence of MCS, a promising large-scale data sensing paradigm plays a vital role for the realization of the new participatory healthcare.

In fact, it became obvious that MCS significantly contributes to the construction of MHCs, which is specifically efficient in such scenarios where an urgent first-aid is needed in cases like a sudden asthma attack for a patient equipped with a sensor-enabled mobile device. To put it in another way, MCS is capable of simplifying the formation of MHCs, which consist of potential passing-by participants suitable for providing instant first-aid. Those users are probably volunteers who use MCS systems and involve voluntarily to MCS participation campaigns.

In addition to provide a base for forming MHCs, MCS exploitation can be extended to attract new volunteers, and strengthen social relationships among volunteers for MHCs that can last. To be more specific, volunteers can actively contribute by feeding the database system with updated data regarding disease's diagnosis and management while moving around in a city, thus enforcing the realization of participatory healthcare. All these features make MCS-based studies a promising and interesting research direction, to the extent that experts are now utilizing it for monitoring infectious disease outbreaks.

Despite the fact that tremendous research efforts have been put in the field of mobile healthcare [5–8], many challenges need to be addressed in a more efficient manner. Many MCS platforms have been proposed in the literature. However, none of them has been encapsulated with a mobile healthcare system. To this end, we introduced COLLEGA, which is basically a middleware that merges MCS with latest community detection paradigms for near real-time and dynamic formation of MHCs, and also continuously injecting updated data suitable for resolving emergencies.

2.2 Community Detection Methods for Mobile Healthcare

Community detection algorithms are prevalent in many real life scenarios. In the last decade or so, they have tremendously been used in various applications like, social network analysis [9], and detecting suspicious events in telecommunication networks [10]. However, there is still a lack of application for relevant algorithms in community detection for forming MHCs.

Detecting communities in mobile healthcare scenarios is non-trivial due to expensive computations required for realizing hidden relationships. This leads us to define a set of requirements under which a system should operate. First, system should be able to construct communities within seconds due to the fact that patients might be in an emergency situation, which in turns means that a quick action should be taken. Second, data arrives continuously in streams and needs instantaneous processing. Third, caching previously generated communities is essential to speedup future processing. Fourth, the form of generated communities should be suitable for an effortless application of data mining algorithms, in order to discover best potential solutions.

Traditional applications of algorithms for community detection have been in action for decades [11, 12]. However, as far as we know, none of those applications have considered collectively the four above mentioned requirements.

Moreover, the running time of those algorithms is typically not linear; therefore, their application in a batch-processing fashion is not suitable for constructing MHCs. Recent trends have tried to reduce running time by implementing those algorithms to run in a multithreaded fashion. However, none of them have considered the scenario where data arrives continuously on the form of streams and needs immediate processing; likewise, as far as we know no speedup strategies like caching have been applied so far in participatory healthcare scenarios.

In order to be able to detect communities, it is a prerequisite to represent actors and relationships of a given scenario as graphs. A graph is a data structure that consists of nodes and edges, where each node models an actor in the scenario, and each edge models a connection between two nodes [13]. However, computations required for detecting communities using the graph paradigm is costly. As a consequence, and because of the need for an enhanced graph computation tools for improving performance, it was essential to introduce new graph-parallel systems, like Pregel [14]. However, these systems did not implicitly consider a streamlined integration with data mining. This, in its turns, led to the introduction of a novel platform called GraphX that is encapsulated with Spark. GraphX simplifies graph computations by expressing graphs using the Spark big data parallel processing framework [3].

Since its introduction, GraphX has been applied to many scenarios including social network analysis [15]. One benefit of GraphX is its adaptability and a precious ability to be executed in a parallel fashion using the core building block of Apache Spark, Resilient Distributed Dataset (RDD), which is a read-only collection of objects distributed on a group of hosts to obtain horizontal scalability and fault tolerance [2]. However, to the best of our knowledge, these methods have never been applied to scenarios specifically related to mobile healthcare that present unique requirements.

Having such information in hand, traditional algorithms for community detection can be implemented with an ease using GraphX. As an example, label propagation algorithm (LPA) is a well-known algorithm in terms of performance [11]. It has been implemented in GraphX using the Pregel framework and can be embedded in any application for community detection. As better explained in the following, for our solution we selected LPA because its running time in a batch-processing scenario have been proved to be near real time, and we wanted to investigate its behavior when implemented using GraphX and in a mobile healthcare scenario.

One more rationale for the selection for GraphX is the ability to apply machine learning algorithms in a straightforward fashion. In fact, on top of the Spark core it is available the MLib that encapsulated many machine learning algorithms. That allows to easily apply machine learning algorithms on a graph constructed using GraphX.

Finally, let us remark that in our scenarios mobile health data will arrive as continuous streams, which means that the discovery of communities and potential participants must be done in a near real time fashion. The ability to extend the static implementation of a community detection algorithm using Spark's Streaming is a major benefit and is expected to perform with a high performance.

3   The COLLEGA Middleware

COLLEGA constitutes a middleware which provides participatory emergency support for moving patients with chronic diseases. It constitutes a comprehensive lifecycle for an emergency scenario, from danger alarm to the construction of MHCs, and to the formation and execution of emergency action plans. Indeed, in COLLEGA mobile emergency scenarios are composed of mobile monitored patients and co-located passing-by participants. Simply put, COLLEGA pre-assumes that mobile patients either have wireless sensors attached to their clothes or implanted under skin for observing vital body health indicators and constructing a Wireless Body Area Network (WBAN). To this end, Patient's smart devices send alarms in case of emergency while moving. On the other side, COLLEGA enables potential passing-by participants to receive those alarms, with information including the type of emergency and helpful information to provide first-aid.

COLLEGA exploits our previous experience in the ParticipAct middleware [16] and the Proteus access control model described in [17]. In addition, new mobile healthcare specific functions are added here as better detailed in the following.

3.1 COLLEGA Architecture

Our COLLEGA architecture constitutes its core modules and their associated workflow as shown in Fig. 1. Each module is devoted to realize a specific function of the mobile healthcare emergency management lifecycle.

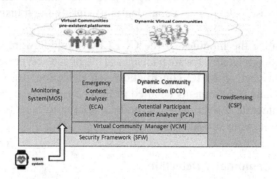

Fig. 1. COLLEGA middleware modules.

The Monitoring System (MOS) is a module that is interfaced with a patient's WBAN for collecting and analyzing sensor's data, thereby sending emergency alerts and coordinating communications with the patient. In addition, MOS is also responsible for suggesting first-aids to patient in relative to off-the-shelf control plans.

The Emergency Context Analyzer (ECA) is responsible for combining data received from MOS module with patient's medical history, probably received from a remote database, then compares them with similar cases stored in a distributed knowledge base, to analyze and classify the severity degree of the emergency situation. Thereafter, ECA selects the most suitable control plan, which contains tolerance limit's values for each event's severity degree. It also chooses the most appropriate actions to be performed for a specific level of severity, the equipment required to accomplish every action and a set of skills that a potential participant should have.

The CrowdSensing module (CSP) encapsulates a variety of mobile crowdsensing-related functionalities. To be more specific, CSP is responsible for discovering user's status, such as user walking and running. Also, it detects user's location by geolocalization functions. Furthermore, it uses geofences to detect user proximity in relative to a specific geographical point. Furthermore, it assigns tasks to users while entering given geofences.

The Participant Context Analyzer (PCA) dynamically selects potential participants from an established MHC. PCA is also responsible for dynamically detecting communities through the Dynamic Community Detection (DCD) sub-module. DCD receives appropriate data from CSP, joins them with corresponding data in the knowledge base, and then applies a community detection algorithm to construct MHCs. To this end, PCA is also responsible to choose the most appropriate participant depending on several factors, including the control plan to be performed.

The Virtual Community Manager (VCM) distributes tasks to the identified participants, gets their acceptance, provides a set of instructions, and asks security support permission to access patient's medical data. Also, VCM gathers data throughout the whole cycle of an emergency situation in order to update the user's medical history and knowledge base.

The core task of the Security Framework (SFW) is to allow the patient to set access control policies, and thereby enforce mechanisms for accessing patient's personal data. Also, SWF assures user's health data confidentiality during the transmission to participant's devices.

In order to realize the modules of the COLLEGA middleware, it is essential to implement and deploy related software packages at client and server sides. In this paper, we focus on the aspect of MHC construction and detection using Spark GraphX. According to our main requirements detailed in Sect. 2.1, we have designed the DCD sub-module and integrate it with the PCA module, aiming to meet those requirements as detailed in the following sub-section.

3.2 COLLEGA Community Detection

We have identified four extreme requirements in MHCs for which any detection algorithm should obey in order to be considered efficient. We believe that those requirements best fit the context of our MHC's formation scenarios. We here list them and rationale their selection.

First, MHCs should be constructed in a near real-time fashion. This means it should only take few seconds to complete the whole process from sending the alert by patient's device, to forming communities, to finding the potential participant who can provide an appropriate first-aid. Second, the algorithm should be able to receive data in streams. The purpose of this constraint is that in our health care scenarios data continuously arrives in streams. This, in turn, means that while participants and patients are moving, they keep sending information and signals to the server which hosts the processing algorithm. Third, the algorithm should be extensible in a way that makes it adaptively update the network community structures based on its cached structures instead of repeating the whole process from scratch. The last requirement is that communities detected using the algorithm should be available in a form that streamline the application of data mining and machine learning algorithms on the constructed graphs [3]. This is because, upon completion of MHCs construction, it is essential to identify the most potential assistance plan, including the identification of the most appropriate participant, finding the nearest hospital that contains medical equipment's relevant to assist that patient, and probably finding the best way to move the patient from current location to the identified hospital. This requires the application of data mining and machine learning techniques and obtaining results within minimal timeframes.

The responsibility of the DCD module is to discover potential nearby participants to provide first-aid. The module comprises three sub-modules deployed on a distributed system. The first sub-module, deployed on patient device, is responsible to generate an alert signal in case that an emergency was detected by the MOS module. The alert is implemented in a formatted packet such that it encapsulates information like an identifier of the health problem type and GPS coordinates of current patient location. The second sub-module is deployed on a remote-server running Spark and implements a community detection algorithm (e.g. LPA). The server-side module will receive the alert, analyze its components, form MHCs and apply data mining and machine learning algorithms on them to discover the best rescue plan. The third sub-module is deployed on the partici- pant's device, and is always listening to alerts. In fact, listening mode is adaptable in accordance with participant's preferences. For example, participant may prefer to receive alerts through messaging services, in order to avoid exhausting the battery and mobile device's resources. After completion of the analysis, the server sends to the potential participant necessary information to commence with the first-aid.

4 Experimental Results

In this section, we present results obtained from applying a community detection algo- rithm using Spark's GraphX. Static LPA has been tested using two implementations. The first one is a conventional (vanilla) implementation of LPA that uses traditional programming modules that have been implemented using Java 1.8 version libraries. The second one, instead, is purely based on Spark's GraphX. We have generated synthetic data that model the relationships between participants and patients. IN particular, gener- ated data consisted of tables, each table contains two columns, and each column contains a set of nodes. This means that each row in the table models the relationship on a patient- participant or a participant-participant base.

Our testing environment consists of one machine hosting Linux Ubuntu 64-bit oper- ating system, with four Intel Core 2.20 GHz processors and 4 GB RAM. In order for the test to be fair with respect to the vanilla LPA concentrated implementation, we have decided to test on a single machine, taking into consideration that the conventional libraries cannot run in a parallel and distributed platform. The goal of our tests is to evaluate the scalability of the two LPA implementations, namely, the evolution of the running time as we increase the network size.

As depicted in Fig. 2, GraphX-based LPA implementation outperforms vanilla LPA implementation in terms of running time, even though both implementations act in a near linear fashion.

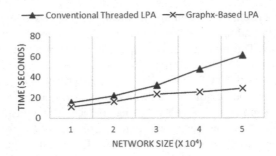

Fig. 2. Comparison between conventional and Spark Graphx implementations of LPA.

We also believe that applying cache mechanisms to the GraphX-based LPA will definitely reduce the running time, which means that formation of MHCs can depends effectively on caching for improving the overall performance and enforcing the near-real time objective. The fact that any application that is constructed using Spark libraries can be executed in a parallel fashion encouraged us to adopt GraphX. The running time shown in the figure will definitely decrease dramatically when executing the algorithm in a cluster or a cloud.

This simplified scenario exhibits the efficiency of adopting Spark and GraphX, for community detection in mobile healthcare scenarios. Add to this the fact that it is a streamlined process to apply a machine learning algorithm on the obtained result in order to identify the most potential participant in case of emergency. For instance, algorithms can be applied to discover the shortest path to the most suitable hospital.

5   Conclusions and Future Work

In this paper, we have introduced the solid COLLEGA middleware and presented the novel function to dynamically discovery potential participants for providing first-aid to co-located patients. Further, we have incorporated a recent technology for the construction of MHCs with COLLEGA. To validate this incorporation, we have tested the middleware with a synthetic data and compared the performance of MHCs construction with a conventional paradigm.

Boosted by obtained results, we are currently exploring other ongoing work directions. First, despite the fact that the incorporated method for MHCs outperforms its predecessors, it is worth noticing that only synthetic testing scenarios have been considered; hence, we plan to test with benchmark data in order to strengthen the theory. In addition, data mining and machine learning algorithms will be applied on the constructed MHCs.

Acknowledgments. This research was supported by the program CAPES- Pesquisador Visitante Especial - 3° Cronograma - Chamadas de Projetos n° 09/2014 and by the Sacher project (no. J32I16000120009) funded by the POR-FESR 2014-20 through CIRI.

References

1. Ganti, R.K., Ye, F., Lei, H.: Mobile crowdsensing: current state and future challenges. IEEE Commun. Magaz. **49**, 32–39 (2011)
2. Zaharia, M., Chowdhury, M., Franklin, M.J., Shenker, S., Stoica, I.: Spark: cluster computing with working sets. In: Presented at the Proceedings of the 2nd USENIX Conference on Hot Topics in Cloud Computing, Boston, MA (2010)
3. Xin, R.S., Gonzalez, J.E., Franklin, M.J., Stoica, I.: GraphX: a resilient distributed graph system on Spark. In: Presented at the First International Workshop on Graph Data Management Experiences and Systems, New York (2013)
4. Rolt, C.R.D., Montanari, R., Brocardo, M.L., Foschini, L., Dias, J.D.S.: COLLEGA middleware for the management of participatory mobile health communities. In: 2016 IEEE Symposium on Computers and Communication (ISCC), pp. 999–1005 (2016)
5. Alali, H., Salim, J.: Virtual communities of practice success model to support knowledge sharing behaviour in healthcare sector. Procedia Technol. **11**, 176–183 (2013)
6. Christo El, M.: Mobile virtual communities in healthcare the chronic disease management case. In: Sabah, M., Jinan, F. (eds.) Ubiquitous Health and Medical Informatics: The Ubiquity 2.0 Trend and Beyond, pp. 258–274. IGI Global, Hershey (2010)
7. Chorbev, I., Sotirovska, M., Mihajlov, D.: Virtual communities for diabetes chronic disease healthcare. Int. J. Telemed. Appl. **2011**, 11 (2011)
8. Morr, C.E.: Mobile virtual communities in healthcare: self-managed care on the move. In: Presented at the Third IASTED International Conference on Telehealth, Montreal, Quebec, Canada (2007)
9. Zhao, Z., Feng, S., Wang, Q., Huang, J.Z., Williams, G.J., Fan, J.: Topic oriented community detection through social objects and link analysis in social networks. Knowl. Based Syst. **26**(164–173), 2 (2012)
10. Akoglu, L., Tong, H., Koutra, D.: Graph based anomaly detection and description: a survey. Data Mining Knowl. Disc. **29**, 626–688 (2015)
11. Raghavan, U.N., Albert, R., Kumara, S.: Near linear time algorithm to detect community structures in large-scale networks. Phys. Rev. E **76**(3 Pt 2), 036106 (2007)
12. Yang, J., McAuley, J., Leskovec, J.: Community detection in networks with node attributes. In: 2013 IEEE 13th International Conference on Data Mining, pp. 1151–1156 (2013)
13. Lei, T., Huan, L.: Community Detection and Mining in Social Media. Morgan & Claypool, San Rafael (2010)
14. Malewicz, G., Austern, M.H., Bik, A.J.C., Dehnert, J.C., Horn, I., Leiser, N., et al.: Pregel: a system for large-scale graph processing. In: Presented at the Proceedings of the 2010 ACM SIGMOD International Conference on Management of data, Indianapolis, Indiana, USA (2010)
15. Lan, S., He, G., Yu, D.: Relationship analysis of network virtual identity based on spark. In: 2016 8th International Conference on Intelligent Human-Machine Systems and Cybernetics (IHMSC), pp. 64–68 (2016)
16. Cardone, G., Cirri, A., Corradi, A., Foschini, L.: The participact mobile crowd sensing living lab: the testbed for smart cities. IEEE Commun. Magaz. **52**, 78–85 (2014)
17. Toninelli, A., Montanari, R., Kagal, L., Lassila, O.: Proteus: a semantic context-aware adaptive policy model. In: Eighth IEEE International Workshop on Policies for Distributed Systems and Networks (POLICY 2007), pp. 129–140 (2007)

Securing Cloud-Based IoT Applications with Trustworthy Sensing

Ihtesham Haider[(✉)] and Bernhard Rinner

Alpen-Adria-Universität, Klagenfurt, Austria
{ihtesham.haider,bernhard.rinner}@aau.at

Abstract. The omnipresence of resource-constrained sensors connected to the cloud has enabled numerous Internet of Things (IoT) applications. However, the trust in these IoT applications is severely compromised by security concerns. We introduce a lightweight and effective security approach for such applications by protecting the sensors. Our approach leverages Physically Unclonable Functions (PUF) on the sensor platform to ensure non-repudiation of sensed data and integrity of sensor hardware and firmware. We compare the performance of different PUF implementations on Atmel, ARM, and FPGA-based sensing platforms, analyze the security properties of the proposed protocols and determine the overhead in terms of latency, storage and logic area. Our evaluation shows that it only incurs insignificant overhead on low-end sensors.

1 Introduction

Ubiquitous sensor networks together with cloud computing and storage have played a vital role in enabling numerous IoT applications permeating in domains such as health-care, environmental monitoring, natural disaster detection, and urban planning. A generic IoT application infrastructure comprises spatially distributed sensor nodes, a cloud-based server that collects the sensed data from the nodes, processes the collected data to extract contextual information that is offered as the service to the end-users. The growing software stack on today's sensor nodes and widespread use of public networks (e.g., Internet) for communications make these cloud-based applications more vulnerable and more attractive for attackers. Thus, the reliability of the services offered by these applications critically depends on the "trustworthiness" of the sensed data.

A typical sensor node comprises a sensing unit (also referred to as a sensor) that is connected to a host processor. A sensing unit typically consists of sensing circuitry and a lightweight MCU (known as the sensor controller), whereas a host processor is mostly a powerful processor that runs an operating system (OS). On top of the OS, the specific applications are deployed. *Sensed data pollution* attacks [1–3], that aim to manipulate and fabricate sensors' readings, can be launched using either software or hardware of the sensor node as illustrated in Fig. 1. An adversary may exploit security bugs (e.g., Android Fake ID and MasterKey vulnerabilities) to inject malware in the host OS, physically tamper with the sensor hardware or falsify sensor data by modifications of the sensor

© ICST Institute for Computer Sciences, Social Informatics and Telecommunications Engineering 2018
A. Longo et al. (Eds.): IISSC 2017/CN4IoT 2017, LNICST 189, pp. 218–227, 2018.
https://doi.org/10.1007/978-3-319-67636-4_23

firmware [3]. Preventing these data pollution attacks is a major challenge in cloud-based sensing applications.

In a traditional holistic security approach, the entire sensor node starting from the applications down to the operating system and the hardware must be secured. A major limitation of this approach is that security is tightly interwoven with the application logic and the increasing complexity of the system components such as OS, network stack, and system libraries which makes it difficult to achieve tight security guarantees about the node. This work follows an alternative approach that makes security protection inherent property of the sensing unit, which we introduced earlier in our concept paper [4]. The "trustworthiness" of sensed data is improved by ensuring non-repudiation of sensed data and integrity of the sensor hardware and firmware as suggested in [3].

Our lightweight and effective approach leverages sensor-based Physically Unclonable Functions (PUF) and the sensor controller for securing the sensors and the sensed data against the sensed data pollution attacks for cloud-based IoT applications. The contributions of this work are twofold: First, we exploit sensor-based PUFs in combination with lightweight security mechanisms to ensure non-repudiation on sensed readings and integrity of sensor's hardware and firmware. Second, we evaluate our scheme for different sensors and compare the performance of different PUF implementations on Atmel, ARM and FPGA-platforms. The marginal overhead in terms of storage, latency and logic area makes our scheme applicable for various resource-limited sensing platforms.

We assume that an adversary (i) can inject malware in the host device OS that can manipulate or fabricate the sensed data, (ii) has access to the sensors to mount any physical (invasive or non-invasive) attacks and (iii) can modify the sensor firmware statically. We argue that there is not enough economic motivation for the attacker to mount sophisticated attacks such as runtime firmware modification on each sensor. The goal here is to ensure that (i) an untrusted OS running on the host device cannot interfere with the sensors' readings and (ii) compromised sensors are unable to contribute sensed data without being detected.

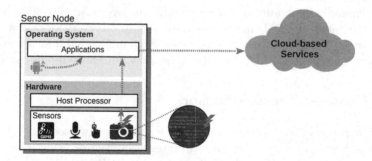

Fig. 1. A high-level sensor node stack, depicting sensed data pollution attacks due to vulnerable host OS, hardware tampering and firmware modification of the sensors.

The rest of the paper is organized as follows: Sect. 2 reviews the state of the art in trustworthy sensing. Section 3 introduces the proposed scheme and provides detailed constructions of the building blocks to achieve non-repudiation of sensed data and integrity of sensor hardware and firmware. Section 4 evaluates our scheme in terms of required logic area, latency and storage. Section 5 concludes this paper.

2   Related Work

Research on trustworthy sensing has mainly focused on the integration of trusted platform modules (TPM) and other secure cryptoprocessors to the sensors or host devices. The anonymous attestation feature of TPM is used to attest the sensed data. Early work on trustworthy sensing [2] was motivated by participatory sensing. TPM was proposed for mobile devices to attest the sensed data. Saroiu and Wolman [1] proposed the integration of TPM into the mobile device sensors which may not be an economical solution for resource constrained embedded applications. Moreover, TPMs are vulnerable to physical attacks. Winkler et al. [5] used TPM to secure embedded camera nodes. Potkonjak et al. [6] proposed an alternative approach for the trusted flow of information in remote sensing scenarios that employed public physically unclonable functions (PPUFs). Despite similar names, PUFs and PPUFs are fundamentally different primitives. PPUFs are hardware security primitives which can be modeled by algorithms of high complexity where as PUFs cannot. The security of PPUF relies on the fact that the PPUF hardware output is many orders faster than its software counterpart. The main drawback of this approach is that current PPUF designs involve complex circuits requiring high measurement accuracy which slows down the authentication process and therefore it is not a scalable solution. Interestingly, some recent research efforts have lead to successful identification of PUF behavior on some sensors. Rosenfeld et al. [7] introduced the idea of a sensor PUF, whereby the PUF response depends on the applied challenge as well as the sensor reading.

The incorporation of TPMs into sensors and host devices requires extensive hardware modifications and introduces significant overhead. Despite the widespread deployment of TPMs in laptops, desktops, and servers for over a decade, TPMs have not yet found their way into sensors or embedded host devices. Protocols based on complex PPUF primitives are slow, and have limited scalability.

3   PUF-Based Trusted Sensors

This section presents our security scheme, which aims for two security objectives: (i) non-repudiation of sensed data and (ii) integrity of sensor firmware and hardware. Non-repudiation of sensed data is ensure by *PUF-based Cert-IBS* module and is implemented in sensor firmware where as the *Verified Boot* ensures the integrity of this firmware. A key element of any security solution is secure key storage. Our scheme leverages a lightweight PUF framework to bind a unique

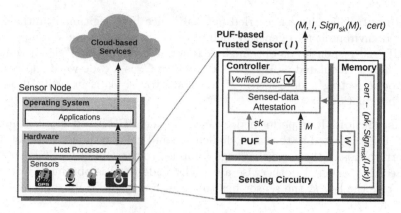

Fig. 2. Our scheme for trustworthy sensing. The readings are signed inside the sensor using a key that is inseperably bound to the sensor by the on chip PUF. The sensor-based security modules are marked in green. (Color figure online)

key to each sensor. All the three components of our scheme: *PUF-based Secure Key Generation & Storage Framework*, *PUF-based Cert-IBS* and *Verified Boot* are realized on the sensor as depicted in Fig. 2 and we refer to the resulting sensor as *PUF-based Trusted Sensor*. Each component requires an enrollment phase, where an interactive protocol is performed between a trusted authority and the sensor before the sensor is deployed in the field.

3.1 PUF-Based Key Generation and Storage Framework

PUFs are lightweight hardware security primitives which typically exhibit a challenge-response behavior. When queried with a challenge c, the PUF generates a response r, that depends on c and the uncontrollable CMOS manufacturing variations of the underlying hardware. Randomness, uniqueness, physical unclonability and tamper resistance properties [8] make PUFs interesting candidates for secure key generation and storage. PUF response is noisy due to variations in the environmental and operating conditions. This noise is measured in terms of intra-Hamming distance (HD^{intra}). The randomness of a PUF response is measure by the Hamming weight (HW). For key generation and storage, PUF response should have zero noise ($HD^{intra} \approx 0\%$) and follow uniform random distribution (HW $\approx 50\%$). Additionally our *PUF-based Cert-IBS* requires the ability to bind an external key to the sensor hardware using PUF. To meet these requirements, we use a PUF-based framework proposed by Tuyls et al. [9] that is able to securely store an external key by masking it with a PUF response. We assume that the PUF is instantiated on the sensor by a legitimate trusted authority. Furthermore, the communication between the PUF and the sensor is secure and is not accessible to the attacker. The framework consists of two phases: enrollment and reconstruction, depicted in Table 1.

Enrollment. This phase is carried out only once by a legitimate authority in a trusted environment to generate helper data W. A challenge c is applied to the PUF and response r is obtained. A random key $k \in \{0,1\}^k$ is chosen, and helper-data is calculated as $W \leftarrow r \oplus C_k$, where C_k is a code-word chosen from the error-correcting code $\mathcal{C}$, with $2^k - 1$ code-words. W is integrity protected public information.

Reconstruction. It is performed every time the PUF-based key is required. The PUF is subjected to the same challenge c and noisy response r' is obtained. If r' corresponds to the same challenge c applied to the same PUF, k is obtained after decoding using W, otherwise an invalid code-word is obtained. Note that to generate the key k, the sensor has to perform only an XOR and a decoding operation.

Table 1. Framework to bind an externally generated key with a PUF.

Enrollment: $W \leftarrow Gen(r,k)$	Reconstruction: $k \leftarrow Rep(r',W)$
Pick a random key: k	$C_{k'} \leftarrow r' \oplus W$
$C_k \leftarrow$ Encoding(k), where	$k \leftarrow$ Decoding($C_{k'}$), if
$\quad C_k \in \mathcal{C}$, the error-correction code	Hamming distance($C_k, C_{k'}$) $\leq t$
$W \leftarrow r \oplus C_k$	t is error-correction capacity of $\mathcal{C}$

3.2 PUF-Based Cert-IBS

Our PUF-based Cert-IBS is based on the definition [10] for constructing a certificate-based IBS scheme using a standard signature scheme (SS). Moreover, it uses the PUF-framework of Sect. 3.1 for secure key storage. We assign each PUF-enabled sensor an identity I which can be any physical identifier such as the sensor's serial number or EPC. The PUF-based Cert-IBS works in two phases: *enrollment*, performed once by the trusted authority before deployment and *sensed data attestation*, performed by the sensor every time it senses fresh data. PUF-based Cert-IBS is a tuple ($MK, UK, SIGN, VER$) of polynomial time algorithms where $MK, UK, SIGN$ and VER refer to master key generation, user key generation, signing and verification algorithms respectively. Let the standard signature scheme $SS := (K, Sign, Ver)$ where K, $Sign$ and Ver are the key generation, signing and verification algorithms. Then the PUF-based Cert-IBS ($MK, UK, SIGN, VER$) is associated to a standard signature scheme SS ($K, Sign, Ver$) as follows:

Enrollment. The trusted authority runs the K of SS as the MK to generate the master key pair: $(mpk, msk) \leftarrow MK(1^k)$. During enrollment, the authority binds a unique key with the PUF-enabled sensor using the user key generation algorithm UK as follows: The sensor presents itself to the authority using identity I. The authority requests the sensor to subject its PUF with challenge c. The sensor obtains the corresponding PUF response r and provides it to the authority who then (i) runs the K of SS and generates a key pair (pk, sk) for the sensor (ii) determines the helper data W by executing $Gen(r, sk)$ of Table 1 and (iii) creates a certificate on the identity and public key of the sensor using signing algorithm $Sign$ of the SS i.e., $cert \leftarrow (pk, Sign_{msk}(pk, I))$. Helper data W and the certificate $cert$ are stored in the sensor memory. The user key usk is given by the PUF-bound secret key sk and the certificate $cert$ (see Fig. 3 (left)).

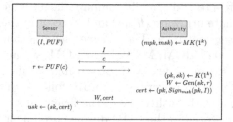 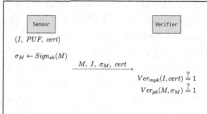

Fig. 3. Enrollment (left) and sensed data attestation (right) phases of PUF-based Cert-IBS scheme

Sensed Data Attestation. Sensed data attestation is performed every time before the sensor outputs a new reading. The private key required for signing is reconstructed at the power-up as $sk \leftarrow Rep(r', W)$ (see Table 1). To sign a new reading M, the sensor uses $Sign$ of SS to obtain $\sigma_M \leftarrow Sign_{sk}(M)$. The PUF-based Cert-IBS signature on the sensed data is given by $SIGN(M) := (I, \sigma_M, cert)$. The verification algorithm VER returns 1 (SUCCESS) if $Ver_{pk}(M, \sigma_M) = Ver_{mpk}(I, cert) = 1$, where Ver is the verification algorithm of SS (see Fig. 3 (right)). If verification of either the certificate or the sensed data fails, the reading is considered corrupt and the protocol is aborted.

The PUF-based Cert-IBS scheme enables a sensor to ensure integrity and authenticity on each reading, verifiable by the cloud-based application server. Any manipulation or fabrication of sensed data will result in failure during PUF-based Cert-IBS verification. The security of the PUF-based Cert-IBS scheme relies on security of PUFs as secure key storage and security of the underlying SS scheme. Using PUFs, the key is derived from device properties upon device start-up. During the state when device is off, the key exists in form of unreadable CMOS manufacturing variations. The side-channel attacks can be thwarted by breaking the correlation between side-channel information and the secret structure of the PUF. The security of PUF-based Cert-IBS scheme is related to the security of underlying SS scheme via Theorem 1. We omit the proof of Theorem 1 since it is similar to the proof of Theorem 3.5 of [10].

Theorem 1. *Let SS be a uf-cma secure standard signature scheme. Let PUF-based Cert-IBS be the corresponding IBS scheme as per construction of Sect. 3.2. Then PUF-based Cert-IBS is a uf-cma secure IBS scheme.*

3.3   Verified Boot

In our scheme, the sensed data attestation is performed in the firmware of the sensor controller (see Fig. 2). Therefore, during the *enrollment* phase of the Verified Boot, the trusted authority binds the legitimate firmware (also responsible for the sensed data attestation) with the sensor I using the on-chip PUF as follows: Given a sensor controller with a two stage boot-chain, i.e., the boot-loader and the firmware, the bootloader is modified to additionally compute the message authentication code (MAC) of the legitimate firmware (h_{FW}) and stores it in the immutable memory available on the sensor controller. The scheme assumes that one-time programmable memory such as OTPROM, MROM or PROM is available on the sensor controller. After the sensor is deployed for sensing, Verified Boot verifies the integrity of the sensor firmware at every power-up as follows: the bootloader generates the key, calculates a fresh hash value of the firmware and compares it with the reference hash value stored in the ROM during enrollment. Verified Boot resists against sensor firmware modification attacks. If a modification in the sensor firmware is detected during power-up, the boot process is aborted.

3.4   Security Properties

The correctness of the trustworthy sensing scheme follows from the correctness of the PUF-based Cert-IBS scheme. Since, any compromise to the trusted authority nullifies the trust and non repudiation guarantees on the sensed data, we emphasize the *offline* nature of the authority in our scheme greatly reduces the risk of compromise. The scheme withstands the sensed data corruption attacks due to (i) compromised host device OS (ii) tampered sensor hardware and (iii) modified sensor firmware. The host OS receives signed sensor readings and the corresponding certificate. In order to inject fabricated data at OS level, an attacker has to produce a valid signature certificate pair i.e., valid PUF-based Cert-IBS signature. A uf-cma secure PUF-based Cert-IBS implies that there is negligible probability that an attacker produces a valid PUF-based Cert-IBS signature. Since the PUF behavior corresponds to underlying hardware, given a tampered sensor hardware, PUF-based key generation implies that this results in generation of invalid secret key leading to generation of invalid signatures. Lastly, the offline attacks to modify the sensor firmware are detected by the Verified Boot.

4   Implementation and Evaluation

This section discusses the overhead incurred by our approach on a sensor in two parts. In Sect. 4.1, we present the implementation results of our PUF-based Key Generation & Storage Framework. Section 4.2 evaluates the total overhead on the sensor incurred by PUF-based Key Generation & Storage Framework, PUF-based Cert-IBS and Verified Boot modules in terms of storage, logic-area and latency.

4.1   PUF-Based Key Generation and Storage Framework

Various PUF sources are inherent to a typical sensor including SRAM PUF, ring oscillator (RO) PUF, and sensor-specific PUFs [7,11,12]. We aim to identify PUF sources that are commonly available on most of the sensors e.g., SRAM PUF and RO PUFs. We implemented PUFs on three platforms of varying complexities: (i) Atmel ATMEGA328P, a lightweight 8-bit MCU, (ii) ARM Cortex M4, a 32-bit MCU, and (iii) Xilinx Zynq7010 SoC with re-programmable logic and a dual core ARM Cortex A9. These platforms are perfectly suitable as sensor controllers for a wide range of sensors. The power-up state of the SRAM cells on the ATMEGA328P and the ARM Cortex M4 show PUF behavior. Figures 4(a) and (b) depicts the error-rate (measured as intra-Hamming distance (HD^{intra})) and the non-uniform distribution (measured as Hamming weight (HW)) of 100 PUF-responses obtained at room temperature. We implemented the RO PUF in FPGA area of Xilinx's Zynq7010 SoC. We characterized the RO PUF for HD^{intra} and HW, from 800 responses obtained over a temperature range of 0–60°C, depicted in the Fig. 4(c). The maximum error-rate $HD^{intra}(max)$ for the three PUFs $\approx 7.2\%$, 9.16%, and 6.97%. So, we designed the framework of Table 1 that can correct 10% error-rate. The error-correcting code determines the number of required PUF response bits and hence the size of PUF, so we experimented with two code: (i) a simple code: BCH(492, 57, 171) and (ii) a concatenated code: Reed Muller(16, 5, 8) ‖ Repetition(5, 1, 5). The resources consumed by SRAM PUF-based framework on ATMEGA328P MCU (Arduino board) and RO PUF-based framework on Xilinx's Zynq7010 SoC (MicroZed board) for 128-bit key are summarized in Table 2.

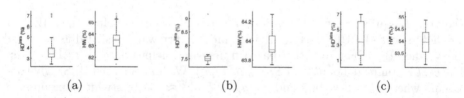

      (a)   (b)   (c)

Fig. 4. PUF characterization of (a) 1 kB SRAM on Atmel ATMEGA328P 8-bit MCU, (b) 15 kB SRAM on ARM Cortex M4 32-bit MCU, and (c) RO PUF comprised of 1040 3-stage ring oscillators implemented in FPGA part of Zynq7010 SoC. The PUF quality parameters for (a) and (b) are calculated over 100 PUF responses at the room temperature and for (c) 800 responses taken over temperature range 0–60°C. The mean and max. error-rate (HD^{intra}) for (a) $\approx 3.4\%$ and 7.2%, (b) $\approx 7.66\%$ and 9.16%, and (c) $\approx 3.6\%$ and 6.97%. The randomness of PUFs (HW(mean)), for (a) $\approx 63.5\%$, (b) $\approx 63.96\%$, and (c) $\approx 53.95\%$.

Table 2. Implementation results of the PUF-based 128-bit key generation and storage framework for the sensors

PUF source	Error correcting code	Area ($\approx$ logic gates)	Latency (Key reconstruction)	Storage Helper data (W)
RO	BCH	2210	≤ 100 ms	**1105** bits
	RM || Rep	3456		1728 bits
SRAM	BCH	NA	≈ 30 ms	**1105** bits
	RM || Rep	NA		2048 bits

4.2 Sensor Overhead

Our prototype PUF-based trusted sensor of Fig. 2 comprises OV5642 image sensor and Zynq7010 SoC as the sensor controller. We evaluate the storage, logic-area and latency overhead and summarize the results in Table 3.

Table 3. Logic-area, latency, and storage requirements of our scheme on a sensor

Area RO PUF only	Latency Sensed data attestation	Storage $W + cert + h_{FW}$
2210 logic gates	6.27 ms	1105 + 480 + 256 bits (≈ 230 bytes)

Storage Requirements. The sensor I needs to store (i) helper data W and certificate $cert$ of PUF-based Cert-IBS and (ii) firmware hash value h_{FW} for the Verified Boot. For RO PUF-based framework, helper data $W \approx 1105$ bits. The $cert$ is comprised of pk and $Sign_{msk}(I, pk)$. We implemented BLS signature scheme where $pk \approx 320$ bits and $Sign_{msk}(I, pk) \approx 160$ bits which amounts to 480 bits. h_{FW} is a 256-bit hash value computed using SHA-256. Therefore, the total storage requirement on a sensor for asymmetric version of our scheme is not more than 1841 bits (≈ 230 bytes).

Latency. PUF-based Key Generation and Verified Boot are performed at start-up and therefore run-time delay overhead is only incurred by the sensed data attestation phase of PUF-based Cert-IBS scheme. For sensed data attestation, we used the open-source *pairing-based cryptography library* and measured the latency of 6.27 ms on ARM cortex A9 core of Zynq7010 SoC. At 640 × 480 resolution, OV5642 can provide up to 15 FPS, which implies that a new frame is available for signing every 66.7 ms $\gg$ 6.27 ms of the signing latency.

Logic-Area Overhead. The logic-area is required only if the RO PUF is implemented. From Table 2, 2210 logic gates are used to generate a 128-bit key.

5   Conclusion

Security concerns in cloud-based IoT applications present severe obstacles for widespread adoption of these applications. In this paper, we presented a PUF-based scheme to secure the sensed data at its source, in order to improve the trust in the services provided by these application. The scheme is proven lightweight resulting in very low overhead wrt. storage ($230B$), and latency ($6.27\,\text{ms}$). The logic area overhead can be avoided by choosing a PUF source inherent of the sensor (e.g., SRAM PUF or sensor PUF). This is significant improvement over TPM-based approach [2] that incurs an overhead of a secure co-processor chip on each sensor and takes $1.92\,\text{s}$ for the attestation.

Acknowledgment. This research has been funded by the Austrian Research Promotion Agency (FFG) under grant number 842432. Michael Höberl has implemented RO PUF and was supported by the FP7 research project MATTHEW under grant number 610436.

References

1. Saroiu, S., Wolman, A.: I am a sensor, and i approve this message. In: Proceedings of Mobile Computing Systems & Applications, pp. 37–42. ACM (2010)
2. Dua, A., Bulusu, N., Feng, W.-C., Hu, W.: Towards trustworthy participatory sensing. In: Proceedings on Hot topics in security, p. 8. USENIX (2009)
3. Kapadia, A., Kotz, D., Triandopoulos, N.: Opportunistic sensing: security challenges for the new paradigm. In: Proceedings of Communication Systems and Networks and Workshops, pp. 1–10. IEEE (2009)
4. Haider, I., Höberl, M., Rinner, B.: Trusted sensors for participatory sensing and iot applications based on physically unclonable functions. In: Proceedings of Workshop on IoT Privacy, Trust, and Security, pp. 14–21. ACM (2016)
5. Winkler, T., Rinner, B.: Securing embedded smart cameras with trusted computing. EURASIP J. Wirel. Commun. Netw. **2011**, 530354 (2011)
6. Potkonjak, M., Meguerdichian, S., Wong, J.L.: Trusted sensors and remote sensing. In: Proceedings on Sensors. IEEE (2010)
7. Rosenfeld, K., Gavas, E., Karri, R.: Sensor physical unclonable functions. In: Proceedings on Hardware-Oriented Security and Trust (HOST). IEEE (2010)
8. Maes, R.: Physically unclonable functions: constructions, properties and applications. Ph.D. dissertation, University of KU Leuven (2012)
9. Tuyls, P., Batina, L.: RFID-tags for anti-counterfeiting. In: Pointcheval, D. (ed.) CT-RSA 2006. LNCS, vol. 3860, pp. 115–131. Springer, Heidelberg (2006). doi:10.1007/11605805_8
10. Bellare, M., Namprempre, C., Neven, G.: Security proofs for identity-based identification and signature schemes. J. Cryptol. **22**(1), 1–61 (2009)
11. Cao, Y., Zhang, L., Zalivaka, S.S., Chang, C., Chen, S.: CMOS image sensor based physical unclonable function for coherent sensor-level authentication. IEEE Trans. Circu. Syst. I Regular Papers **62**(11), 2629–2640 (2015)
12. Rajendran, J., Tang, J., Karri, R.: Securing pressure measurements using Sensor-PUFs. In: Proceedings of Circuits and Systems, pp. 1330–1333. IEEE (2016)

Secure Data Sharing and Analysis in Cloud-Based Energy Management Systems

Eirini Anthi$^{(\boxtimes)}$, Amir Javed, Omer Rana, and George Theodorakopoulos

School of Computer Science and Informatics, Cardiff University, Cardiff, UK
{anthies,javeda7}@cardiff.ac.uk

Abstract. Analysing data acquired from one or more buildings (through specialist sensors, energy generation capability such as PV panels or smart meters) via a cloud-based Local Energy Management System (LEMS) is increasingly gaining in popularity. In a LEMS, various smart devices within a building are monitored and/or controlled to either investigate energy usage trends within a building, or to investigate mechanisms to reduce total energy demand. However, whenever we are connecting externally monitored/controlled smart devices there are security and privacy concerns. We describe the architecture and components of a LEMS and provide a survey of security and privacy concerns associated with data acquisition and control within a LEMS. Our scenarios specifically focus on the integration of Electric Vehicles (EV) and Energy Storage Units (ESU) at the building premises, to identify how EVs/ESUs can be used to store energy and reduce the electricity costs of the building. We review security strategies and identify potential security attacks that could be carried out on such a system, while exploring vulnerable points in the system. Additionally, we will systematically categorize each vulnerability and look at potential attacks exploiting that vulnerability for LEMS. Finally, we will evaluate current counter measures used against these attacks and suggest possible mitigation strategies.

Keywords: Internet of Things · Security and privacy · Smart grids

1 Introduction

Smart grids can be defined as a network of intelligent entities that are capable of bidirectional communication and can autonomously operate and interact with each other to deliver power to the end users. Over the years smart grids have been used to address the high energy consumption of commercial building or set of buildings. As it was reported by the United Nations Environment Program that residential and commercial buildings consume approximately 60% of the world's electricity. In addition to using 40% of global energy, 25% of global water, and 40% of global resources. Interestingly, because of the high energy consumption, buildings are also one of the major contributors to greenhouse gas production [22,38], but also offer the greatest potential for achieving significant greenhouse gas emission reductions,

© ICST Institute for Computer Sciences, Social Informatics and Telecommunications Engineering 2018
A. Longo et al. (Eds.): IISSC 2017/CN4IoT 2017, LNICST 189, pp. 228–242, 2018.
https://doi.org/10.1007/978-3-319-67636-4_24

with numbers projected to increase [34, 52]. For these reasons improving energy efficiency of buildings has received a lot of attention globally [53]. Smart grids based energy management systems have been used to reduce the energy demand of a building or set of buildings however, these systems have their own challenges. Such as they have central point of failure and scalability issues due to limited memory [3]. Researchers over the years have suggested a cloud based energy management system that is not only scalable, it does not have a single point of failure and because of its on demand allocation of resources, it uses only the energy required for the energy management system. Keeping these challenges in mind and to overcome them, a cloud based demand response system was proposed that introduced data centric communication and topic based communication models [20]. Their model was based on a master and slave architecture, in which the smart meters and energy management system at home acted as slave where as the utility acted as masters. The authors advocated that a reliable and scalable energy management system can be built using their model. Energy pricing is considered to be one of the relevant factor as the energy consumption cost is determined by it. Taking this into consideration, an energy management system was built by considering the energy pricing to be dynamic [23]. While building this model, the authors considered the peak demand of the building and incorporated the dynamic pricing while handling customer requests. While designing a cloud based energy management system [39] proposed an architecture for control, storage, power management and resource allocation of micro-grids and to integrate cloud based application for micro-grids with external one. The bigger and distributed the smart grid infrastructure becomes, the more difficult it is to analyse real time data from smart meters. Yang et al. [54] suggested that a cloud based system is most appropriate to handle the analysis of real-time energy data from smart meters. In another approach, power monitoring and early warning system facilities were provided using a cloud platform [17]. A mobile agent architecture for cloud based energy management system was proposed to handle customer request more efficiently [47]. Focusing on the energy demand a dynamic cloud based demand response model was proposed to periodically forecast demand and by dynamically managing available resources to reduce the peak demand [43]. The shift of micro-grid based energy management system to cloud based energy management system does overcome many challenges faced by conventional smart grid based energy management system. However, whenever we expose a model to the internet, security and privacy concerns are raised. In this paper we address these issues for the cloud based energy management system and particularly for the Internet of Things (IoT) devices that are integrated into it. The analysis is done by a live example of a cloud based Local Energy Management System (LEMS) and later extended to general cloud based energy management system. The LEMS is developed and deployed on cloud (i) to flatten the demand profile of the building facility and reduce its peak, based on analysis that can be carried out at the building or in its vicinity (rather than at a data center); (ii) to enable the participation of the building manager in the grid balancing services market through demand side management and response.

Contribution. In this paper we describe the architecture of a Cloud-based Energy Management System (LEMS), that is developed to reduce the energy demand of a commercial building or set of buildings in the United Kingdom. We will further give an overview of the LEMS operation, using which a building manager can reduce the energy cost using intelligent devices such as smart chargers, EVs/ESUs present at the building site. We then provide a systematic overview of the major cyber attacks against LEMS and the associated data capture devices involved. The main aims of this paper are:

- Give an architectural overview of LEMS and its operations.
- Identify cyber attacks LEMS.
- Provide an overview of counter measure/mitigation strategies for these attacks and identify any research gaps.

The structure of the paper is as follows: Sect. 2 discusses the LEMS architecture and give an overview of its operations. Section 3 gives an overview of attacks identified for cloud based energy management system and presents current counter measures. Section 4 concludes the paper.

2 Cloud Based Local Energy Management Systems

In order to give a systematic security overview of a cloud based energy management system we deployed a cloud based local energy system and used it as a case study to address the security concerns. The proposed energy management system can be divided into three parts: (a) the IoT devices that are present at the edge of the network, (b) the main LEMS algorithm deployed in the cloud, and (c) the GUI which is used to control the LEMS. The architecture of Local energy Management System (LEMS) is presented in Fig. 1. The main objective of LEMS is to manage the building demand by using various IoT devices at building premises by sending power set points through a Gateway to Electric Vehicle (EV) chargers and Energy Storage Units (ESUs).

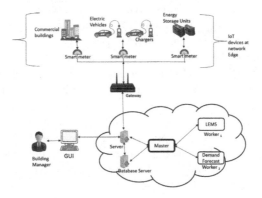

Fig. 1. Architecture of cloud based local energy management system

IoT Devices at the Network Edge: The cloud based energy management system and our LEMS, depend on smart devices such as: smart meters, chargers, electric vehicles, energy storage units, to gather information from the environment/buildings and to control the energy flow. Smart meters measure the energy consumption of the commercial building at a 15 min interval. The chargers are capable to charge but also discharge an electric vehicle, in order to efficiently manage the energy demand of the connected buildings. The electric vehicles and energy storage unites reserve energy, that can be supplied to the buildings whenever is needed to reduce the energy cost or demand.

The LEMS Algorithm and the GUI: The heart of the LEMS consists of a demand forecasting tool and a scheduling algorithm. The rationale to add a forecasting tool, was to be able to predict in advance what the building's energy demand, so that a schedule can be created to reduce this expected demand. The demand forecast tool estimates the electricity demand of the building for a particular time period. The demand forecasting tool made use of a neural network (from the Weka toolkit [32]) using historical data (collected from actual building use) and weather data within the proximity of the building. The LEMS scheduling algorithm operates in timesteps during which the system is considered static (changes are only discovered at the end of the timestep). A time step is defined as a time interval after which the LEMS read the data from each components such as building, EVs/ESUs, etc. For our case study we have kept the timestep duration to be 15 min. It was concluded that this timestep duration is an acceptable trade-off between a dynamic (semi-real time) and a reliable operation that allows the frequent capture of the building conditions and minimizes the risk of communication lags. Data about EVs located at the building, such as their battery capacity, state of charge (SoC), expected disconnection times, charging/discharging power rate, charging/discharging schedule and available discharge capacity, is requested from the EV charging stations upon the connection of every EV. Information regarding the available capacity, state of charge (SoC), charging/discharging power rate and charging/discharging schedule is requested from every ESU. This information is stored in a database, and is accessed from the LEMS on a regular basis (every 15 min) in order to define the future power set points for the chargers.

   The LEMS is deployed on the CometCloud [5] system. CometCloud enables federation between heterogeneous computing platforms that can support complete LEMS work, such as a local computational cluster with a public cloud (such as Amazon AWS). There are two main components in CometCloud: a *master* and (potentially multiple) the *worker* node(s). In its software architecture, CometCloud comprises mainly three layers: the programming layer, an automatic management layer and a federation or infrastructure layer. The programming layer defines the task that needs to be executed, the set of dependencies between tasks that enables a user to define the number of resources that are available along with any constraints on the usage of those resources. Each task in this instance is associated with the types of LEMS operation supported, or whether a demand forecast needs to be carried out. In the automatic management layer the policy and objectives are specified by the user that help in allocating the resource to carry out the task. In addition to allocation of resources, this layer also keeps a track of all task that are generated for workers are executed or not [6]. In the federation layer a look-up system is built so that content locality is maintained and a search can be carried out using wildcards [30]. Furthermore, a "CometSpace" is defined that can be accessed by all resources in the federation [26]. Essentially, CometCloud uses this physically distributed, but logically shared, tuple space to share tasks between different resources that are included in a resource federation. The main task of the master node is to prepare a task that is to be executed and give information about the data required to process the task. The second component is the worker, which receives request from the master, executes the job and sends the results to the place specified by the master. In our framework there are two workers – one that will be running the LEMS algorithm that will generate the schedule and the second that will forecast energy demand for the next day, to generate the charging and discharging of the electric vehicles.

There are two cloud-hosted servers that receive requests from a graphical user interface, and based on the requests call the appropriate function via the master. The second server manages a database which contains information about building data, EVs and weather attributes around the building. The database is used to store historic data about power consumption, energy pricing, and more, for each building. Information regarding the weather is also used to forecast (energy) the energy demand for the next day. There is an intermediary gateway, which intercepts all signals from the cloud server and forwards the requests to the EVs to either charge or discharge.

The energy management system is designed for various purposes such as to reduce demand, reduce energy cost etc. The LEMS that we had developed maximizes its utility to the building manager by adjusting its operational target (objective) according to the system status and condition. Furthermore, it was designed to create two scheduling algorithms for the management of the EVs and the ESUs, namely Peak Shaving Schedule and Demand Response Schedule respectively. Each algorithm serves one objective and the LEMS shifts from one scheduling strategy to another depending on the objective of the building manager. The peak shaving algorithm aims to flatten the aggregate demand profile of the building facility. This is achieved by filling the valleys and shaving the peaks of the demand profile using the controllable loads (EVs, ESUs) of the building facility. The LEMS calculates the charging/discharging schedules of the EVs and ESUs, and sends them the corresponding power set points at the beginning of every timestep. For the demand response algorithm a demand response signal is send by the building manager to either reduce or increase its aggregate demand in the next time step (of 15 min). Triggered by the arrival of such a request, the LEMS overrides the charging/discharging schedules of the available controllable assets.

3 Security Concerns of Cloud Based Energy Management System - LEMS as Case Study

Energy systems designed to manage the energy consumption of commercial buildings have certain security challenges to combat. These include the system availability at all times and ensuring that the power is not lost or stolen. As these systems are migrating regularly to the cloud, their complexity increases. Whilst designing such systems, it is important to employ various security mechanisms to defend them against cyber attacks. However, regardless of that, there will always be vulnerabilities ready to be exploited by cyber criminals.

Researchers in the past have suggested many strategies to protect these cloud based energy management systems. Emphasizing on the cloud security, a client-server based model was proposed by Wang et al. [50]. The main idea of this model is that all the data processing and important tasks would be performed on a secure cloud platform, and the client would only be responsible for collecting data. Simman et al. [44] looked at security risks and concerns for public, private and hybrid cloud platforms that can be used to deploy the energy management system. The authors concluded that private cloud is more suitable for deploying energy management system as they are less prone to malware and are easily containable. However hosting and maintaining a private cloud is more expensive than public cloud. Ugale et al. [48] focused on the security of the data stored on cloud by proposing a distributed verification protocol. Maheshwari et al. [28] proposed that by using public key infrastructure one can mitigate issues relating to fault tolerance and can detect any intrusion in the system. While most research has been on the security of the cloud, Wen et al. [51] focused on the security of the smart grids that are integral part of the energy management system. The authors proposed that by encrypting smart meter data on the cloud, its privacy is being preserved, as only authorised people can access it. Although the research that has already been conducted to secure cloud and data stored is important, it is also significant to investigate the security of other components that are integral parts of the energy management system. The security concerns that are addressed are looking at the kind of attacks that are used to bring down a cloud based energy management system.

The term Internet of Things (IoT) is used to describe a structure of interconnected devices, which provides automation and various other functionalities [1]. A cloud based energy management system and our LEMS depends on various smart objects such as: smart meters, chargers, electric vehicles, etc., to gather information from the environment/buildings and to control the energy flow. Although these devices provide great opportunities in the concept of Smart Grids, they come with tremendous security risks [18,46,58].

The architectural structure of IoT can be divided into three key layers [10]. The Perception Layer, Network Layer, and Middle-ware layer. The Perception Layer consists of different kinds of data sensors such as RFID. The Network Layer refers to the data transmission process, where information gathered from the perception layer gets transferred to an information processing system via communication networks, such as: the Internet, Mobile Network, etc. [57]. Finally the Middle-ware layer consists of information processing systems such as cloud storage infrastructures. Each one of these layers presents its own security issues to combat.

While evaluating the architecture of a cloud based energy management system for vulnerabilities, we have identified a number of cyber attacks that can bring down the system. We will focus on discussing in detail the attacks targeting the Network Layer of the IoT system associated with the LEMS. Finally, we will present the current counter measures against these attacks and also suggest the most suitable strategies to defend our energy management system.

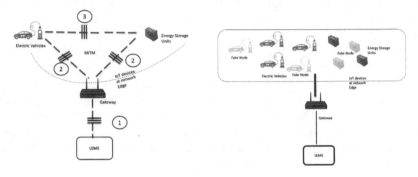

(a) An attacker can eavesdrop on on the communication channels between 1) the gateway and the LEMS, 2) the gateway and the IoT system, and 3) among the IoT devices.

(b) An attacker forges a number of identities to act as legal nodes (impersonate EV/ESUs) on the system, so that its energy consumption levels will be increased.

Fig. 2. Data leakage and spoofing attacks

Data Leakage: As one of the key features of a smart grid based energy management system is bidirectional communication, an attacker could eavesdrop on information from the communication channels between: (a) the gateway and LEMS, (b) the gateway and the IoT system, and (c) among the IoT devices (i.e. between the smart charger and the electric vehicle) [10] as per Fig. 2a. If the Secure Sockets Layer (SSL)/Transport Layer Security (TLS) protocol [7,12] is not employed and therefore the data that gets transmitted is not encrypted, an unauthorized party could simply intercept it by performing passive network sniffing on the operating channel [2,19]. If the SSL/TLS protocol is employed, and therefore the transmitted data is encrypted, an eavesdropping attacker can observe it to identify traffic patterns and hence gain information about the functionality of the system. For example, the smart energy storage units that are used in the LEMS send information to the gateway about their energy status every 15 min. The adversary could use this information to identify when and how the energy management system is going to adjust the energy requirements of the buildings and therefore could alter the scheduling algorithm sent to the energy storage units. Once the scheduling algorithm is altered, the cyber criminal can create a situation where the ESU's and EV's are charging at peak hours resulting in increasing the energy demand at these hours. This will increase the energy demand and cost for the company and defeat the purpose of deploying an energy management system.

Additionally, an attacker can perform a Man-In-The-Middle (MITM) attack. With this attack the original connection between the two parties gets split into two new ones: one connection between the first party/device and the attacker and another one between the attacker and the second party/device. When the original connection is finally compromised, the attacker is able to act as a proxy and therefore read, insert, and modify data in the intercepted communication [33]. In cases where the attacker has managed to compromise the communication channels, using any of the above discussed methods, they could gain access to important information such as: IDs from the electrical vehicles, electrical signals/pulse from the batteries, meter readings etc. This could significantly impact the energy management functionality of the LEMS and the energy cost. For instance, if an unauthorised party interfered (spoofed, manipulated, inserted, or deleted) with the unique IDs of the batteries of the electrical vehicles, then the LEMS would receive false information from the gateway and it would not be able to adjust correctly the building's energy demand.

To defend the energy management system, the SSL/TLS protocols should always be used to establish a secure channel for communication among all the parties/devices in the LEMS. Nevertheless, this protocol is not enough to prevent MITM attacks. Consequently, techniques such as certificate pinning [16], should also be employed to authenticate the devices on the grid. This ensures that each device checks the servers certificate against a known copy stored in its firmware [11]. However, although this is an efficient way of preventing MITM attacks it is not completely immune, as an adversary could disable the certificate pinning procedure, and manage to intercept the communication [31]. As an alternative to SSL/TLS, managed certificate whitelisting was recently proposed [9] to authenticate devices, specifically in energy automation systems. Even though this approach appears to be promising, its security aspects haven't been fully explored. Finally, to protect against traffic analysis, [27] proposes a re-encryption algorithm that can be used to randomise the transmitted cipher text, without affecting the decryption process. This prevents the attacker from linking in and out data by comparing the transmitted packets.

Spoofing: Sybil attack is a type of spoofing attack in which IoT devices on the LEMS are particularly vulnerable [56]. During such attacks, attackers can manipulate fake identities to compromise the effectiveness of the IoT as per Fig. 2b. For instance, in the energy management system, such an attack could forge a massive number of identities to act as legal nodes and request more energy from the LEMS. This could severely affect the energy cost and latency of the system.

Various methods to detect and defend against Sybil attacks have already been implemented and can be employed on the LEMS. For instance, SVELTE, is a novel Intrusion Detection System designed specifically for IoT devices, which is inherently protected against Sybil attacks [41]. Alternatively, Zhang et al. [56]

discuss some cryptography-based schemes MSD (crypto-MSD), that can also defend against these attacks. Finally, the use of a unique shared symmetric key for each node on the system with the base station/gateway is another way to defend against it [42,49,59].

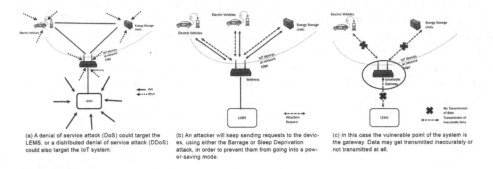

(a) A denial of service attack (DoS) could target the LEMS, or a distributed denial of service attack (DDoS) could also target the IoT system.

(b) An attacker will keep sending requests to the devices, using either the Barrage or Sleep Deprivation attack, in order to prevent them from going into a power-saving mode.

(c) In this case the vulnerable point of the system is the gateway. Data may get transmitted inaccurately or not transmitted at all.

Fig. 3. DDoS, energy bleeding, and gateway attacks

Disruption of Service (DoS/DDoS): are the most common kind of attacks that can occur in a network and can severely impact the internet of things [46]. These reduce, interrupt, or completely eliminate the network's communications, and range from jamming to more sophisticated attacks [35]. In any network and specifically in an energy management system, *device availability* is crucial. As DoS attacks target to destroy the availability of communication among them, they can have serious reverberations on the system [46]. DoS attacks can be initialised remotely and they are very hard to detect before the network/service becomes unavailable. This is why they are considered to be one of the most serious networking threats [19,46]. DoS attacks can also evolve to distributed DoS (DDoS) attacks and in this case the attacker could take down the LEMS, as per Fig. 3.

Given the way our management energy system is designed, we can have two scenarios of DoS/DDoS attacks. A DoS attack could target the LEMS system and a DDoS attack could also target the IoT devices on the grid. In the first case, the communication between the LEMS and the IoT would be lost and there would be no way to control the energy flow on the energy management system. The second scenario is more severe and therefore we will describe it in more depth.

Consider that an attacker identifies an exploitable vulnerability in the smart energy storage units used in the energy management system, which would allow them to charge and discharge them whenever they want. They can then create an exploit that will help them locate and take control of all these vulnerable devices on the LEMS (bot herder) [8]. At this point the adversary would be able to constantly discharge the batteries, resulting in wasting huge amounts of energy and a possible blackout of the system. As our energy management system is connected to the National Grid, the hacker could potentially take control of it too. As a result, this would lead to serious financial losses and not only. A recent study by Dlamini et al. [8] showed that this scenario could also result in loss of lives.

Although various mechanisms against DoS attacks have been proposed, none of them can provide full protection against them all. Raymond et al. [40], discusses currently used protection methods against DoS in Wireless Sensor Networks. Moreover, Garcia et al. [13,14] present various DoS countermeasures such as: DTLS, IKEv2, HIP, and Diet HIP, for IP-based Internet of Things. Finally [19] proposes a DoS detection architecture for 6LoWPAN network with great potential. It is necessary to underline that due to the severity of DoS attacks, there is a need to research better preventive measures and defensive mechanisms [29].

Energy Bleeding: In sensor networks like the cloud based energy management system, the ability of the devices to enter power-saving modes (e.g. various sleep and hibernation modes) is important to preserve the network's longevity, the lifetime of these devices, and reduce the overall power consumption [15,36,37]. In this section two major attacks that target this functionality of the devices will be discussed: sleep deprivation and barrage attack. Specifically, an attacker can use them to forbid these devices from going into power-saving mode by continually sending traffic to them and hence exhausting their battery resources [21], as per Fig. 3b. These are also known as *sleep deprivation torture attacks* [45]. Both of them, if used against the LEMS, could cause severe energy and therefore financial losses.

During the barrage attack the targeted device is being bombarded with requests that seem to be legitimate. The goal is to waste the device's limited power supply by preventing it from going into sleep mode and making it perform complex energy demanding operations. In sleep deprivation attack, malicious nodes on the network, send requests to the victim device only as often as necessary to keep it switched on. Although the goal of this attack is the same as the barrage attack, the sleep deprivation attack does not make the target nodes perform energy intense operations [36]. Barrage attack has been proven to exhaust faster the battery resources of the targeted nodes [36], but at the same time it is very easy to detect as opposed to sleep deprivation attack. For this reason we consider sleep deprivation to be more a more serious threat [21].

Pirreti et al. [36] showed that sleep deprivation attack can impact severely networks like the LEMS. They demonstrated that if an attacker manages to compromise as few as 20 devices on a 400 node network, they will be able to double its power consumption. Additionally, they showed that a single malicious node can attack approximately 150 devices at the same time. Therefore this attack can significantly affect the energy consumption levels of the system. To protect the energy management system from sleep deprivation attack, we can use any of the currently implemented mechanisms. For instance, Pirretti et al. [36], extensively compares and evaluates three different defence schemes against sleep deprivation attack that can be applied in sensor networks. These include the random vote scheme, the round robin scheme, and the hash-based scheme.

Finally, another recent study [4] proposes a framework based on distributed collaborative mechanism, that efficiently detects sleep deprivation torture.

Insecure Gateways: One of the most basic components of our energy management system is the gateway, which is responsible for transmitting information from the IoT devices to the LEMS and vice versa. As the LEMS adjusts the energy flow on the system according to the information it receives from the gateway, we need to examine its reliability by exploring possible issues associated with it and current solutions. The gateway can be considered to be untrustworthy if it does not transmit any data to the LEMS/IoT, or if it transmits it inaccurately [25], as per Fig. 3. Reasons why a gateway could be faulty consist of complications to wireless media, software issues and hardware defects. This could lead to increase in communication delays, waste of bandwidth, increased power consumption, data loss, and communication failures on the system [25,55]. Various network attacks such as the ones described in data leakage and distributed denial of service section can also be responsible for making the gateway unreliable. Consequences of an unreliable gateway on the LEMS include mainly inefficient management of the energy, financial losses, and data loss.

As the gateway plays such an important role in the energy management system, we need to employ measures that will help us detect as quickly as possible issues associated with it. An inexpensive and promising way to identify such problems is by using the side channel monitoring technique (SCM) [24]. SCM uses existing nodes as observers to monitor the gateway's packet transmission behavior. If any abnormalities are noticed, they will be reported back to LEMS. Although this technique is efficient, it can be easily detected by attackers and the reports could also be manipulated or intercepted. Therefore, as the detection of issues regarding the gateway is not guaranteed, multipath routing could also be employed to increase the probability of the data being delivered from the Gateway to LEMS and to the IoT [25]. Finally, in case that multiple unreliable gateways appear on the LEMS and the multipath routing also fails, to extend its functionality, the whole system could switch from using Wi-Fi to using the relatively reliable 3G network for data communication [25]. However, the cost of this solution is significantly high.

4   Conclusion

With the advancement of technology a gradual shift of energy management systems to the cloud has been seen, to overcome computational challenges faced by conventional energy management system. However, as we expose each component to the internet, to move to the cloud, the complexity and security of the system increases. In this paper we have given an overview of a cloud based energy management system by using a live example of a cloud based local energy management system (LEMS).

The aim of LEMS is to reduce the aggregated energy demand of a commercial building by using a set of electric vehicles and energy storage units available at building sites. Furthermore, we have addressed security concerns for

Table 1.

LEMS vulnerabilities		
Risks	Attacks	Target
Data leakage	Data sniffing and MITM	Transmitted data
Spoofing	Sybil attack	System blackout
Disruption of service	DoS/DDoS	System availability
Energy bleeding	Barrage and sleep deprivation	System's energy resources
Hardware issues	Faulty gateways	Transmitted data

the algorithm in the cloud as well as for the attached IoT devices. Each concern
is explored by creating an attack scenario to identify vulnerabilities and best
countermeasures for each attack is presented for that scenario.

In a cloud based energy management system, five major risks were identified
and included: Data Leakage, Spoofing, Disruption of Service, Energy Bleeding,
and Hardware issues, as per Table 1. For each one of this risks, we described
in detail the attacks associated with it and current defence mechanisms. We
concluded that, although various measures to defend against these attacks have
been proposed, none can fully guarantee the protection of the system. However,
we hope this paper will act as a guideline to build a robust and lightweight
security architecture to secure it.

Acknowledgment. This work was carried out in the InnovateUK/EPSRC-funded
"Ebbs and Flows of Energy Systems" (EFES) project.

References

1. Ashton, K.: That 'internet of things' thing. RFiD J. **22**(7), 97–114 (2009)
2. Barcena, M.B., Wueest, C.: Insecurity in the internet of things. In: Security
   Response, Symantec (2015)
3. Bera, S., Misra, S., Rodrigues, J.J.: Cloud computing applications for smart grid:
   a survey. IEEE Trans. Parallel Distrib. Syst. **26**(5), 1477–1494 (2015)
4. Bhattasali, T., Chaki, R., Sanyal, S.: Sleep deprivation attack detection in wireless
   sensor network. arXiv preprint arXiv:1203.0231 (2012)
5. Diaz-Montes, J., AbdelBaky, M., Zou, M., Parashar, M.: CometCloud: enabling
   software-defined federations for end-to-end application workflows. IEEE Internet
   Comput. **19**(1), 69–73 (2015)
6. Diaz-Montes, J., Xie, Y., Rodero, I., Zola, J., Ganapathysubramanian, B.,
   Parashar, M.: Exploring the use of elastic resource federations for enabling large-
   scale scientific workflows. In: Proceedings of Workshop on Many-Task Computing
   on Clouds, Grids, and Supercomputers (MTAGS), pp. 1–10 (2013)
7. Dierks, T.: The transport layer security (TLS) protocol version 1.2 (2008)
8. Dlamini, M., Eloff, M., Eloff, J.: Internet of things: emerging and future scenarios
   from an information security perspective. In: Southern Africa Telecommunication
   Networks and Applications Conference (2009)

9. Falk, R., Fries, S.: Managed certificate whitelisting-a basis for internet of things security in industrial automation applications. In: SECURWARE 2014, p. 178 (2014)

10. Farooq, M., Waseem, M., Khairi, A., Mazhar, S.: A critical analysis on the security concerns of internet of things (IoT). Int. J. Comput. Appl. **111**(7), 1–6 (2015)

11. Fossati, T., Tschofenig, H.: Transport layer security (TLS)/datagram transport layer security (DTLS) profiles for the internet of things. Transport (2016)

12. Frier, A., Karlton, P., Kocher, P.: The ssl 3.0 protocol, vol. 18, p.2780. Netscape Communications Corporation (1996)

13. Garcia-Morchon, O., Kumar, S., Struik, R., Keoh, S., Hummen, R.: Security considerations in the IP-based internet of things (2013)

14. Heer, T., Garcia-Morchon, O., Hummen, R., Keoh, S.L., Kumar, S.S., Wehrle, K.: Security challenges in the IP-based internet of things. Wirel. Personal Commun. **61**(3), 527–542 (2011)

15. Hummen, R., Wirtz, H., Ziegeldorf, J.H., Hiller, J., Wehrle, K.: Tailoring end-to-end IP security protocols to the internet of things. In: 21st IEEE International Conference on Network Protocols (ICNP), pp. 1–10. IEEE (2013)

16. Jha, A., Sunil, M.: Security considerations for internet of things. L&T Technology Services (2014)

17. Ji, L., Lifang, W., Li, Y.: Cloud service based intelligent power monitoring and early-warning system. In: Innovative Smart Grid Technologies-Asia (ISGT Asia), pp. 1–4. IEEE (2012)

18. Jing, Q., Vasilakos, A.V., Wan, J., Lu, J., Qiu, D.: Security of the internet of things: perspectives and challenges. Wirel. Netw. **20**(8), 2481–2501 (2014)

19. Kasinathan, P., Pastrone, C., Spirito, M.A., Vinkovits, M.: Denial-of-service detection in 6LoWPAN based internet of things. In: IEEE 9th International Conference on Wireless and Mobile Computing, Networking and Communications (WiMob), pp. 600–607. IEEE (2013)

20. Kim, H., Kim, Y.-J., Yang, K., Thottan, M.: Cloud-based demand response for smart grid: architecture and distributed algorithms. In: IEEE International Conference on Smart Grid Communications (SmartGridComm), pp. 398–403. IEEE (2011)

21. Krishnaswami, J.: Denial-of-service attacks on battery-powered mobile computers. Ph.D. thesis, Virginia Polytechnic Institute and State University (2004)

22. Laustsen, J.: Energy efficiency requirements in building codes, energy efficiency policies for new buildings. Int. Energy Agency (IEA) **2**, 477–488 (2008)

23. Li, X., Lo, J.-C.: Pricing and peak aware scheduling algorithm for cloud computing. In: Innovative Smart Grid Technologies (ISGT), IEEE PES, pp. 1–7. IEEE (2012)

24. Li, X., Lu, R., Liang, X., Shen, X.: Side channel monitoring: packet drop attack detection in wireless ad hoc networks. In: IEEE International Conference on Communications (ICC), pp. 1–5. IEEE (2011)

25. Li, X., Lu, R., Liang, X., Shen, X., Chen, J., Lin, X.: Smart community: an internet of things application. IEEE Commun. Mag. **49**(11) (2011)

26. Li, Z., Parashar, M.: A computational infrastructure for grid-based asynchronous parallel applications. In: Proceedings of the 16th International Symposium on High Performance Distributed Computing, pp. 229–230. ACM (2007)

27. Lin, X., Lu, R., Shen, X., Nemoto, Y., Kato, N.: SAGE: a strong privacy-preserving scheme against global eavesdropping for eHealth systems. IEEE J. Sel. Areas Commun. **27**(4), 365–378 (2009)

28. Maheshwari, K., Lim, M., Wang, L., Birman, K., van Renesse, R.: Toward a reliable, secure and fault tolerant smart grid state estimation in the cloud. In: Innovative Smart Grid Technologies (ISGT), IEEE PES, pp. 1–6. IEEE (2013)

29. Mayer, C.P.: Security and privacy challenges in the internet of things. Electron. Commun. EASST **17**, 1–12 (2009)

30. Montes, J.D., Zou, M., Singh, R., Tao, S., Parashar, M.: Data-driven workflows in multi-cloud marketplaces. In: IEEE 7th International Conference on Cloud Computing, pp. 168–175. IEEE (2014)

31. Moonsamy, V., Batten, L.: Mitigating man-in-the-middle attacks on smartphones-a discussion of SSL pinning and DNSSec. In: Proceedings of the 12th Australian Information Security Management Conference, pp. 5–13. Edith Cowan University (2014)

32. University of Waikato: Weka 3 - data mining with open source machine learning software in Java (2017). http://www.cs.waikato.ac.nz/ml/weka/. Accessed 13 Jan 2017

33. OWASP: Man-in-the-middle attack (2016). https://www.owasp.org/index.php/Man-in-the-middle_attack/. Accessed 18 Apr 2016

34. Pérez-Lombard, L., Ortiz, J., Pout, C.: A review on buildings energy consumption information. Energy Build. **40**(3), 394–398 (2008)

35. Perrig, A., Stankovic, J., Wagner, D.: Security in wireless sensor networks. Commun. ACM **47**(6), 53–57 (2004)

36. Pirretti, M., Zhu, S., Vijaykrishnan, N., McDaniel, P., Kandemir, M., Brooks, R.: The sleep deprivation attack in sensor networks: analysis and methods of defense. Int. J. Distrib. Sens. Netw. **2**(3), 267–287 (2006)

37. Poslad, S., Hamdi, M., Abie, H.: Adaptive security and privacy management for the internet of things (ASPI 2013). In: Proceedings of the 2013 ACM Conference on Pervasive and Ubiquitous Computing Adjunct Publication, pp. 373–378. ACM (2013)

38. United Nations Environment Programme: Why buildings (2016). http://www.unep.org/sbci/AboutSBCI/Background.asp. Accessed 11 Jan 2017

39. Rajeev, T., Ashok, S.: A cloud computing approach for power management of microgrids. In: Innovative Smart Grid Technologies-India (ISGT India), IEEE PES, pp. 49–52. IEEE (2011)

40. Raymond, D.R., Midkiff, S.F.: Denial-of-service in wireless sensor networks: attacks and defenses. IEEE Pervasive Comput. **7**(1), 74–81 (2008)

41. Raza, S., Wallgren, L., Voigt, T.: SVELTE: real-time intrusion detection in the internet of things. Ad Hoc Netw. **11**(8), 2661–2674 (2013)

42. Saxena, M.: Security in wireless sensor networks-a layer based classification. Department of Computer Science, Purdue University (2007)

43. Simmhan, Y., Aman, S., Kumbhare, A., Liu, R., Stevens, S., Zhou, Q., Prasanna, V.: Cloud-based software platform for big data analytics in smart grids. Comput. Sci. Eng. **15**(4), 38–47 (2013)

44. Simmhan, Y., Kumbhare, A.G., Cao, B., Prasanna, V.: An analysis of security and privacy issues in smart grid software architectures on clouds. In: IEEE International Conference on Cloud Computing (CLOUD), pp. 582–589. IEEE (2011)

45. Stajano, F., Anderson, R.: The resurrecting duckling: security issues for ubiquitous computing. Computer **35**(4), supl22–supl26 (2002)

46. Suo, H., Wan, J., Zou, C., Liu, J.: Security in the internet of things: a review. In: International Conference on Computer Science and Electronics Engineering (ICCSEE), vol. 3, pp. 648–651. IEEE (2012)

47. Tang, L., Li, J., Wu, R.: Synergistic model of power system cloud computing based on mobile-agent. In: 3rd IEEE International Conference on Network Infrastructure and Digital Content (IC-NIDC), pp. 222–226. IEEE (2012)

48. Ugale, B.A., Soni, P., Pema, T., Patil, A.: Role of cloud computing for smart grid of India and its cyber security. In: Nirma University International Conference on Engineering (NUiCONE), pp. 1–5. IEEE (2011)

49. Wang, Y., Attebury, G., Ramamurthy, B.: A survey of security issues in wireless sensor networks (2006)

50. Wang, Y., Deng, S., Lin, W.-M., Zhang, T., Yu, Y.: Research of electric power information security protection on cloud security. In: International Conference on Power System Technology (POWERCON), pp. 1–6. IEEE (2010)

51. Wen, M., Lu, R., Zhang, K., Lei, J., Liang, X., Shen, X.: PaRQ: a privacy-preserving range query scheme over encrypted metering data for smart grid. IEEE Trans. Emerg. Top. Comput. 1(1), 178–191 (2013)

52. Weng, T., Agarwal, Y.: From buildings to smart buildings—sensing and actuation to improve energy efficiency. IEEE Des. Test 29(4), 36–44 (2012)

53. Wijayasekara, D., Linda, O., Manic, M., Rieger, C.: Mining building energy management system data using fuzzy anomaly detection and linguistic descriptions. IEEE Trans. Ind. Inform. 10(3), 1829–1840 (2014)

54. Yang, C.-T., Chen, W.-S., Huang, K.-L., Liu, J.-C., Hsu, W.-H., Hsu, C.-H.: Implementation of smart power management and service system on cloud computing. In: 9th International Conference on Ubiquitous Intelligence & Computing and 9th International Conference on Autonomic & Trusted Computing (UIC/ATC), pp. 924–929. IEEE (2012)

55. Zanella, A., Bui, N., Castellani, A., Vangelista, L., Zorzi, M.: Internet of things for smart cities. IEEE Internet Things J. 1(1), 22–32 (2014)

56. Zhang, K., Liang, X., Lu, R., Shen, X.: Sybil attacks and their defenses in the internet of things. IEEE Internet Things J. 1(5), 372–383 (2014)

57. Zhang, Y.: Technology framework of the internet of things and its application. In: International Conference on Electrical and Control Engineering (ICECE), pp. 4109–4112. IEEE (2011)

58. Zhao, K., Ge, L.: A survey on the internet of things security. In: 9th International Conference on Computational Intelligence and Security (CIS), pp. 663–667. IEEE (2013)

59. Zia, T., Zomaya, A.: Security issues in wireless sensor networks. In: International Conference on Systems and Networks Communications (ICSNC 2006), p. 40. IEEE (2006)

IoT and Big Data: An Architecture with Data Flow and Security Issues

Deepak Puthal[1(✉)], Rajiv Ranjan[2], Surya Nepal[3], and Jinjun Chen[4]

[1] School of Computing and Communications, University of Technology Sydney,
Ultimo, Australia
deepak.puthal@gmail.com
[2] School of Computing Science, Newcastle University, Newcastle upon Tyne, UK
rranjans@gmail.com
[3] CSIRO Data61, Canberra, Australia
Surya.Nepal@data61.csiro.au
[4] Swinburne Data Science Research Institute, Swinburne University of Technology,
Melbourne, Australia
jinjun.chen@gmail.com

Abstract. The Internet of Things (IoT) introduces a future vision where users, computer, computing devices and daily objects possessing sensing and actuating capabilities cooperate with unprecedented convenience and benefits. We are moving towards IoT trend, where the number of smart sensing devices deployed around the world is growing at a rapid speed. With considering the number of sources and types of data from smart sources, the sensed data tends to new trend of research i.e. big data. Security will be a fundamental enabling factor of most IoT applications and big data, mechanisms must also be designed to protect communications enabled by such technologies. This paper analyses existing protocols and mechanisms to secure the IoT and big data, as well as security threats in the domain. We have broadly divided the IoT architecture into several layers to define properties, security issues and related works to solve the security concerns.

Keywords: Internet of Things · Big data · Security · Security threats · Quality of Service

1 Introduction

IoT is a widely-used expression but still a fuzzy one, due to the large number of concepts brought together to a concept. The IoT appears a vision of a future source of data where sensing device, possessing computing and sensorial capabilities can communicate with other devices using Internet protocol. Such applications are expected to bring a large total of sensing and actuating devices, and in significance these costs will be a major factor. On the other hand, cost restrictions dictate constraints in terms of the resources available in sensing platforms, such as memory and computational power. Overall, such factors motivate the design and adoption of communications and security mechanisms

© ICST Institute for Computer Sciences, Social Informatics and Telecommunications Engineering 2018
A. Longo et al. (Eds.): IISSC 2017/CN4IoT 2017, LNICST 189, pp. 243–252, 2018.
https://doi.org/10.1007/978-3-319-67636-4_25

optimized for constrained sensing platforms, capable of providing its functionalities efficiently and reliably.

Several of these applications are approaching the bottleneck of current data streaming infrastructures and require real-time processing of very high-volume and high-velocity data streams (also known as big data streams). The complexity of big data is defined through 5Vs: (1) volume– referring to terabytes, petabytes, or even exabytes (1000^6 bytes) of stored data, (2) variety– referring to unstructured, semi-structured and structured data from different sources like sensors, surveillance, image or video, medical records etc., (3) velocity– referring to the high speed at which the data is handled in/out for stream processing, (4) variability– referring to the different characteristics and data value where the data stream is handled, (5) veracity– referring to the quality of data. These features introduce huge open doors and enormous difficulties for big data stream computing. A big data stream is continuous in nature and it is important to perform real-time analysis as the lifetime of the data is often very short (data is accessed only once) [1, 2, 6, 7]. As the volume and velocity of the data is so high, there is not enough space to store and process; hence, the traditional batch computing model is not suitable.

Even though big data stream processing has become an important research topic in the current era, data stream security has received little attention from researchers [1, 2]. Some of these data streams are analysed and used in very critical applications (e.g. surveillance data, military applications, etc.), where data streams need to be secured to detect malicious activities. The problem is exacerbated when thousands to millions of small sensors in self-organising wireless networks become the sources of the data stream. How can we provide the security for big data streams? In addition, compared to conventional store-and-process, these sensors will have limited processing power, storage, bandwidth, and energy.

Big data in IoT environment is gaining lots of interest from global researcher. By focusing current research trend, we have given the data flow between the layers including research issues in IoT generated big data architecture. The main contributions of the paper can be summarized as follows:

- We have proposed IoT generated big data architecture while defining layer wise properties of IoT.
- Followed by, we have highlighted the security threats, issues and solutions of individual IoT layers.
- Finally, we have highlighted the security issues of big data in IoT.

The rest of this paper is organized as follows. Section 2 gives the background IoT layers and their features. Section 3 describes security threats of individual layers in IoT architecture. Section 4 presents the security issues and requirements in IoT generated big data streams. Section 5 concludes the paper.

2 IoT Architecture

The connection of physical things to the Internet makes it possible to access remote sensor data and to control the physical world from a distance. The IoT is based on this vision. A smart object, which is the building block of the IoT, is just another name for an embedded system that is connected to the Internet [9]. Al-Fuqaha et al. in [10] clearly defined the individual elements of IoT, which includes identification, sensing, communication, computation, services, and semantics. There is another technology that points in the same direction as RFID technology. The novelty of the IoT is not in any new disruptive technology, but in the pervasive deployment of smart objects. IoT system architecture must guarantee the operations of IoT, which bridges the gap between the physical and the virtual worlds. Since things may move geographically and need to interact with others in real-time mode, IoT architecture should be adaptive to make devices interact with other things dynamically and support unambiguous communication of events [11]. We broadly divided the complete architecture of IoT into three different layers, such as source smart sensing device, communication (Networks) layer and cloud data centre as shown in Fig. 1. These layers can be related to the service layer of IoT, where service layer and interface layer are integrated into the data centre in our architecture. The service level architecture of IoT consists of four different layers with functionality such as sensing layer, network layer, service layer, and interfaces layer [11, 12].

- Sensing layer: This layer is integrated with available hardware objects (sensors, RFID, etc.) to sense/control statuses of things.
- Network layer: This layer supports the infrastructure for networking over wireless or wired connections.
- Service layer: This layer creates and manages services requirements according to the user's need.
- Interfaces layer: This layer provides interaction methods to users and applications.

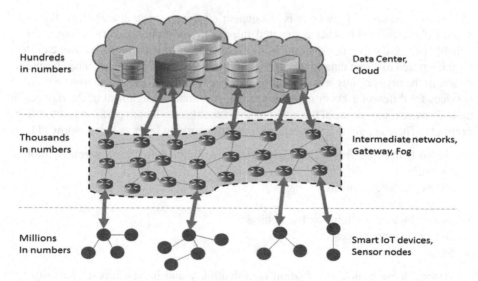

Fig. 1. Layer wise IoT architecture from IoT device to cloud data centre.

2.1 Sensing Layer

IoT is expected to be a world-wide physical inner-connected network, in which things are connected seamlessly and can be controlled remotely. In this layer, more and more devices are equipped with RFID or intelligent sensors, connecting things becomes much easier [13]. Individual objects in IoT hold a digital identity which helps to track easily in the domain. The technique of assigning a unique identity to an object is called a universal unique identifier (UUID). UUID is critical to successful services deployment in a huge network like IoT. The identifiers might refer to names and addresses. There are a few aspects that need to be considered in the sensing layer such as deployment (devices need to deployed randomly or incrementally), heterogeneity (devices have different properties), communication (needs to communicate with each other in order to get access), network (devices maintain different topology for data transmission process), cost, size, resources and energy consumption. As the use of IoT increases day by day, many hardware and software components are involved in it. IoT should have these two important properties: energy efficiency and protocols [11].

- *Energy efficiency:* Sensors should be active all the time to acquire real-time data. This brings the challenge to supply power to sensors; high energy efficiency allows sensors to work for a longer period.
- *Protocols:* Different things existing in IoT provide multiple functions of systems. IoT must support the coexistence of different communications such as ZigBee, 6LoWPAN etc.

2.2 Networking Layer

The role of the networking layer is to connect all things together and allow things to share information with other connected things. In addition, the networking layer is capable of aggregating information from existing IT infrastructures [4], data can then be transmitted to cloud data centre for the high-level complex services. The communication in the network might involve the Quality of Service (QoS) to guarantee reliable services for different users or applications [5]. Automatic assignment of the devices in an IoT environment is one of the major tasks, it enables devices to perform tasks collaboratively. There are some issues related to the networking layer as listed below [11]:

- Network management technologies including managing fixed, wireless, mobile networks
- Network energy efficiency
- Requirements of QoS
- Technologies for mining and searching
- Data and signal processing
- Security and privacy

Among these issues, information confidentiality and human privacy security are critical because of the IoT device deployment, mobility, and complexity. For information confidentiality, the existing encryption technology used in WSNs can be extended and deployed in IoT. Granjal et al. [3] divided the communication layer for IoT applications into five different parts: Physical layer, MAC layer, Adaptation layer, network/routing layer, application layers. They also mentioned the associated protocols for energy efficiency as shown in Fig. 2.

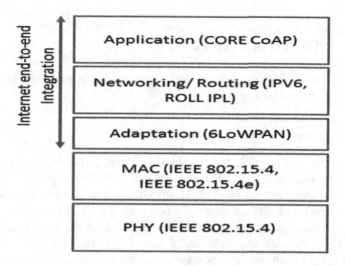

Fig. 2. Communication protocol in IoT.

2.3 Service Layer

A main activity in the service layer involves the service specifications for middleware, which are being developed by various organisations. A well-designed service layer will be able to identify common application requirements.

The service layer relies on the middleware technology, which provides functionalities to integrate services and applications in IoT. The middleware technology provides a cost-effective platform, where the hardware and software platforms can be reused. The services in the service layer run directly on the network to effectively locate new services for an application and retrieve metadata dynamically about services. Most of specifications are undertaken by various standards developed by different organisations. However, a universally accepted service layer is important for IoT. A practical service layer consists of a minimum set of the common requirements of applications, application programming interfaces (APIs), and protocols supporting required applications and services.

2.4 Interface Layer

In IoT, a large number of devices are involved; those devices can be provided by different vendors and hence do not always comply with same standards. The compatibility issue among the heterogeneous things must be addressed for the interactions among things. Compatibility involves information exchanging, communication, and events processing. There is a strong need for an effective interface mechanism to simplify the management and interconnection of things. An interface profile (IFP) is a subset of service standards that allows a minimal interaction with the applications running on application layers. The interface profiles are used to describe the specifications between applications and services.

3   Security Threats of Each Layer

This subsection lists the security threats and security issues is each individual layer as divided in the above subsections.

3.1   Sensing Layer

The sensing layer is responsible for frequency selection, carrier frequency generation, signal detection, modulation, and data encryption [3, 14]. An adversary may possess a broad range of attack capabilities. A physically damaged or manipulated node used for attack may be less powerful than a normally functioning node. IoT devices use wireless communication because the network's ad hoc, large-scale deployment makes anything else impractical. As with any radio-based medium, there exists the possibility of jamming in IoT. In addition, devices may be deployed in hostile or insecure environments where an attacker has easy physical access. Network jamming and source device tampering are the major types of possible attack in the sensing layer. The features of sensing layers follow from Fig. 2.

Jamming: Interference with the radio frequencies nodes are using and

Tampering: Physical compromise of nodes.

3.2   Network Layer

The security mechanisms designed to protect communications with the previously discussed protocols must provide appropriate assurances in terms of *confidentiality,* *integrity, authentication* and *non-repudiation* of the information flows. Other relevant security requirements are *privacy, anonymity, liability* and *trust,* which will be fundamental for the social acceptance of most of the future IoT applications employing Internet integrated sensing devices. According to the communication protocol in IoT, we divided in five different layer as shown in Fig. 2.

MAC Layer. The MAC layer manages, besides the data service, other operations, namely accesses to the physical channel, validation of frames, guaranteed time slots, node association and security. The standard distinguishes sensing devices by its capabilities and roles in the network. A full-function device (FFD) can coordinate a network of devices, while a reduced-function device (RFD) is only able to communicate with other devices (of RFD or FFD types). By using RFD and FFD, IEEE 802.15.4 support topologies such as peer-to-peer, star and cluster networks [15].

Network Layer. One fundamental characteristic of the Internet architecture is that it enables packets to traverse interconnected networks using heterogeneous link-layer technologies, and the mechanisms and adaptations required to transport IP packets over particular link-layer technologies with appropriate specifications. With a similar goal, the IETF IPv6 over Low-power Wireless Personal Area Networks (6LoWPAN) working group was formed in 2007 to produce a specification enabling the transportation of IPv6 packets over low-energy IEEE 802.15.4 and similar wireless communication environments. 6LoWPAN is currently a key technology to support Internet communications in the IoT, and one that has changed a previous perception of IPv6 as being impractical for low energy wireless communication environments. No security mechanisms are currently defined in the context of the 6LoWPAN adaptation layer, but the relevant documents include discussions on the security vulnerabilities, requirements and approaches to consider for network layer security.

Routing Layer. The Routing Over Low-power and Lossy Networks (ROLL) working group of the IETF was formed with the goal of designing routing solutions for IoT applications. The current approach to routing in 6LoWPAN environments is materialized in the Routing Protocol for Low power and Lossy Networks (RPL) [16] Protocol. The information in the *Security* field indicates the level of security and the cryptographic algorithms employed to process security for the message. What this field doesn't include is the security-related data required to process security for the message, for example a Message Integrity Code (MIC) or a signature. Instead, the security transformation itself states how the cryptographic fields should be employed in the context of the protected message.

Application Layer. As previously discussed, application-layer communications are supported by the CoAP [17] protocol, currently being designed by the Constrained RESTful Environments (CoRE) working group of the IETF. We next discuss the operation of the protocol as well as the mechanisms available to apply security to CoAP communications. The CoAP Protocol [17] defines bindings to DTLS (Datagram Transport-Layer Security) [18] to secure CoAP messages, along with a few mandatory minimal configurations appropriate for constrained environments.

3.3 Service Layer (Middleware Security)

Due to the very large number of technologies normally in place within the IoT paradigm, a type of middleware layer is employed to enforce seamless integration of devices and data within the same information network. Within such middleware, data must be exchanged respecting strict protection constraints. IoT applications are vulnerable to security attacks for several reasons: first, devices are physically vulnerable and are often left unattended; second, is difficult to implement any security countermeasure due to the large scale and the decentralised paradigm; finally, most of the IoT components are devices with limited resources, that can't support complex security schemes [19]. The major security challenge in IoT middleware is to protect data from data integrity, authenticity, and confidentiality attacks [20].

Both the networking and security issues have driven the design and the development of the VIRTUS Middleware, an IoT middleware relying on the open XMPP protocol to provide secure event driven communications within an IoT scenario [19]. Leveraging the standard security features provided by XMPP, the middleware offers a reliable and secure communication channel for distributed applications, protected with both authentication (through TLS protocol) and encryption (SASL protocol) mechanisms.

Security and privacy are responsible for confidentiality, authenticity, and nonrepudiation. Security can be implemented in two ways – (i) secure high-level peer communication which enables higher layers to communicate among peers in a secure and abstract way and (ii) secure topology management which deals with the authentication of new peers, permissions to access the network and protection of routing information exchanged in the network [21]. The major IoT security requirements are data authentication, access control, and client privacy [8]. Several recent works tried to address the presented issues. For example, [22] deals with the problem of task allocation in IoT.

4   Security Issues in IoT Generated Big Data Streams

Applications dealing with large data sets obtained via simulation or actual real-time sensor networks/social network are increasing in abundance [23]. The data obtained from real-time sources may contain certain discrepancies which arise from the dynamic nature of the source. Furthermore, certain computations may not require all the data and hence this data must be filtered before it can be processed. By installing adaptive filters that can be controlled in real-time, we can filter out only the relevant parts of the data thereby improving the overall computation speed.

Nehme et al. [24] proposed a system, StreamShield, designed to address the problem of security and privacy in the data stream. They have clearly highlighted the need for two types of security in data stream i.e. (1) the "data security punctuations" (dsps) describing the data-side security policies, and (2) the "query security punctuations" (qsps) in their paper. The advantages of such a stream-centric security model include flexibility, dynamicity and speed of enforcement. A stream processor can adapt to not only data-related but also to security-related selectivity, which helps reduce waste of resources, when few subjects have access to streaming data.

There are several applications where sensor nodes work as the source of the data stream. Here we list several applications such as real-time health monitoring applications (Health care), industrial monitoring, geo-social networking, home automation, war front monitoring, smart city monitoring, SCADA, event detection, disaster management and emergency management.

From all the above applications, we found data needs to be protected from malicious attacks to maintain originality of data before it reaches a data processing centre [25]. As the data sources is sensor nodes, it is always important to propose lightweight security solutions for data streams [25].

These applications require real-time processing of very high-volume data streams (also known as *big data stream*). The complexity of big data is defined through 5Vs i.e. *volume, variety, velocity, variability, veracity*. These features present significant opportunities and challenges for big data stream processing. Big data stream is continuous in nature and it is important to perform the real-time analysis as the life time of the data is often very short (applications can access the data only once) [1, 2]. So, it is important to perform security verification of big data streams prior to data evaluation. Following are the important points to consider during data streams security evaluation.

- Security verification is important in data stream to avoid malicious data.
- Another important issue, security verification should perform in near real-time.
- Security verification should not degrade the performance of stream processing engine (SPE). i.e. security verification speed should synchronize with SPE.

5 Conclusion

A glimpse of the IoT may be already visible in current deployments where networks of smart sensing devices are being interconnected with a wireless medium, and IP-based standard technologies will be fundamental in providing a common and well accepted ground for the development and deployment of new IoT applications. According to the 5Vs features of big data, the current data stream heading towards the new term as big data stream where sources are the IoT smart sensing devices. Considering that security may be an enabling factor of many of IoT applications, mechanisms to secure data stream using data in flow for the IoT will be fundamental. With such aspects in mind, this paper an exhaustive analysis on the security protocols and mechanisms available to protect big data streams on IoT applications.

References

1. Puthal, D., Nepal, S., Ranjan, R., Chen, J.: A dynamic prime number based efficient security mechanism for big sensing data streams. J. Comput. Syst. Sci. **83**(1), 22–42 (2017)
2. Puthal, D., Nepal, S., Ranjan, R., Chen, J.: DLSeF: a dynamic key length based efficient real-time security verification model for big data stream. ACM Trans. Embedded Comput. Syst. **16**(2), 51 (2016)
3. Granjal, J., Monteiro, E., Sá Silva, J.: Security for the internet of things: a survey of existing protocols and open research issues. IEEE Commun. Surv. Tutor. **17**(3), 1294–1312 (2015)
4. Tien, J.: Big data: unleashing information. J. Syst. Sci. Syst. Eng. **22**(2), 127–151 (2013)
5. Boldyreva, A., Fischlin, M., Palacio, A., Warinschi, B.: A closer look at PKI: security and efficiency. In: Okamoto, T., Wang, X. (eds.) PKC 2007. LNCS, vol. 4450, pp. 458–475. Springer, Heidelberg (2007). doi:10.1007/978-3-540-71677-8_30
6. Puthal, D., Nepal, S., Ranjan, R., Chen, J.: A dynamic key length based approach for real-time security verification of big sensing data stream. In: Wang, J., Cellary, W., Wang, D., Wang, H., Chen, S.-C., Li, T., Zhang, Y. (eds.) WISE 2015. LNCS, vol. 9419, pp. 93–108. Springer, Cham (2015). doi:10.1007/978-3-319-26187-4_7
7. Puthal, D., Nepal, S., Ranjan, R., Chen, J.: DPBSV- an efficient and secure scheme for big sensing data stream. In: 14th IEEE International Conference on Trust, Security and Privacy in Computing and Communications, pp. 246–253 (2015)
8. Weber, R.: Internet of things-new security and privacy challenges. Comput. Law Secur. Rev. **26**(1), 23–30 (2010)

9. Kopetz, H.: Internet of things. In: Kopetz, H. (ed.) Real-Time Systems. Real-Time Systems Series. Springer, Boston (2011). doi:10.1007/978-1-4419-8237-7_13

10. Al-Fuqaha, A., et al.: Internet of things: a survey on enabling technologies, protocols, and applications. IEEE Commun. Surv. Tutor. **17**(4), 2347–2376 (2015)

11. Li, S., Xu, L., Zhao, S.: The internet of things: a survey. Inf. Syst. Front. **17**(2), 243–259 (2015)

12. Xu, L., He, W., Li, S.: Internet of things in industries: a survey. IEEE Trans. Industr. Inf. **10**(4), 2233–2243 (2014)

13. Ilie-Zudor, E., et al.: A survey of applications and requirements of unique identification systems and RFID techniques. Comput. Ind. **62**(3), 227–252 (2011)

14. Wang, Y., Attebury, G., Ramamurthy, B.: A survey of security issues in wireless sensor networks. IEEE Commun. Surv. Tutor. **8**(2), 2–23 (2006)

15. IEEE Standard for Local and Metropolitan Area Networks—Part 15.4: Low-Rate Wireless Personal Area Networks (LR-WPANs) Amendment 1: MAC Sublayer, IEEE Std. 802.15.4e-2012 (Amendment to IEEE Std. 802.15.4–2011), (2011), pp. 1–225 (2012)

16. Thubert, P.: Objective function zero for the routing protocol for low-power and lossy networks (RPL). RFC 6550 (2012)

17. Bormann, C., Castellani, A., Shelby, Z.: Coap: an application protocol for billions of tiny internet nodes. IEEE Internet Comput. **16**(2), 62 (2012)

18. Zheng, T., Ayadi, A., Jiang, X.: TCP over 6LoWPAN for industrial applications: an experimental study. In: 4th IFIP International Conference on New Technologies, Mobility and Security (NTMS), pp. 1–4 (2011)

19. Conzon, D., Bolognesi, T., Brizzi, P., Lotito, A., Tomasi, R., Spirito, M.: The virtus middleware: an XMPP based architecture for secure IoT communications. In: 21st International Conference on Computer Communications and Networks, pp. 1–6 (2012)

20. Sicari, S., Rizzardi, A., Grieco, L., Coen-Porisini, A.: Security, privacy and trust in internet of things: the road ahead. Comput. Netw. **76**, 146–164 (2015)

21. Bandyopadhyay, S., Sengupta, M., Maiti, S., Dutta, S.: A survey of middleware for internet of things. In: Özcan, A., Zizka, J., Nagamalai, D. (eds.) CoNeCo/WiMo -2011. CCIS, vol. 162, pp. 288–296. Springer, Heidelberg (2011). doi:10.1007/978-3-642-21937-5_27

22. Colistra, G., Pilloni, V., Atzori, L.: The problem of task allocation in the internet of things and the consensus-based approach. Comput. Netw. **73**, 98–111 (2014)

23. Fox, G., et al.: High performance data streaming in service architecture. Technical report, Indiana University and University of Illinois at Chicago (2004)

24. Nehme, R., Lim, H., Bertino, E., Rundensteiner, E.: StreamShield: a stream-centric approach towards security and privacy in data stream environments. In: ACM SIGMOD International Conference on Management of data, pp. 1027–1030 (2009)

25. Chen, P., Wang, X., Wu, Y., Su, J., Zhou, H.: POSTER: iPKI: identity-based private key infrastructure for securing BGP protocol. In: ACM CCS, pp. 1632–1634 (2015)

IoT Data Storage in the Cloud: A Case Study in Human Biometeorology

Brunno Vanelli[1], A.R. Pinto[1], Madalena P. da Silva[1], M.A.R. Dantas[1],
M. Fazio[2(✉)], A. Celesti[2], and M. Villari[2,3]

[1] Federal University of Santa Catarina, Florianópolis, Santa Catarina, Brazil
mario.dantas@ufsc.br
[2] University of Messina, Messina, Italy
{mfazio,acelesti,mvillari}@unime.it
[3] IRCCS Centro Neurolesi "Bonino Pulejo", Messina, Italy

Abstract. The IoT (Internet of Things) has emerged to increase the
potentiality of pervasive monitoring devices. However, the implementation and integration of IoT devices, data storage and the development
of applications are still considered challenging. This paper presents an
infrastructure for aggregating and storing data from different sources
from IoT devices to the cloud. In order to evaluate the infrastructure
regarding the quality in storage, it has been implemented and verified
in an AAL (Ambient Assisted Living) case scenario, the main application being Human Biometeorology. The evaluation of metrics related to
sending, receiving and storing data demonstrate that the experimental
environment is completely reliable and appropriate for the case study in
question.

Keywords: AAL · Cloud computing · Human biometeorology · IoT

1 Introduction

The emergence of WSNs (Wireless Sensor Networks) enabled the pervasive monitoring of environments. However, the main weakness of the WSNs is that communications are restricted to the monitoring site (due to short-range radios and
energy constraints). The necessary modifications to the WSNs in order to actually be introduced on a large scale in the IT industry (Information Technology)
is to connect them to the Internet and extend their limited computation and
storage capabilities. Thus, the IoT (Internet of Things) has emerged to fill this
gap and provide interconnected devices able to interact with the environment [1].

The implementation and integration of IoT devices, data storage and
the development of applications is very challenging. This paper presents an
infrastructure for aggregating and storing data collected from different IoT
devices into the cloud. It make use of consolidated technologies, such as ZigBee
to interconnect monitoring devices, and Azure, to implement a NoSQL Database
(DB) into the cloud.

© ICST Institute for Computer Sciences, Social Informatics and Telecommunications Engineering 2018
A. Longo et al. (Eds.): IISSC 2017/CN4IoT 2017, LNICST 189, pp. 253–262, 2018.
https://doi.org/10.1007/978-3-319-67636-4_26

In order to evaluate the proposed infrastructure and the quality of the storage service in, the paper deals with an AAL (Ambient Assisted Living) scenario and, in particular, it addresses an Human Biometeorology application as use case. The evaluation of metrics related to sending, receiving and storing data demonstrate that the experimental environment is completely reliable and appropriate for the case study in question.

This paper is organized as follows: Sect. 2 introduces the reference scenario and the motivations at the base of this work. Section 3 discusses the state of the art on the main topic related to our work. Section 4 presents the architecture we propose and related technologies. We describe our evaluation results in Sect. 5. Finally, Sect. 6 presents our conclusions and future work.

2   Reference Scenario and Motivations

This section presents the motivational scenario, the experimental environment and the results of evaluation of infrastructure proposal. The hardware, software and technologies used in the experiments, are shown in Fig. 1.

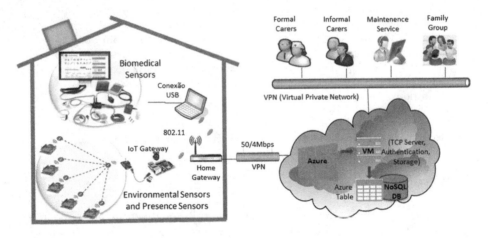

Fig. 1. Experimental infrastructure

The Human Biometeorology is the science that studies the impact of atmospheric influence on health and well-being of humans. There are many proposals in the literature that correlate weather conditions with health, including thermal comfort [2] morbidities [3] mortality [3,4], fetal health [5], among many others. The vast majority of the proposed uses data from the health information providers and climate to correlate and make inferences about the impacts of climate variables with some morbidities of a country, region or group of people [6].

Although the aforementioned research to generate indicators for the management of health, they need to be refined, since there is difference in the accuracy of the values of the meteorological variables read in external versus internal environment [3]. As people live most of the time indoors and many of them are likely to trigger some kind of respiratory disease, it is strongly recommended to monitor the weather conditions in the internal environment. The values of the meteorological variables associated with the user context (i.e. clinical status, patient/family history) become valuable indicators for decision-making by health care providers.

Using technology to support the Human Biometeorology, this article implements the IoT to monitor environmental conditions (dry bulb temperature, dew point temperature, relative humidity, light), the patient's clinical conditions (biomedical signals) and user detection in rooms of an AAL (Ambient Assisted Living) ubiquitous. In the experiments, it was designed a scenario where the patient is remotely assisted by health caregivers and the devices often send data to the cloud relating to biomedical signals, environmental conditions and presence.

Data from the AAL are stored in the cloud and can be consumed by third party applications (formal caregiver/informal, maintenance and family group). The data collected on the case scenario is often crucial for proper monitoring of the patient, hence it should offer reliability and quality in the storage infrastructure proposal.

3   Related Work

The search for related work was conducted on two main topics, that are (1) the adoption of ubiquitous computing to monitor environmental conditions and correlate the meteorological variables with human biometeorology, and (2) data storage solutions for IoT data into the Cloud.

About the first topic, we noticed that many monitoring biomedical signals using body sensor networks and monitoring elderly activities in AAL environments use the ZigBee technology. Indeed, ZigBee presents good performance in monitoring the ambient air quality in order to improve and support the users' health [8,9,11–13]. For these reasons, we adopted ZigBee in our experimentation (as we will discuss later).

About the second topic, we noticed a great interest of the scientific community in designing new solutions for IoT and cloud integration. This paper [14] presents a two-layer architecture based on a hybrid storage system able to support a Platform as a Service (PaaS) federated Cloud scenario. Generalized architectures which use Cloud computing and Big Data for effective storage and analysis of data generated are discussed in [10,15]. This paper proposes [16] a parallel storage algorithm for the classification of data The experiment shows that it classifies the original heterogeneous data flow according to the data type to realize parallel processing, which greatly improves the storage and access efficiency. In this paper [17], the two technologies, cloud computing and IoT, are introduced and analyzed. Then, an intelligent storage management system is designed combining of cloud computing and IoT. The designed system is divided into four layers: perception layer, network layer, service layer, and application layer. And the system's function modules and database design are also described. The system processes stronger applicability and expansion functions, and all of them can be extendedly applied to other intelligent management systems based on cloud calculating and IoT. Our solution is mainly focused on a storage service for IoT data exploiting consolidated technologies, such as ZigBee and Microsoft Azure.

4   Storage Service in the Cloud for IoT Data Management

Figure 2 presents the reference architecture for the IoT data storage service in the cloud. The architecture is composed of three layers, described below.

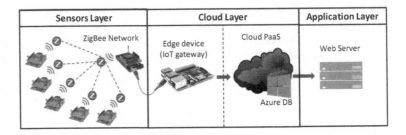

Fig. 2. Reference architecture for IoT data storage service in the cloud

The **Sensors Layer** is responsible for perceiving the environment, collect and transmit the data to the IoT gateway. In our implementation, at this layer we exploit ZigBee networks, because they allow the standalone and scalar configuration, and provide a low-cost and low-power solution. However, any other module or physical medium can be used, as long the devices all agree upon how the data will be handed to the gateway. In particular, each ZigBee network is configured with star topology, where the master node coordinates the process of sending slaves through requests. The slaves collect data from sensors (temperature, humidity, light intensity and presence) according to the master's requests.

The **Cloud Layer** implements remote resource over the Internet and in cloud datacenters. It includes an *edge device* (e.g., IoT gateway), whose function is to convert data received from the **Sensor Layer** (temperature, humidity, presence and brightness) in data suitable for the **Application Layer**. The Cloud Platform as a Service (PaaS) provides tools for data storage and retrieval over cloud datacenters, in order to benefit of the main advantages of cloud computing in terms of scalability and elasticity. In particular, data are stored in a NoSQL database that is Azure DB.

The **Application Layer** implements the business applications necessary to manage and process AAL data. At this stage of our work, we exploit a web server at the application layer that processes requests for data storage and retrieval.

To store and provide fast retrieval of information generated by the various devices connected to the cloud, it is proposed a storage mechanism based on NoSQL operating architecture, available on Azure called Azure Tables. Unlike storage systems based on relational paradigm, NoSQL databases have as one of its most notable features the non-relational data schema, often allowing more flexible data storage. The Azure tables allow the creation of key-pair tuples (records) with different number of attributes (columns) to be stored in the same entity. Thus, the Azure Tables is able to offer flexible and low-cost storage and efficient searches.

Basic Scheme for Data Storage.
The Azure Table imposes some restrictions on the indexing of stored data. In short, an entity must have two indexed fields: *PartitionKey* and *RowKey*. Additionally, the Azure Table automatically generates a timestamp indicating the last date that the entity was created or changed, for control purposes. The indices of the entities are created using the combination of the PartitionKey with the RowKey, which must be unique across the table. The PartitionKey indicates the partition in the table, and other fields like RowKey are often used to refine the search. Each entity can have up to 255 properties (including the three required) and can store user information such as data strings and integers. According to the manufacturer of the product, the retrieval of information is facilitated when, in the schema definition, the primary information for the search are aimed at these fields because their indexing is already automatically using the combination PartitionKey/RowKey. Searching other fields is possible, but may have some limitations due to the flexibility of the scheme, and is computationally more expensive. On this basis, we defined the basic scheme for storing data of different devices based on a single entity and using the device identifier information, device type and date of the event, to compose the entity's records keys. Thus, each device will be required to provide this information to the composition of the keys and will be free to store in each record the number of attributes you need (e.g., a temperature and humidity sensor will send two pieces of information to each reading, while a location sensor can send, for example, latitude, longitude and altitude). Table 1 shows an example with data on the hypothetical scheme adopted. The PartitionKey field will store the device type (in the example can be: ENE LOC or TP) concatenated with the device identifier (E1, E2, C1, C2, S1). This approach facilitates the retrieval of data from specific sensors. For instance, a query could be made to get all the data related to the ENE sensors, or refine the search to all ENE_E1 sensors. The field RowKey will contain temporal information about the event. The mandatory field Timestamp is an internal information system, and stores the time of the last recording information in the entity. This field can be used for reading but cannot be changed. For this reason, it was decided to store the event occurrence time in the RowKey field, since the time of occurrence of the event and the arrival time to the storage system in the cloud can be distinguished due to delays, in both the network and the queue storage server, or even batch updates. This way, when retrieving data, the query could specify both the sensors and timespan required for the application.

Table 1. Data schema adopted

PartitionKey	RowKey	Timestamp	info	potencia	lat	long	pressao	temp
ENE_E1	T3	06/24/16 19:01:56	Sensor de cons...	13				
ENE_E1	T2	06/24/16 19:02:22	Sensor de cons...	12				
ENE_E1	T1	06/24/16 19:02:13	Sensor de cons...	10				
ENE_E2	T2	06/24/16 19:03:52	Sensor de cons...	7				
ENE_E2	T1	06/24/16 19:02:35	Sensor de cons...	8				
LOC_C1	T2	06/24/16 19:08:45	Localização de t...		-27.108414	-48.8414		
LOC_C1	T1	06/24/16 19:08:56	Localização de t...		-26.896977	-49.08414		
TP_S1	T2	06/24/16 19:10:48	Sensor de temp...				20	22
TP_S1	T1	06/24/16 19:10:06	Sensor de temp...				20	19

5   Experimental Results

In this section, we present the experimentation we performed, providing details on our implementation of the IoT storage service on the cloud, and discussing evaluation results.

5.1   Implementation Details

The AAL (Ambient Assisted Living) comprises the ZigBee sensor network and bio-medical sensors. In order to send data to the cloud, it was used a Home Gateway, a TP-Link with Link Internet an Internet link of 50 Mbps/4 Mbps to guarantee access the cloud. TheZigBee network was configured to standard 802.15.4 with star topology consisting of 12 slave nodes and a coordinator node. The slave nodes are composed of 6 DHT11 sensor - humidity and temperature, 3 LDR sensor - light and 3 PIR sensor - presence. The ZigBee network is composed by 12 modules XBee Antenna 1Mw Serie 1. Each module is connected to aXBee shield, which in turn is embedded in the Arduino Uno board.

In the experiment, we used sensors for pulse and oxygen in blood, body temperature, blood pressure,airflow and electrocardiogram sensor (EGC). The collection of data from the sensors was done through the open-source Arduino Software (IDE) - ARDUINO 1.0.6. The data are captured and transmitted via serial communication of the user terminal to the Home Gateway, this in turn sends the data to the web server for storage in the cloud. The frequency of data transmission depends on the type of sensing, that is, pulse and oxygen in blood, body temperature – every 5 min; bloodpressure – every 2 h; airflow and electrocardiogram sensor (EGC) – continuously for periods of set times).

After establishing the connection, the host (i.e., IoT gateway) needs to authenticate to the web server. The authentication process assigns the credentials of the host and grants permission for the storage table(s). To store the data, each host can invoke the storage functions. For each data type sensed, there is a storage function and invocation, and each host must pass the right parameters according to the type of data sensed. After this process, the script automatically sends a data storage request to the respective table in the database. Considering the organization of the data schema defined in Sect. 4, searches by device type, device identifier, or time will be easier and there will be a better use of Azure Table mandatory keys, since these fields carry the most used information such as filter in the consultations to be held. Authentication services and storage were made in the Azure using a virtual machine, standard DS1 v2 (1 core, 3.5 GB memory), with Linux operating system. For this scenario have been implemented some tables, the main ones being the tables for authentication of hosts, storage environmental conditions and storage of biomedical signals.

5.2 Evaluation Results

We evaluated received packets from the IoT Gateway at the web server, and sent packets from the server for the Azure Storage platform. In Fig. 3, it is possible to see that all packets have been received and sent without error. This is justified by the TCP/IP protocol reliability in the exchange of messages.

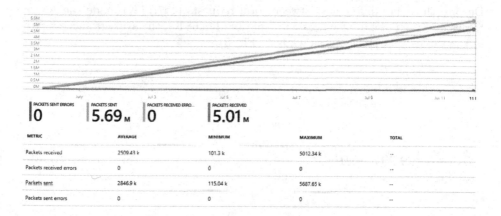

PACKETS SENT ERRORS	PACKETS SENT	PACKETS RECEIVED ERRO...	PACKETS RECEIVED
0	5.69 M	0	5.01 M

METRIC	AVERAGE	MINIMUM	MAXIMUM	TOTAL
Packets received	2509.43 k	101.3 k	5012.34 k	..
Packets received errors	0	0	0	..
Packets sent	2846.9 k	115.04 k	5687.65 k	..
Packets sent errors	0	0	0	..

Fig. 3. Monitoring transmission data

Figure 4 illustrates the monitoring Azure Tables metrics: *TotalRequests, Success, ClientOtherError and ClientTimeoutError*. The *TotalRequests* metric summarizes the number of requests made to the storage service. This number includes successful and failed requests and requests that generated errors. The *Success* metric indicates the number of successful requests to the storage service. The *ClientOtherError* metric monitors authenticated requests that failed as expected. This error can represent many of status codes and HTTP 300–400 level conditions as NotFound and ResourceAlreadyExists. The *ClientTimeoutError* metric monitors authenticated requests with time limits that returned an HTTP status code 500. If the client network timeout or request timeout is set to a value lower than expected by the storage service, this will be expected

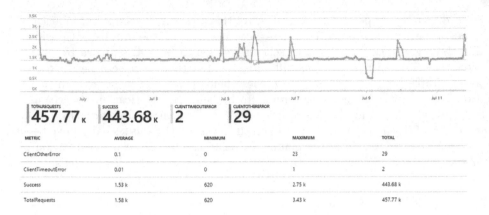

Fig. 4. Metrics requests for data storage service

time limit. Otherwise, it will be reported as a ServerTimeoutError. Through Fig. 7 can be identified, insignificant, but existing errors by timeout and others. Despite the small difference between total requests (457.77 K) made the Azure tables and the number of successful requests (443.68 K), the average success rate in the tables data storage was 99.99% (Fig. 5).

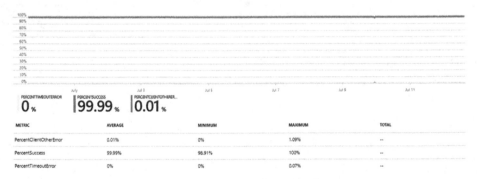

Fig. 5. Percentages of carried requests the data storage service

Consistent with the metrics monitoring Fig. 4, Fig. 5 shows the metrics with the percentage of success and errors of requests to the storage service. In the monitored period, the minimum percentage of successful requests came in 98.91%, maximum of 100% and average of 99.99%. The percentage of requests that failed with a timeout error, got maximum value of 0.07%. This number includes the client time and server. The percentage of requests that have failed with a ClientOtherError was a maximum of 1.09%.

Figure 6 shows the latency (in milliseconds) of successful requests made to the storage service. This amount includes the processing time required in the Azure storage to read the request, send the response and receive the confirmation response.

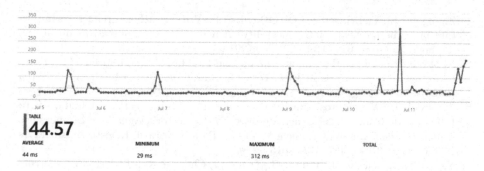

Fig. 6. Time in well successful requests to storage service

6   Conclusions

This paper presented an infrastructure for IoT data gathering and storage service in a NoSQL cloud DB. To evaluate the proposed solution, we implemented the system considering an AAL reference scenario. The setting was applied to human biometeorology where a patient, assisted remotely, frequently sends environmental data, presence and biomedical signals to the cloud. The available data in the cloud can be consumed by third party applications (health caregivers, family members, equipment maintenance operator or the user himself). However, in order to achieve the desired behavior for monitoring applications, it is necessary to verify both the quality in transmission and in data storage. The storage service is based on Azure.

To evaluate the quality, several metrics were selected for the purpose of showing the number and percentage of successful requests to the storage service as well as possible errors and the response time in storage operations carried out successfully. The results show that the experimental environment is reliable and appropriate for the considered case of study.

As future proposals, we intend to scale the AAL equipments, implement new functions in the storage service and work with machine learning, to support human analysis by health caregiver about persisted data.

Acknowledgements. We would like to thanks to Microsoft Research for Azure Award.

References

1. Botta, A., de Donato, W., Persico, V., Pescapé, A.: Integration of cloud computing and internet of things: a survey. Future Gener. Comput. Syst. **56**, 684–700 (2016)
2. Thom, E.C.: The discomfort index. Weatherwise **12**, 57–60 (1959)
3. Quinn, A., Tamerius, J.D., Perzanowski, M., Jacobson, J.S., Goldstein, I., Acosta, L., Shaman, J.: Predicting indoor heat exposure risk during extreme heat events. Sci. Total Environ. **490**, 686–693 (2014)

4. Zhang, K., Li, Y., Schwartz, J.D., O'Neill, M.S.: What weather variables are important in predicting heat-related mortality? A new application of statistical learning methods. Environ. Res. **132**, 350–359 (2014)
5. Ngo, N.S., Horton, R.M.: Climate change and fetal health: the impacts of exposure to extreme temperatures in New York City. Environ. Res. **144**(Pt A), 158–164 (2016)
6. Azevedo, J.V.V., Santos, A.C., Alves, T.L.B., Azevedo, P.V., Olinda, R.A.: Influência do Clima na Incidência de Infecção Respiratória Aguda em Crianças nos Municípios de Campina Grande e Monteiro, Paraíba, Brasil. Revista Brasileira de Meteorologia **30**(4), 467–477 (2015)
7. Yang, C.-T., Liao, C.-J., Liu, J.-C., Den, W., Chou, Y.-C., Tsai, J.-J.: Construction and application of an intelligent air quality monitoring system for healthcare environment. J. Med. Syst. **38**(2), 15 (2014)
8. Sun, F.M., Fang, Z., Zhao, Z., Xu, Z.H., Tan, J., Chen, D.L., Du, L.D., Qian, Y.M., Hui, H.Y., Tian, L.L.: A wireless ZigBee router with P-H-T sensing for health monitoring. In: IEEE International Conference on Green Computing and Communications and IEEE Internet of Things and IEEE Cyber, Physical and Social Computing, GreenCom-iThings-CPSCom 2013, art. no. 682338, pp. 1773–1778 (2013)
9. Nam, J.-W., Kim, H.-T., Min, B.-B., Kim, K.-H., Kim, G.-S., Kim, J.-C.: Ventilation control of subway station using USN environmental sensor monitoring system. In: International Conference on Control, Automation and Systems, art. 6106440, pp. 305–308 (2011)
10. Fazio, M., Celesti, A., Puliafito, A., Villari, M.: Big data storage in the cloud for smart environment monitoring. Procedia Comput. Sci. **52**(2015), 500–506 (2015)
11. Jayakumar, D., Omana, J., Sivakumar, M., Senthil, B.: A safe guard system for mine workers using wireless sensor networks. Int. J. Appl. Eng. Res. **10**(8), 21429–21441 (2015)
12. Sung, W.-T., Chen, J.-H., Wang, H.-C.: Wisdom health care environment systems for monitoring and automated control via RBF function. Appl. Mech. Mater. **157–158**, 315–318 (2012)
13. Li, H., Zhao, L., Ling, P.: Wireless control of residential HVAC systems for energy efficient and comfortable homes. ASHRAE Trans. **116**(PART 2), 355–367 (2010)
14. Fazio, M., Celesti, A., Villari, M., Puliafito, A.: The need of a hybrid storage approach for IoT in PaaS cloud federation. In: 28th International Conference on Advanced Information Networking and Applications Workshops, pp. 779–784 (2014)
15. Behera, R.K., Gupta, S., Gautam, A.: Big-data empowered cloud centric internet of things. In: International Conference on Man and Machine Interfacing, pp. 1–5 (2015)
16. Yan, Z.: The application of mobile cloud in heterogeneous data storage in web of things system. In: 7th International Conference on Intelligent Computation Technology and Automation, pp. 773–776 (2014)
17. Kang, J., Yin, S., Meng, W.: An Intelligent storage management system based on cloud computing and internet of things. In: Patnaik, S., Li, X. (eds.) Proceedings of International Conference on Computer Science and Information Technology. AISC, vol. 255, pp. 499–505. Springer, New Delhi (2014). doi:10.1007/978-81-322-1759-6_57

Author Index

Printed in the United States
By Bookmasters